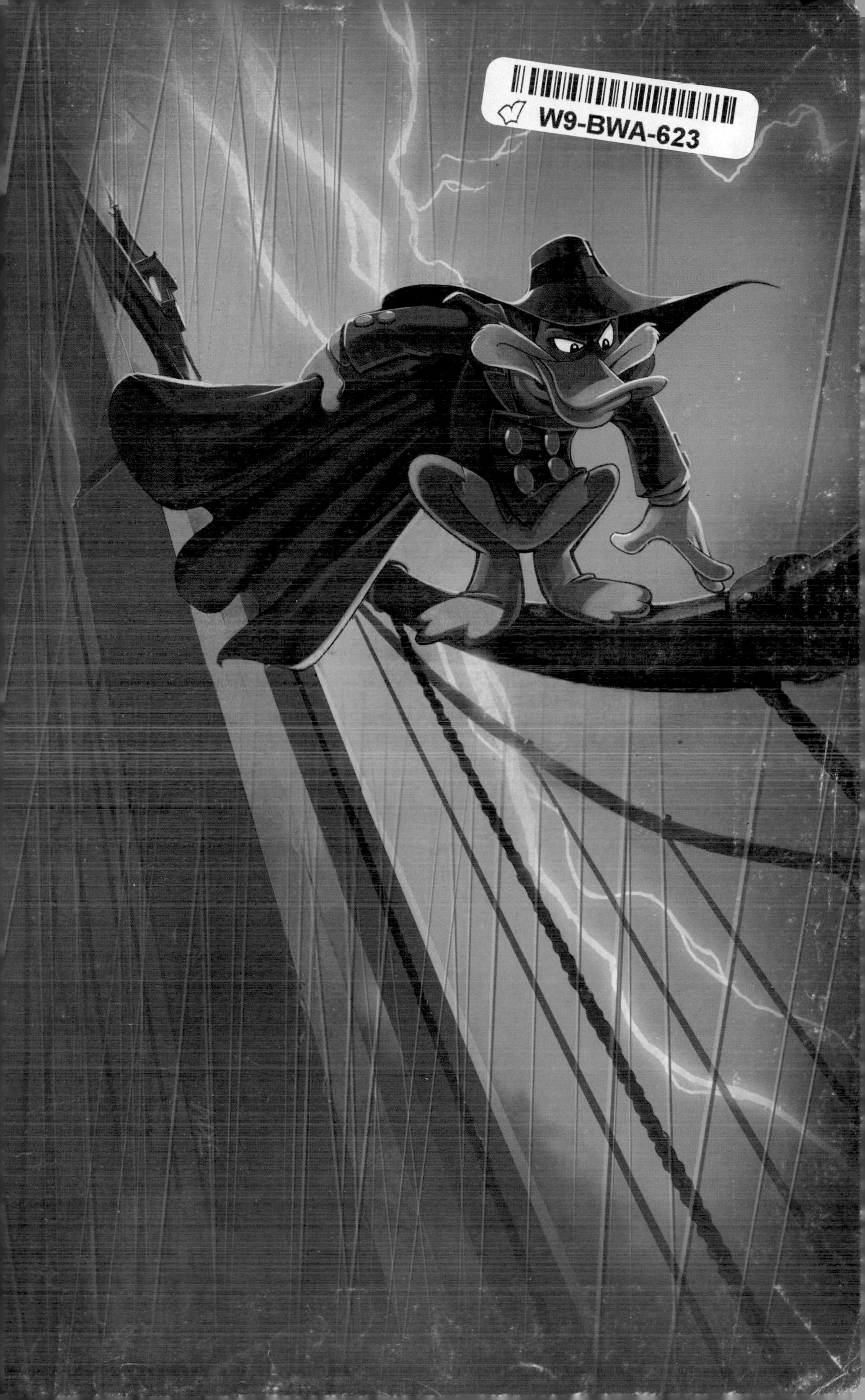

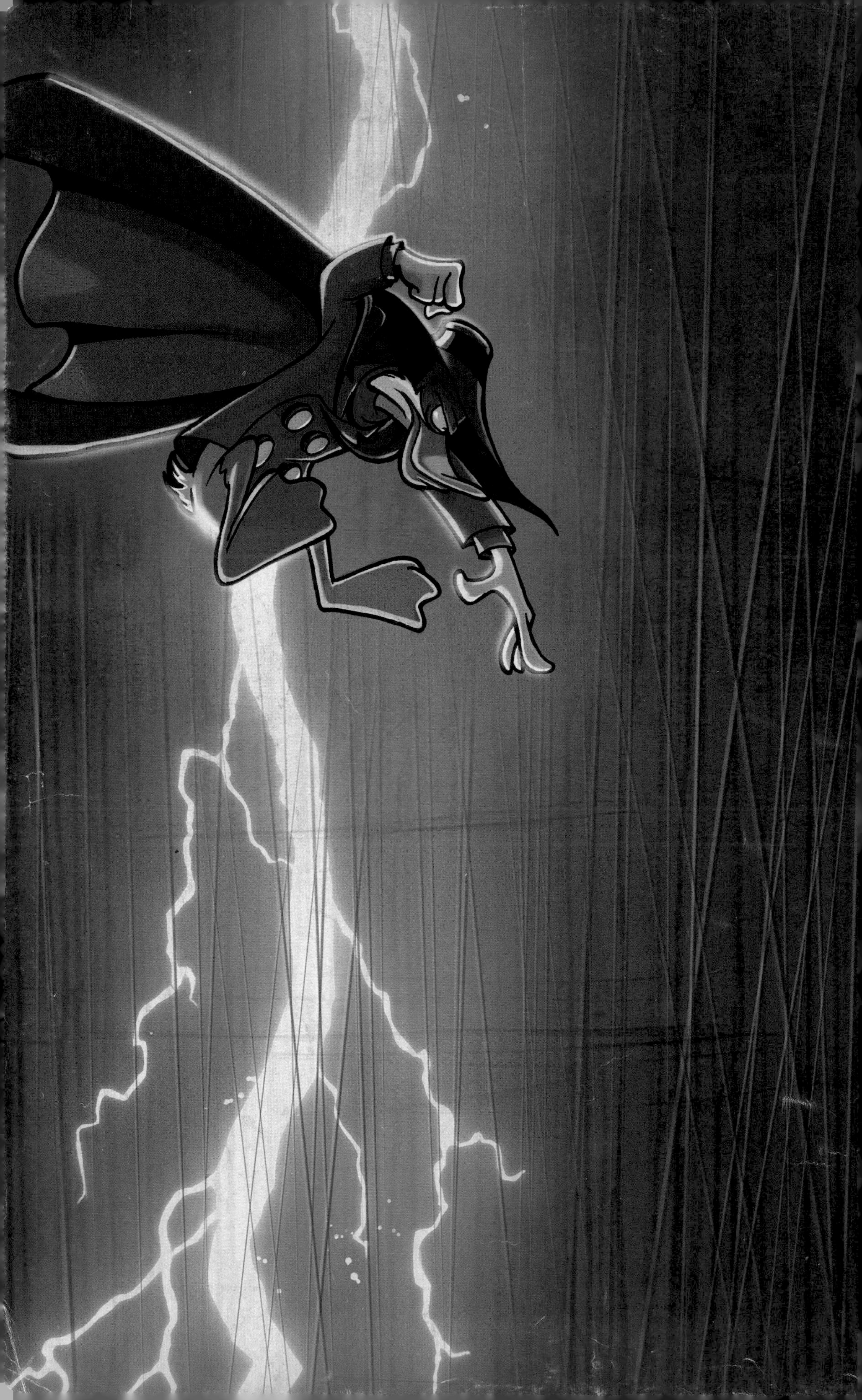

WRITER:
IAN BRILL

ARTIST:
JAMES SILVANI

COLORIST:
ANDREW DALHOUSE

LETTERER: DERON BENNETT

COVER:
MAGIC EYE STUDIOS

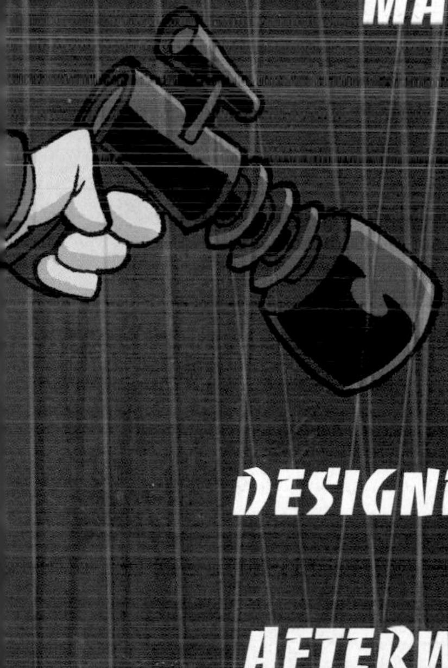

EDITOR:
CHRISTOPHER BURNS

DESIGNER: ERIKA TERRIQUEZ

AFTERWORD BY TAD STONES

SPECIAL THANKS:
JESSE POST, STEVE BEHLING, BRYCE VANKOOTEN AND
ROB TOKAR OF DISNEY PUBLISHING AND TAD STONES
FOR BRINGING DARKWING TO LIFE.

ONE

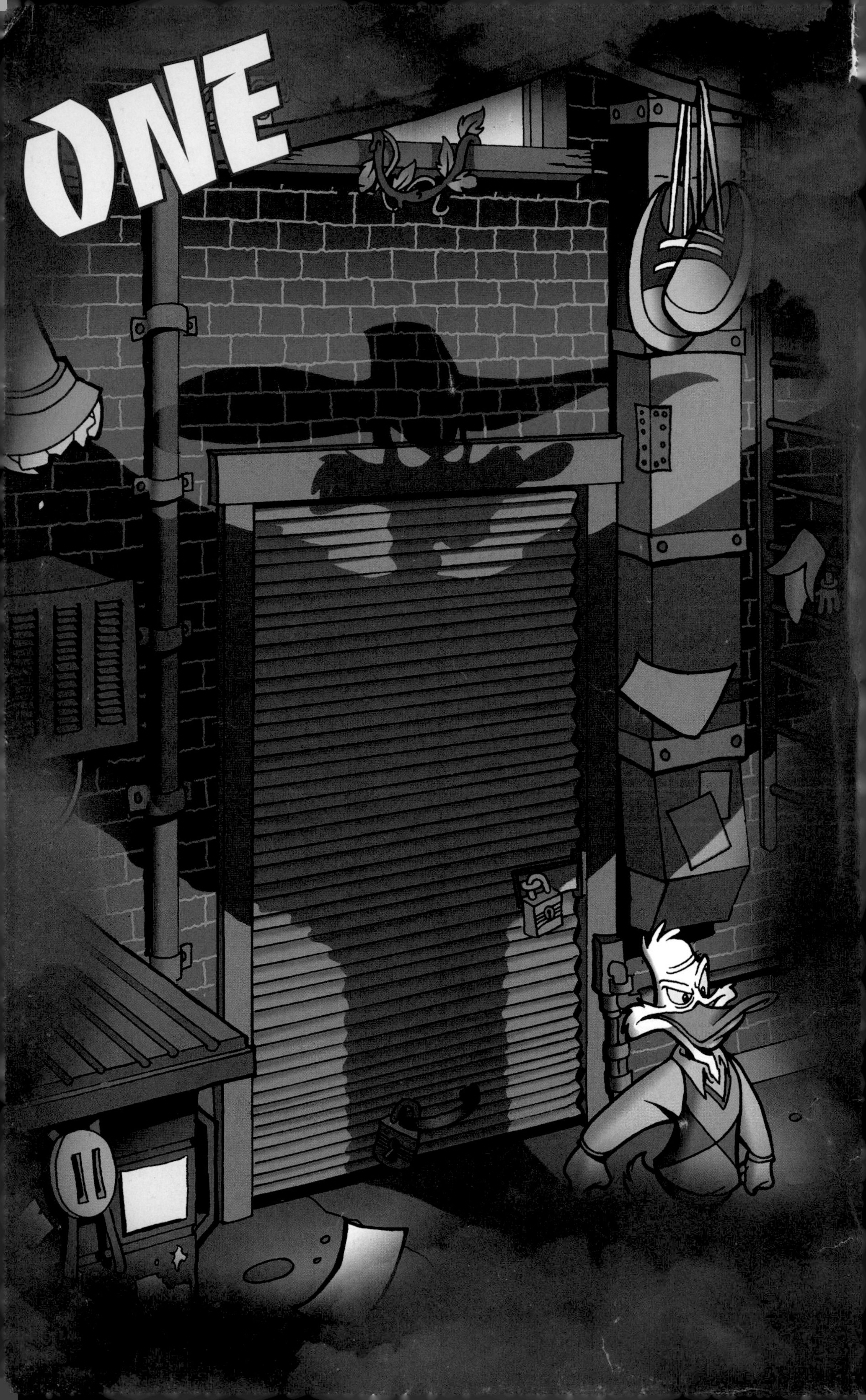

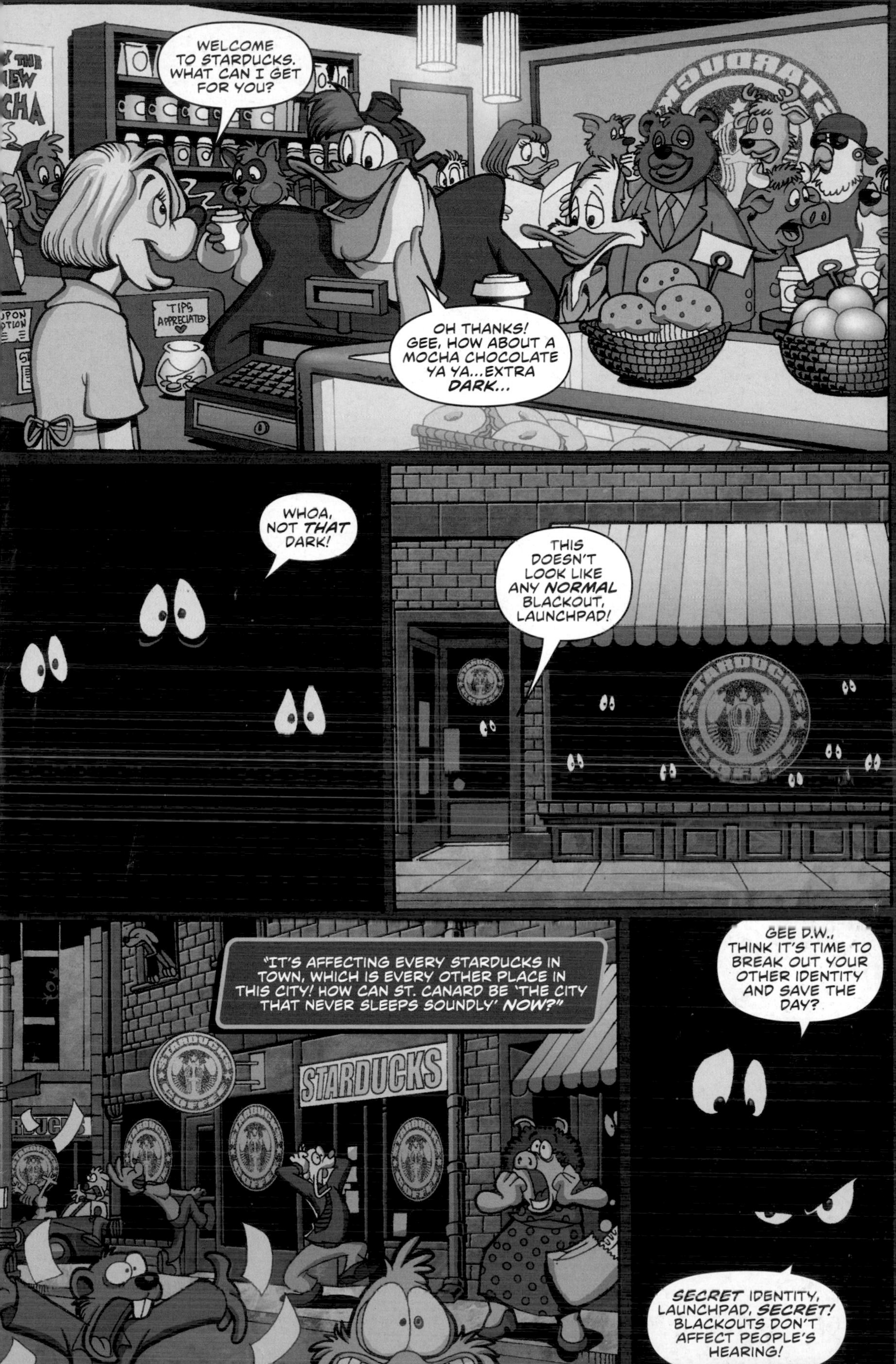
WELCOME TO STARDUCKS. WHAT CAN I GET FOR YOU?
TIPS APPRECIATED
OH THANKS! GEE, HOW ABOUT A MOCHA CHOCOLATE YA YA...EXTRA DARK...
WHOA, NOT THAT DARK!
THIS DOESN'T LOOK LIKE ANY NORMAL BLACKOUT, LAUNCHPAD!
"IT'S AFFECTING EVERY STARDUCKS IN TOWN, WHICH IS EVERY OTHER PLACE IN THIS CITY! HOW CAN ST. CANARD BE 'THE CITY THAT NEVER SLEEPS SOUNDLY' NOW?"
STARDUCKS
GEE D.W., THINK IT'S TIME TO BREAK OUT YOUR OTHER IDENTITY AND SAVE THE DAY?
SECRET IDENTITY, LAUNCHPAD, SECRET! BLACKOUTS DON'T AFFECT PEOPLE'S HEARING!

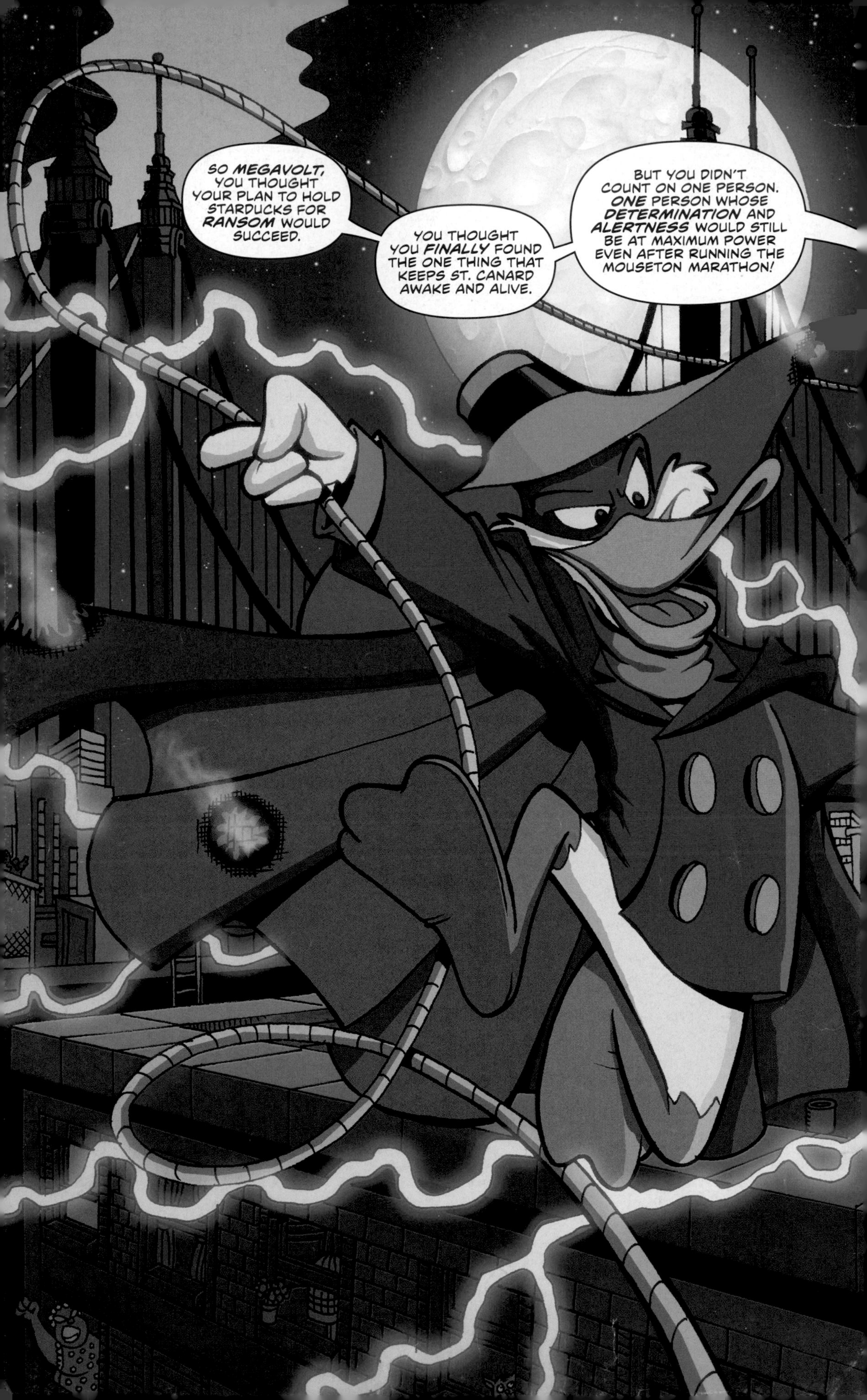
SO MEGAVOLT, YOU THOUGHT YOUR PLAN TO HOLD STARDUCKS FOR RANSOM WOULD SUCCEED.
YOU THOUGHT YOU FINALLY FOUND THE ONE THING THAT KEEPS ST. CANARD AWAKE AND ALIVE.
BUT YOU DIDN'T COUNT ON ONE PERSON. ONE PERSON WHOSE DETERMINATION AND ALERTNESS WOULD STILL BE AT MAXIMUM POWER EVEN AFTER RUNNING THE MOUSETON MARATHON!

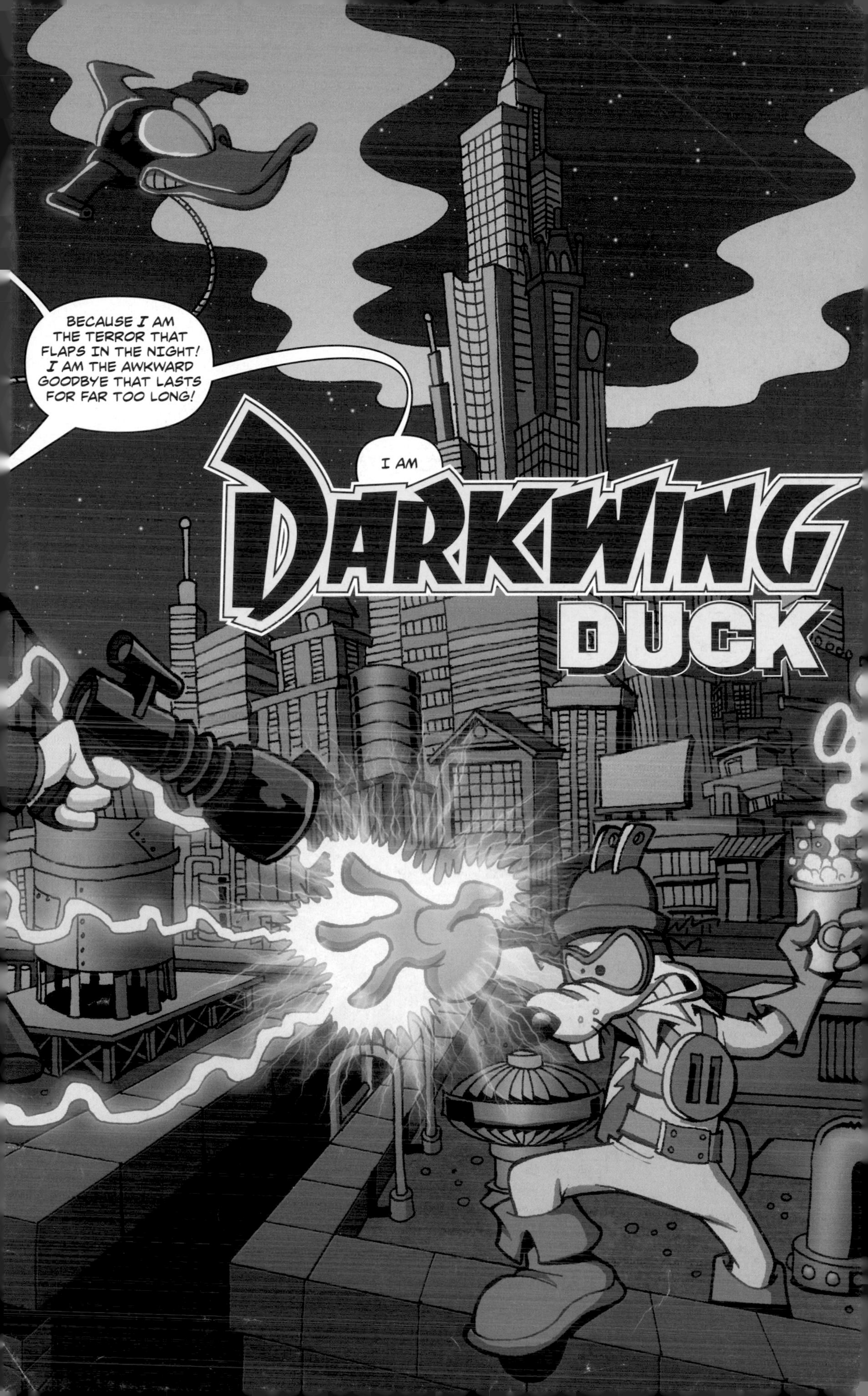

BECAUSE I AM THE TERROR THAT FLAPS IN THE NIGHT! I AM THE AWKWARD GOODBYE THAT LASTS FOR FAR TOO LONG!
I AM
DARKWING DUCK

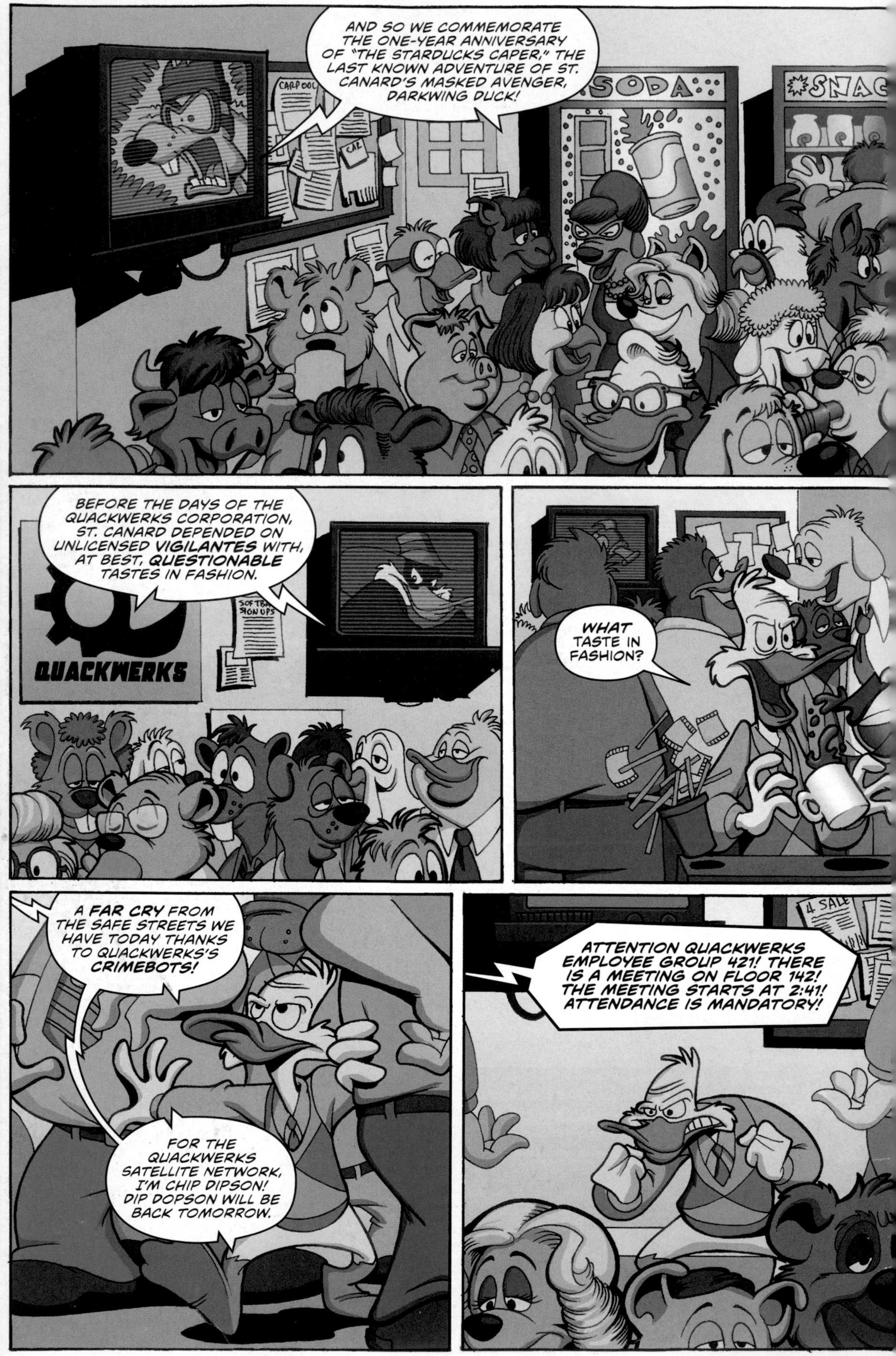
AND SO WE COMMEMORATE THE ONE-YEAR ANNIVERSARY OF "THE STARDUCKS CAPER," THE LAST KNOWN ADVENTURE OF ST. CANARD'S MASKED AVENGER, DARKWING DUCK!
SODA
SNAC
CARPOOL
BEFORE THE DAYS OF THE QUACKWERKS CORPORATION, ST. CANARD DEPENDED ON UNLICENSED VIGILANTES WITH, AT BEST, QUESTIONABLE TASTES IN FASHION.
QUACKWERKS
WHAT TASTE IN FASHION?
A FAR CRY FROM THE SAFE STREETS WE HAVE TODAY THANKS TO QUACKWERKS'S CRIMEBOTS!
FOR THE QUACKWERKS SATELLITE NETWORK, I'M CHIP DIPSON! DIP DOPSON WILL BE BACK TOMORROW.
ATTENTION QUACKWERKS EMPLOYEE GROUP 421! THERE IS A MEETING ON FLOOR 142! THE MEETING STARTS AT 2:41! ATTENDANCE IS MANDATORY!
4 SALE

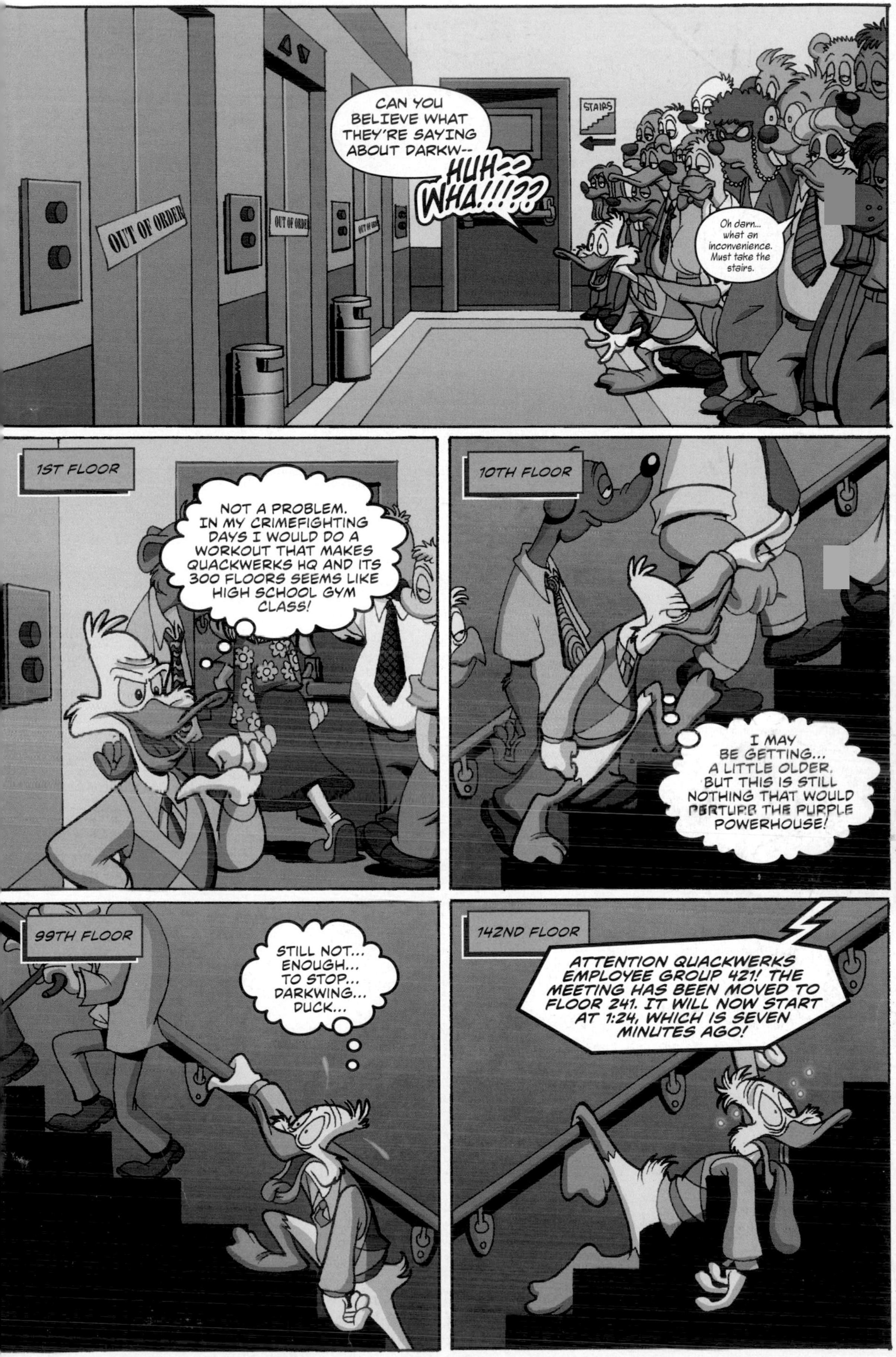
STAIRS
OUT OF ORDER
OUT OF ORDER
OUT OF ORDER
CAN YOU BELIEVE WHAT THEY'RE SAYING ABOUT DARKW--
HUH--? WHA!!!??
Oh darn... what an inconvenience. Must take the stairs.
1ST FLOOR
NOT A PROBLEM. IN MY CRIMEFIGHTING DAYS I WOULD DO A WORKOUT THAT MAKES QUACKWERKS HQ AND ITS 300 FLOORS SEEMS LIKE HIGH SCHOOL GYM CLASS!
10TH FLOOR
I MAY BE GETTING... A LITTLE OLDER, BUT THIS IS STILL NOTHING THAT WOULD PERTURB THE PURPLE POWERHOUSE!
99TH FLOOR
STILL NOT... ENOUGH... TO STOP... DARKWING... DUCK...
142ND FLOOR
ATTENTION QUACKWERKS EMPLOYEE GROUP 421! THE MEETING HAS BEEN MOVED TO FLOOR 241. IT WILL NOW START AT 1:24, WHICH IS SEVEN MINUTES AGO!

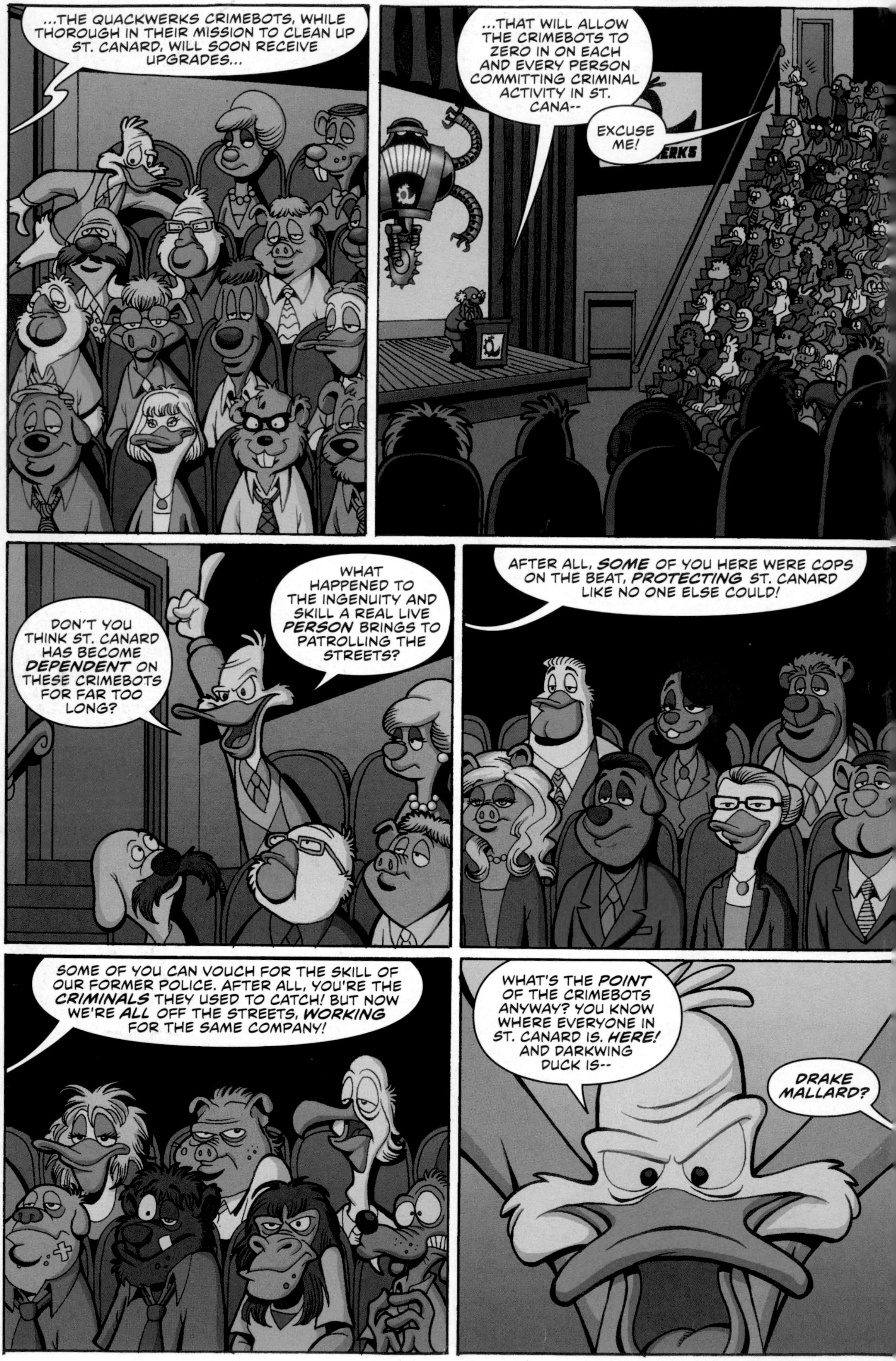
...THE QUACKWERKS CRIMEBOTS, WHILE THOROUGH IN THEIR MISSION TO CLEAN UP ST. CANARD, WILL SOON RECEIVE UPGRADES...
...THAT WILL ALLOW THE CRIMEBOTS TO ZERO IN ON EACH AND EVERY PERSON COMMITTING CRIMINAL ACTIVITY IN ST. CANA--
EXCUSE ME!
WERKS
DON'T YOU THINK ST. CANARD HAS BECOME *DEPENDENT* ON THESE CRIMEBOTS FOR FAR TOO LONG?
WHAT HAPPENED TO THE INGENUITY AND SKILL A REAL LIVE *PERSON* BRINGS TO PATROLLING THE STREETS?
AFTER ALL, *SOME* OF YOU HERE WERE COPS ON THE BEAT, *PROTECTING* ST. CANARD LIKE NO ONE ELSE COULD!
SOME OF YOU CAN VOUCH FOR THE SKILL OF OUR FORMER POLICE. AFTER ALL, YOU'RE THE *CRIMINALS* THEY USED TO CATCH! BUT NOW WE'RE *ALL* OFF THE STREETS, *WORKING* FOR THE SAME COMPANY!
WHAT'S THE *POINT* OF THE CRIMEBOTS ANYWAY? YOU KNOW WHERE EVERYONE IN ST. CANARD IS. *HERE!* AND DARKWING DUCK IS--
DRAKE MALLARD?

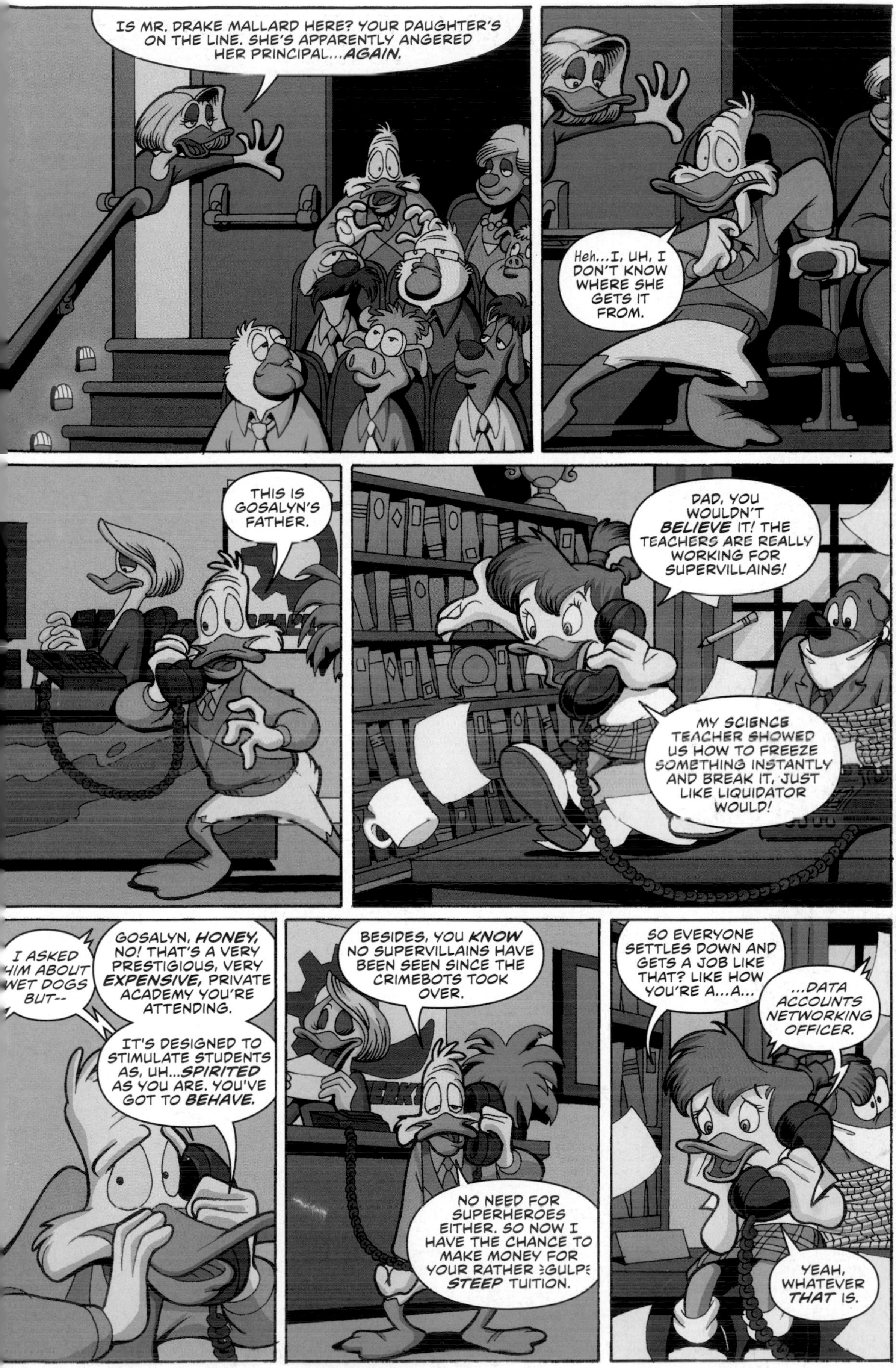
IS MR. DRAKE MALLARD HERE? YOUR DAUGHTER'S ON THE LINE. SHE'S APPARENTLY ANGERED HER PRINCIPAL...AGAIN.
Heh...I, UH, I DON'T KNOW WHERE SHE GETS IT FROM.
THIS IS GOSALYN'S FATHER.
DAD, YOU WOULDN'T BELIEVE IT! THE TEACHERS ARE REALLY WORKING FOR SUPERVILLAINS!
MY SCIENCE TEACHER SHOWED US HOW TO FREEZE SOMETHING INSTANTLY AND BREAK IT, JUST LIKE LIQUIDATOR WOULD!
I ASKED HIM ABOUT WET DOGS BUT--
GOSALYN, HONEY, NO! THAT'S A VERY PRESTIGIOUS, VERY EXPENSIVE, PRIVATE ACADEMY YOU'RE ATTENDING.
IT'S DESIGNED TO STIMULATE STUDENTS AS, UH...SPIRITED AS YOU ARE. YOU'VE GOT TO BEHAVE.
BESIDES, YOU KNOW NO SUPERVILLAINS HAVE BEEN SEEN SINCE THE CRIMEBOTS TOOK OVER.
NO NEED FOR SUPERHEROES EITHER. SO NOW I HAVE THE CHANCE TO MAKE MONEY FOR YOUR RATHER :GULP: STEEP TUITION.
SO EVERYONE SETTLES DOWN AND GETS A JOB LIKE THAT? LIKE HOW YOU'RE A...A...
...DATA ACCOUNTS NETWORKING OFFICER.
YEAH, WHATEVER THAT IS.

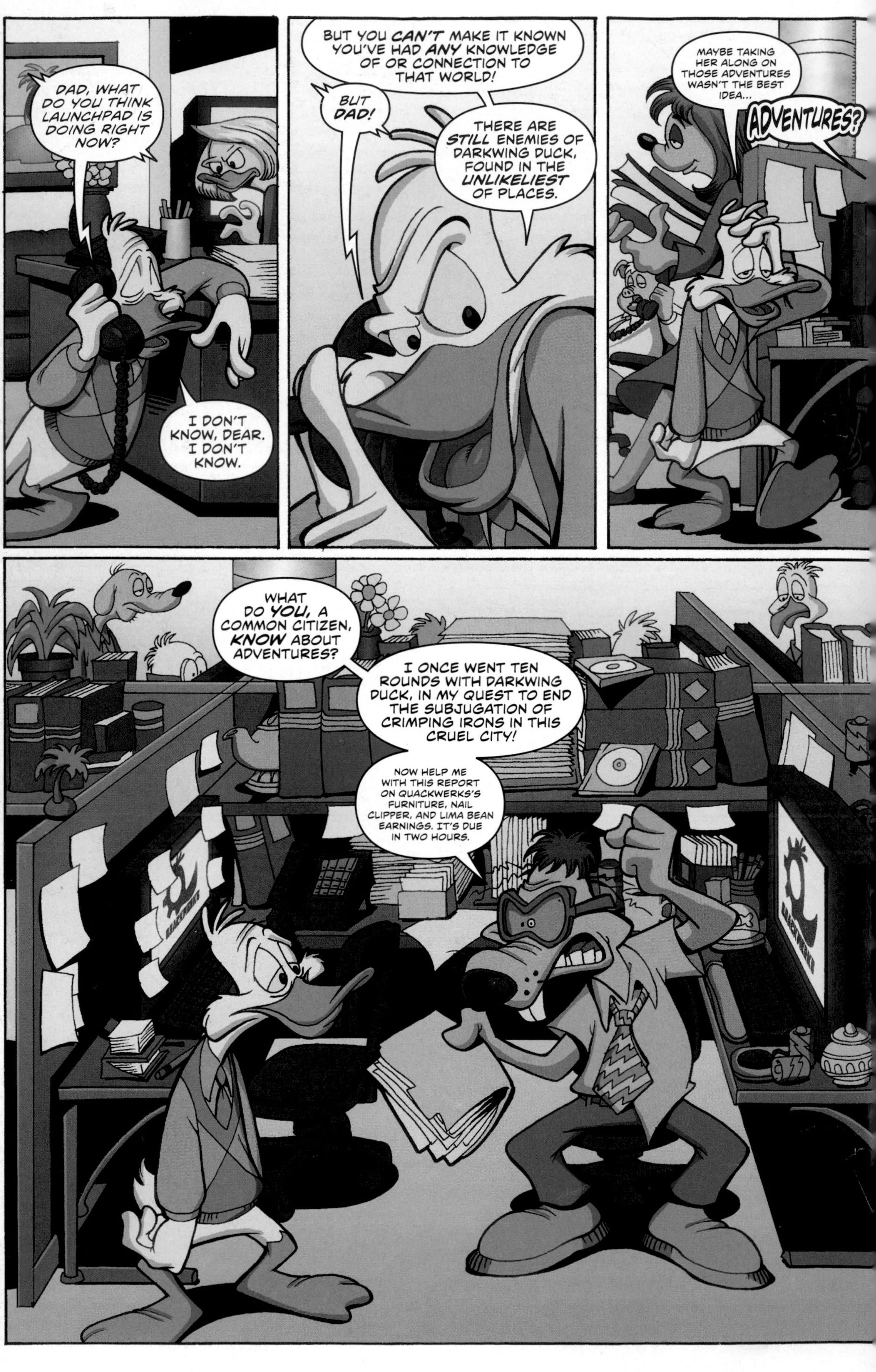
DAD, WHAT DO YOU THINK LAUNCHPAD IS DOING RIGHT NOW?
I DON'T KNOW, DEAR. I DON'T KNOW.
BUT YOU CAN'T MAKE IT KNOWN YOU'VE HAD ANY KNOWLEDGE OF OR CONNECTION TO THAT WORLD!
BUT DAD!
THERE ARE STILL ENEMIES OF DARKWING DUCK, FOUND IN THE UNLIKELIEST OF PLACES.
MAYBE TAKING HER ALONG ON THOSE ADVENTURES WASN'T THE BEST IDEA...
ADVENTURES?
WHAT DO YOU, A COMMON CITIZEN, KNOW ABOUT ADVENTURES?
I ONCE WENT TEN ROUNDS WITH DARKWING DUCK, IN MY QUEST TO END THE SUBJUGATION OF CRIMPING IRONS IN THIS CRUEL CITY!
NOW HELP ME WITH THIS REPORT ON QUACKWERKS'S FURNITURE, NAIL CLIPPER, AND LIMA BEAN EARNINGS. IT'S DUE IN TWO HOURS.

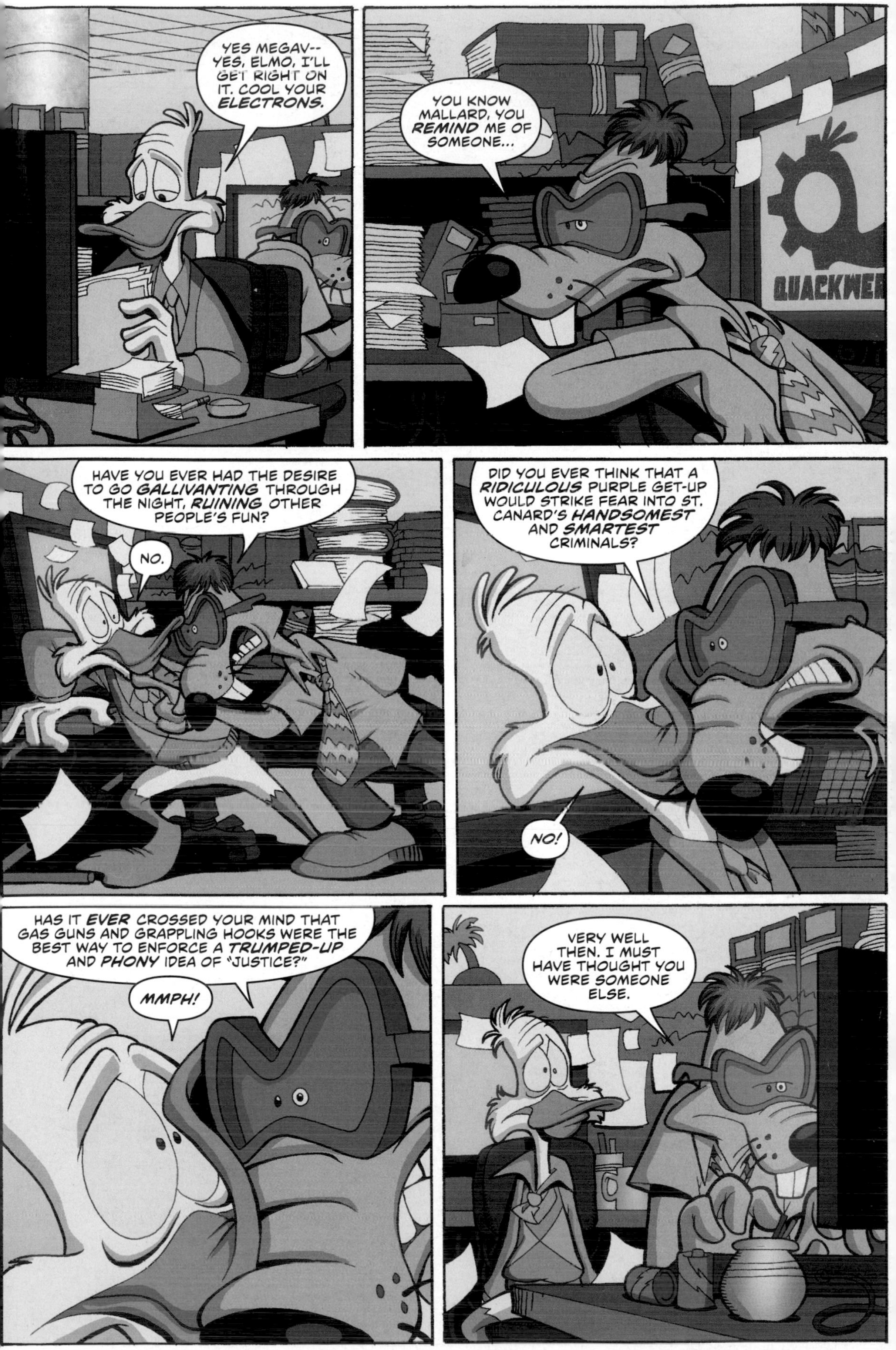
YES MEGAV-- YES, ELMO, I'LL GET RIGHT ON IT. COOL YOUR ELECTRONS.
YOU KNOW MALLARD, YOU REMIND ME OF SOMEONE...
QUACKWER
HAVE YOU EVER HAD THE DESIRE TO GO GALLIVANTING THROUGH THE NIGHT, RUINING OTHER PEOPLE'S FUN?
NO.
DID YOU EVER THINK THAT A RIDICULOUS PURPLE GET-UP WOULD STRIKE FEAR INTO ST. CANARD'S HANDSOMEST AND SMARTEST CRIMINALS?
NO!
HAS IT EVER CROSSED YOUR MIND THAT GAS GUNS AND GRAPPLING HOOKS WERE THE BEST WAY TO ENFORCE A TRUMPED-UP AND PHONY IDEA OF "JUSTICE?"
MMPH!
VERY WELL THEN. I MUST HAVE THOUGHT YOU WERE SOMEONE ELSE.

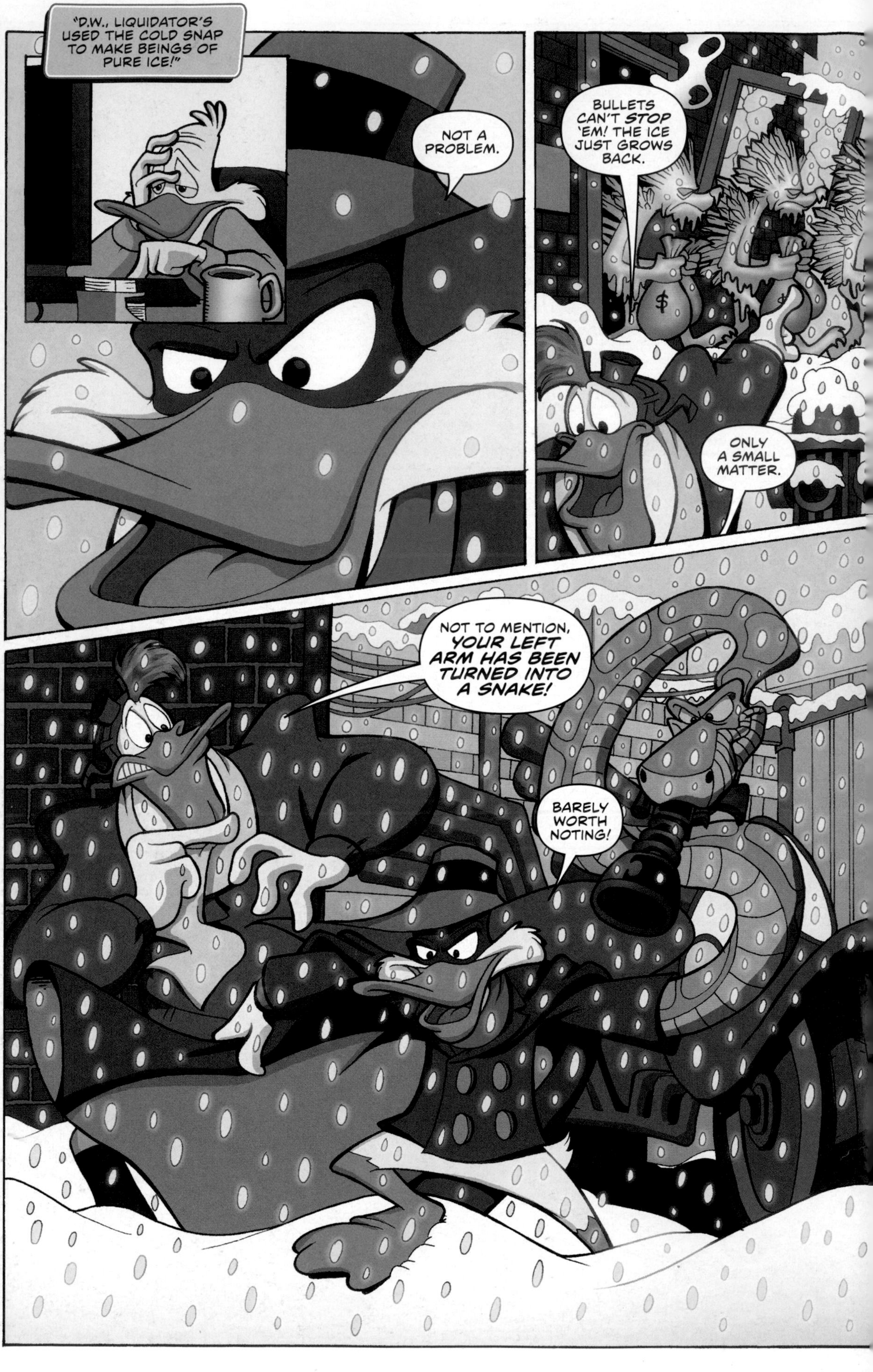
"D.W., LIQUIDATOR'S USED THE COLD SNAP TO MAKE BEINGS OF PURE ICE!"
NOT A PROBLEM.
BULLETS CAN'T STOP 'EM! THE ICE JUST GROWS BACK.
ONLY A SMALL MATTER.
NOT TO MENTION, YOUR LEFT ARM HAS BEEN TURNED INTO A SNAKE!
BARELY WORTH NOTING!

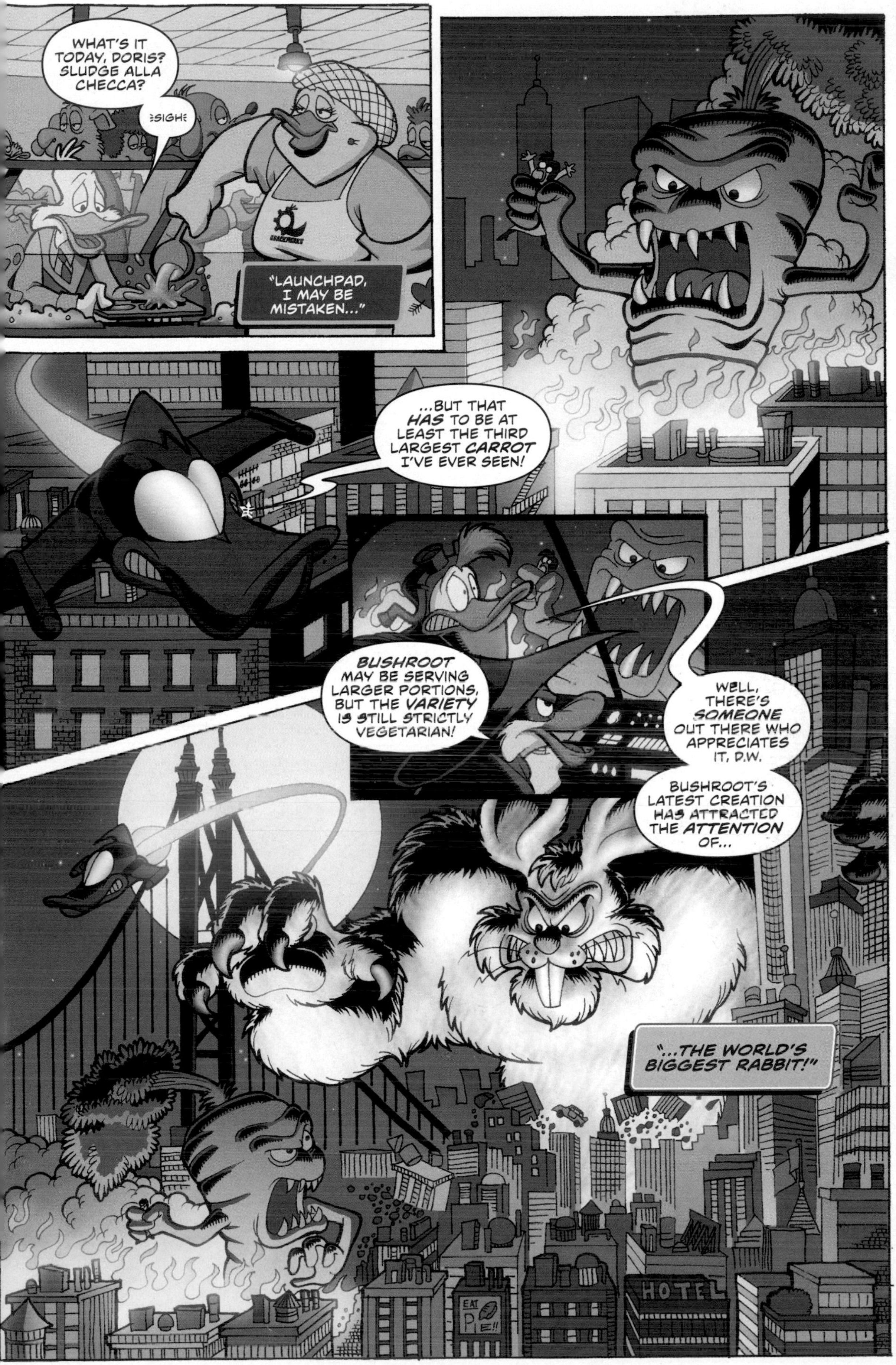
WHAT'S IT TODAY, DORIS? SLUDGE ALLA CHECCA?
SIGH
"LAUNCHPAD, I MAY BE MISTAKEN..."
...BUT THAT HAS TO BE AT LEAST THE THIRD LARGEST CARROT I'VE EVER SEEN!
BUSHROOT MAY BE SERVING LARGER PORTIONS, BUT THE VARIETY IS STILL STRICTLY VEGETARIAN!
WELL, THERE'S SOMEONE OUT THERE WHO APPRECIATES IT, D.W.
BUSHROOT'S LATEST CREATION HAS ATTRACTED THE ATTENTION OF...
"...THE WORLD'S BIGGEST RABBIT!"
HOTEL
EAT PIE!!

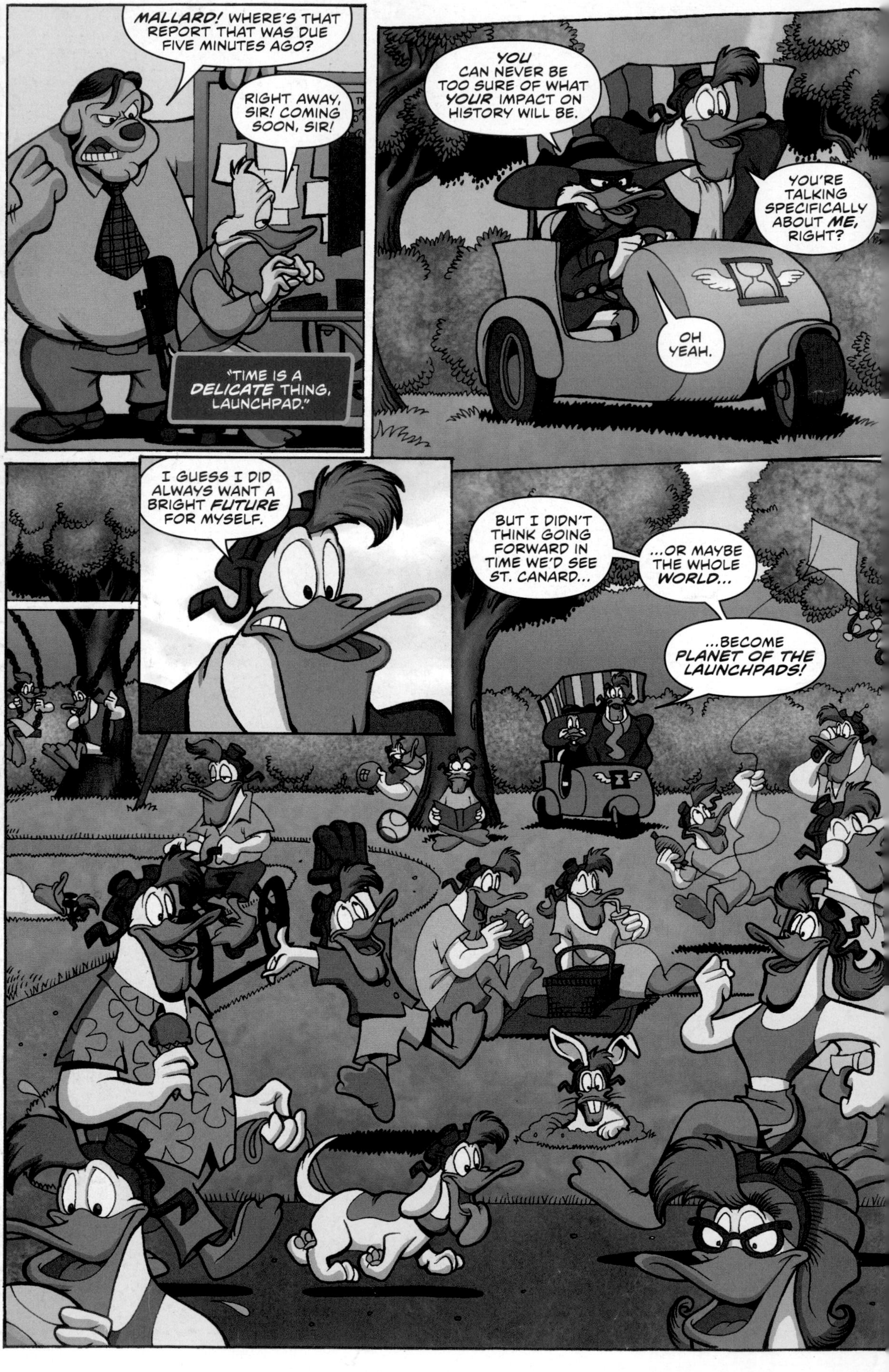
MALLARD! WHERE'S THAT REPORT THAT WAS DUE FIVE MINUTES AGO?
RIGHT AWAY, SIR! COMING SOON, SIR!
"TIME IS A DELICATE THING, LAUNCHPAD."
YOU CAN NEVER BE TOO SURE OF WHAT YOUR IMPACT ON HISTORY WILL BE.
YOU'RE TALKING SPECIFICALLY ABOUT ME, RIGHT?
OH YEAH.
I GUESS I DID ALWAYS WANT A BRIGHT FUTURE FOR MYSELF.
BUT I DIDN'T THINK GOING FORWARD IN TIME WE'D SEE ST. CANARD...
...OR MAYBE THE WHOLE WORLD...
...BECOME PLANET OF THE LAUNCHPADS!

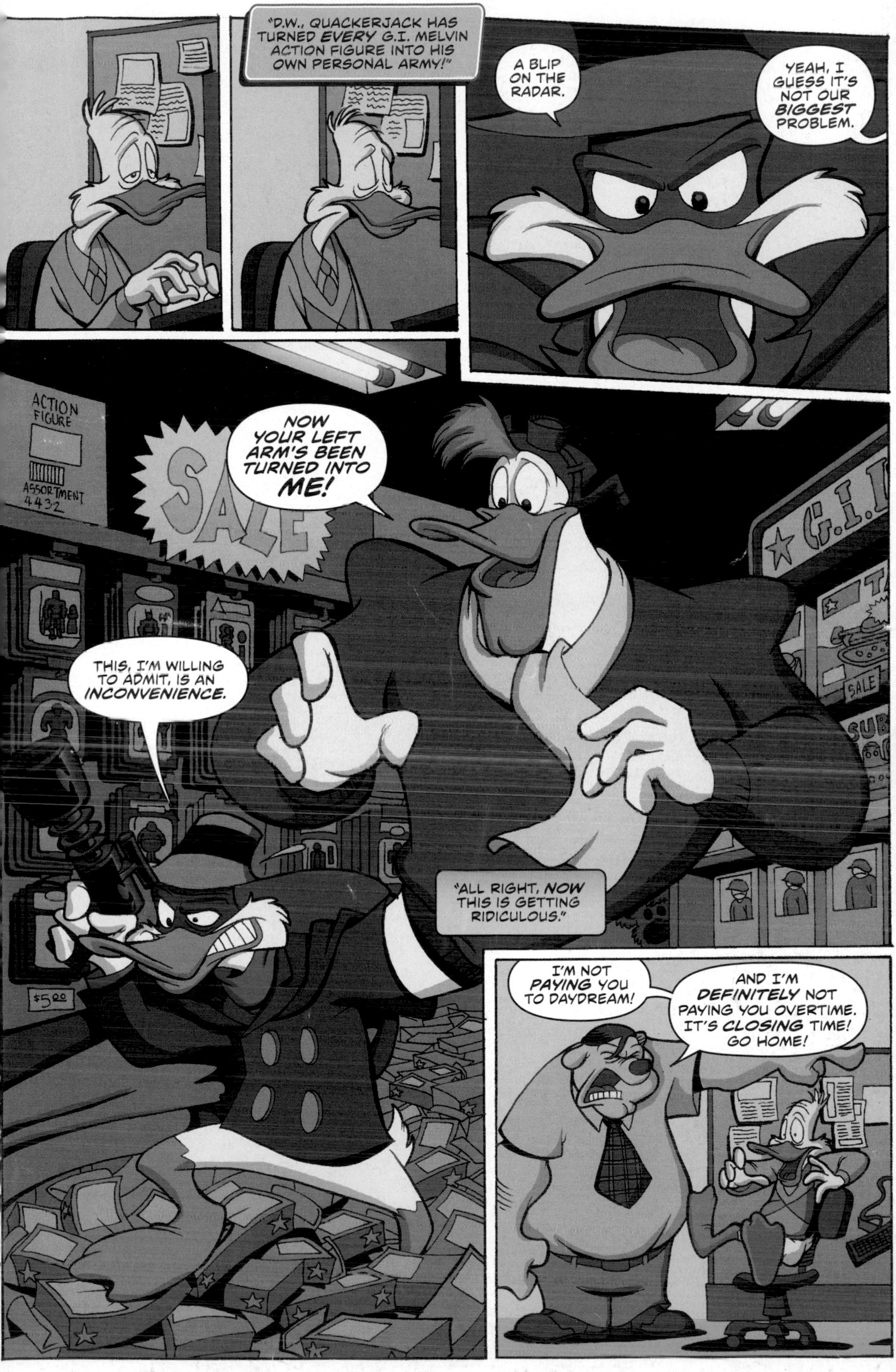
"D.W., QUACKERJACK HAS TURNED *EVERY* G.I. MELVIN ACTION FIGURE INTO HIS OWN PERSONAL ARMY!"
A BLIP ON THE RADAR.
YEAH, I GUESS IT'S NOT OUR *BIGGEST* PROBLEM.
ACTION FIGURE
ASSORTMENT 4432
SALE
NOW YOUR LEFT ARM'S BEEN TURNED INTO ***ME!***
THIS, I'M WILLING TO ADMIT, IS AN *INCONVENIENCE.*
$5.00
"ALL RIGHT, *NOW* THIS IS GETTING RIDICULOUS."
I'M NOT *PAYING* YOU TO DAYDREAM!
AND I'M *DEFINITELY* NOT PAYING YOU OVERTIME. IT'S *CLOSING* TIME! GO HOME!

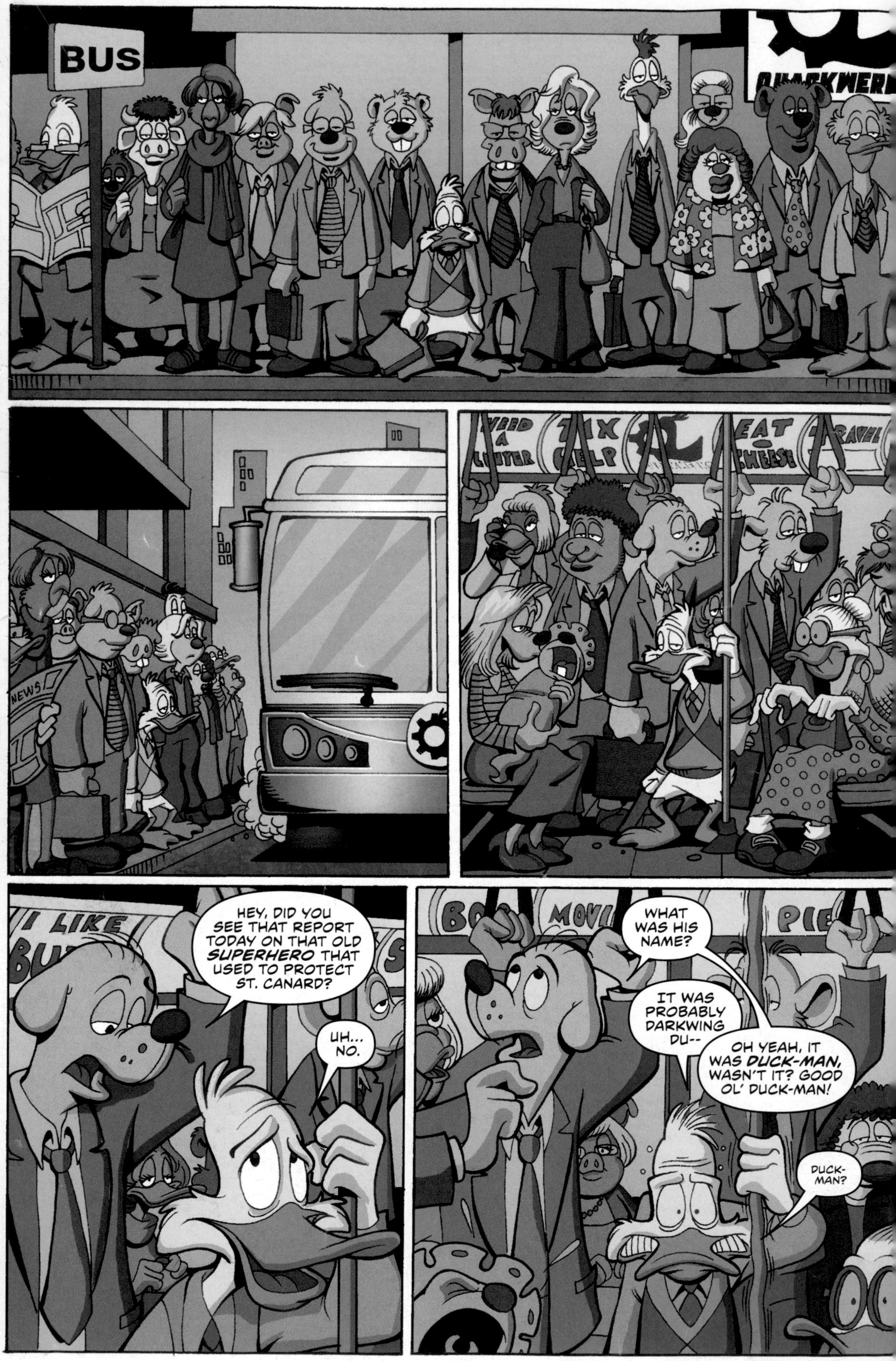
BUS
QUACKWERKS
NEWS
I LIKE
HEY, DID YOU SEE THAT REPORT TODAY ON THAT OLD SUPERHERO THAT USED TO PROTECT ST. CANARD?
UH... NO.
WHAT WAS HIS NAME?
IT WAS PROBABLY DARKWING DU--
OH YEAH, IT WAS DUCK-MAN, WASN'T IT? GOOD OL' DUCK-MAN!
DUCK-MAN?

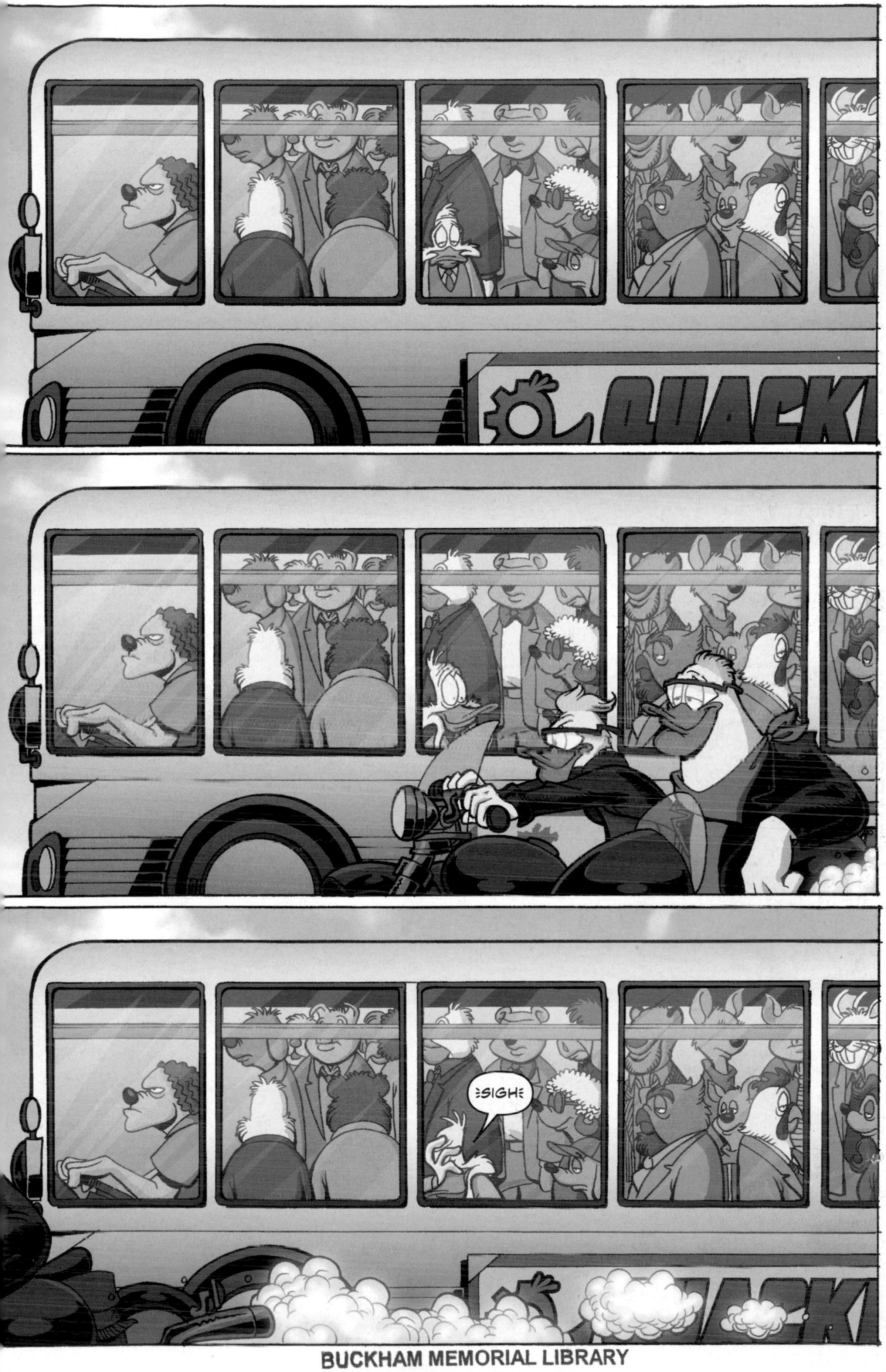
SIGH

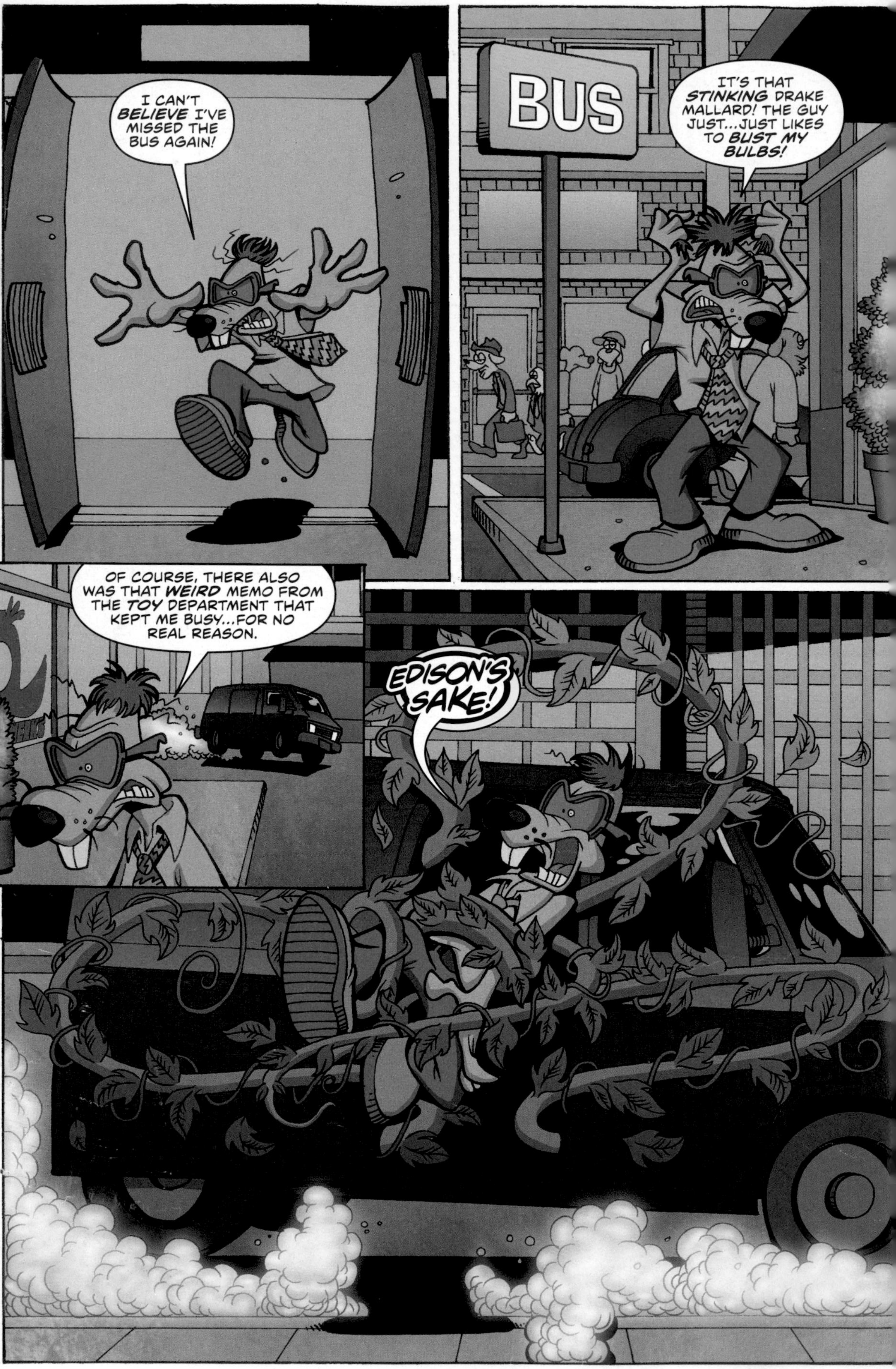
I CAN'T BELIEVE I'VE MISSED THE BUS AGAIN!
BUS
IT'S THAT STINKING DRAKE MALLARD! THE GUY JUST...JUST LIKES TO BUST MY BULBS!
OF COURSE, THERE ALSO WAS THAT WEIRD MEMO FROM THE TOY DEPARTMENT THAT KEPT ME BUSY...FOR NO REAL REASON.
EDISON'S SAKE!

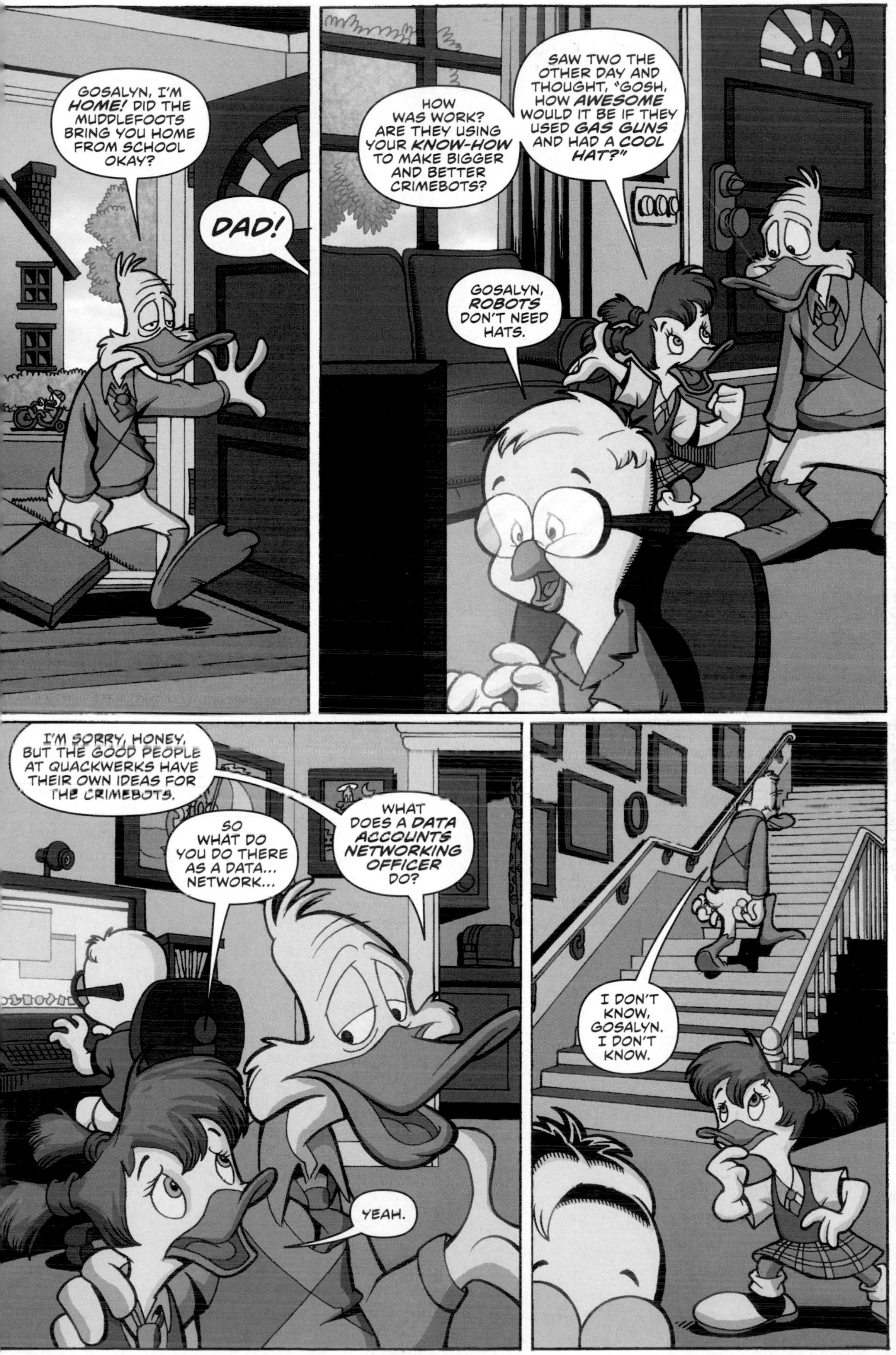
GOSALYN, I'M HOME! DID THE MUDDLEFOOTS BRING YOU HOME FROM SCHOOL OKAY?
DAD!
HOW WAS WORK? ARE THEY USING YOUR KNOW-HOW TO MAKE BIGGER AND BETTER CRIMEBOTS?
SAW TWO THE OTHER DAY AND THOUGHT, "GOSH, HOW AWESOME WOULD IT BE IF THEY USED GAS GUNS AND HAD A COOL HAT?"
GOSALYN, ROBOTS DON'T NEED HATS.
I'M SORRY, HONEY, BUT THE GOOD PEOPLE AT QUACKWERKS HAVE THEIR OWN IDEAS FOR THE CRIMEBOTS.
SO WHAT DO YOU DO THERE AS A DATA... NETWORK...
WHAT DOES A DATA ACCOUNTS NETWORKING OFFICER DO?
YEAH.
I DON'T KNOW, GOSALYN. I DON'T KNOW.

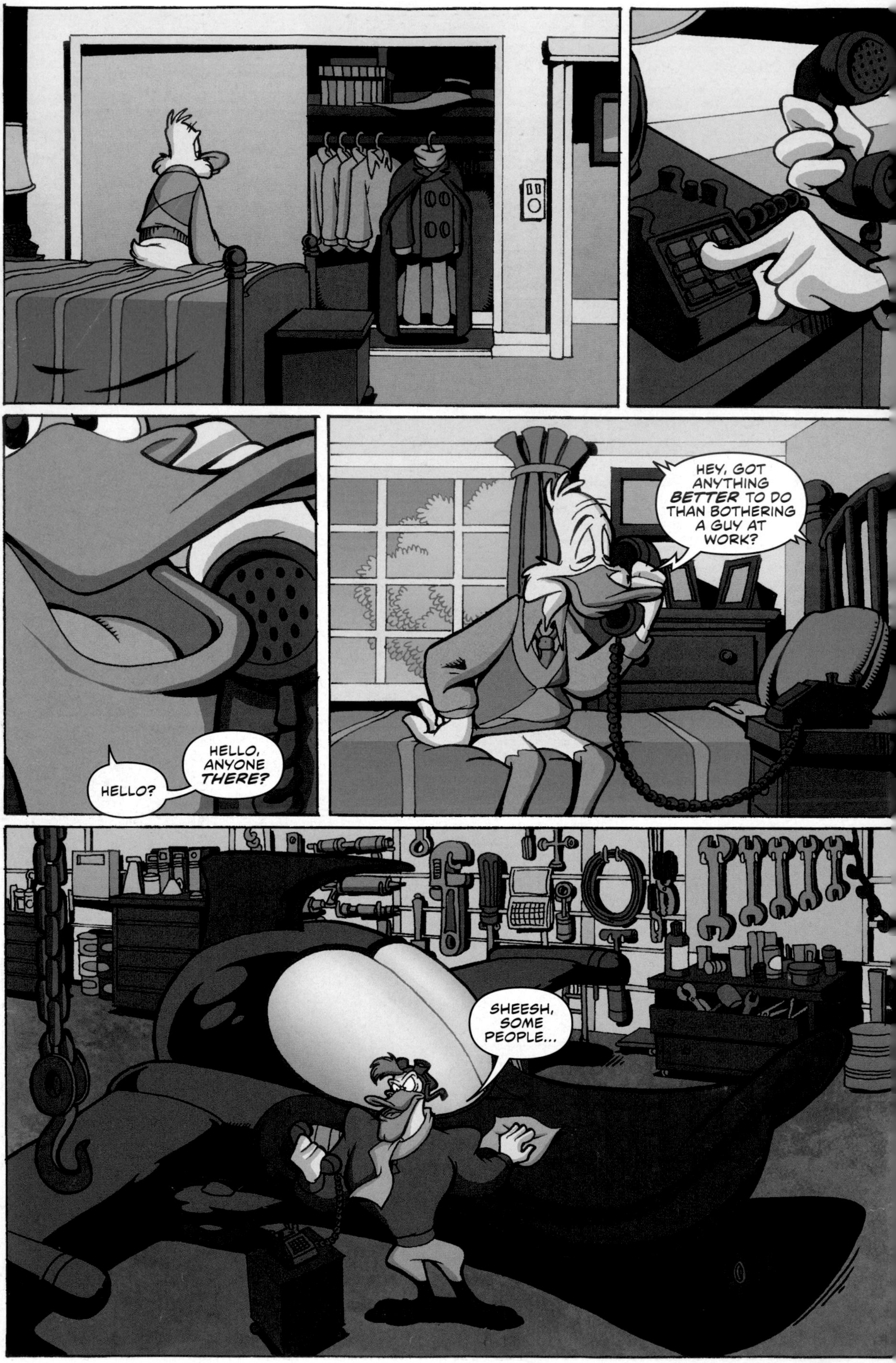
HELLO?
HELLO, ANYONE THERE?
HEY, GOT ANYTHING BETTER TO DO THAN BOTHERING A GUY AT WORK?
SHEESH, SOME PEOPLE...

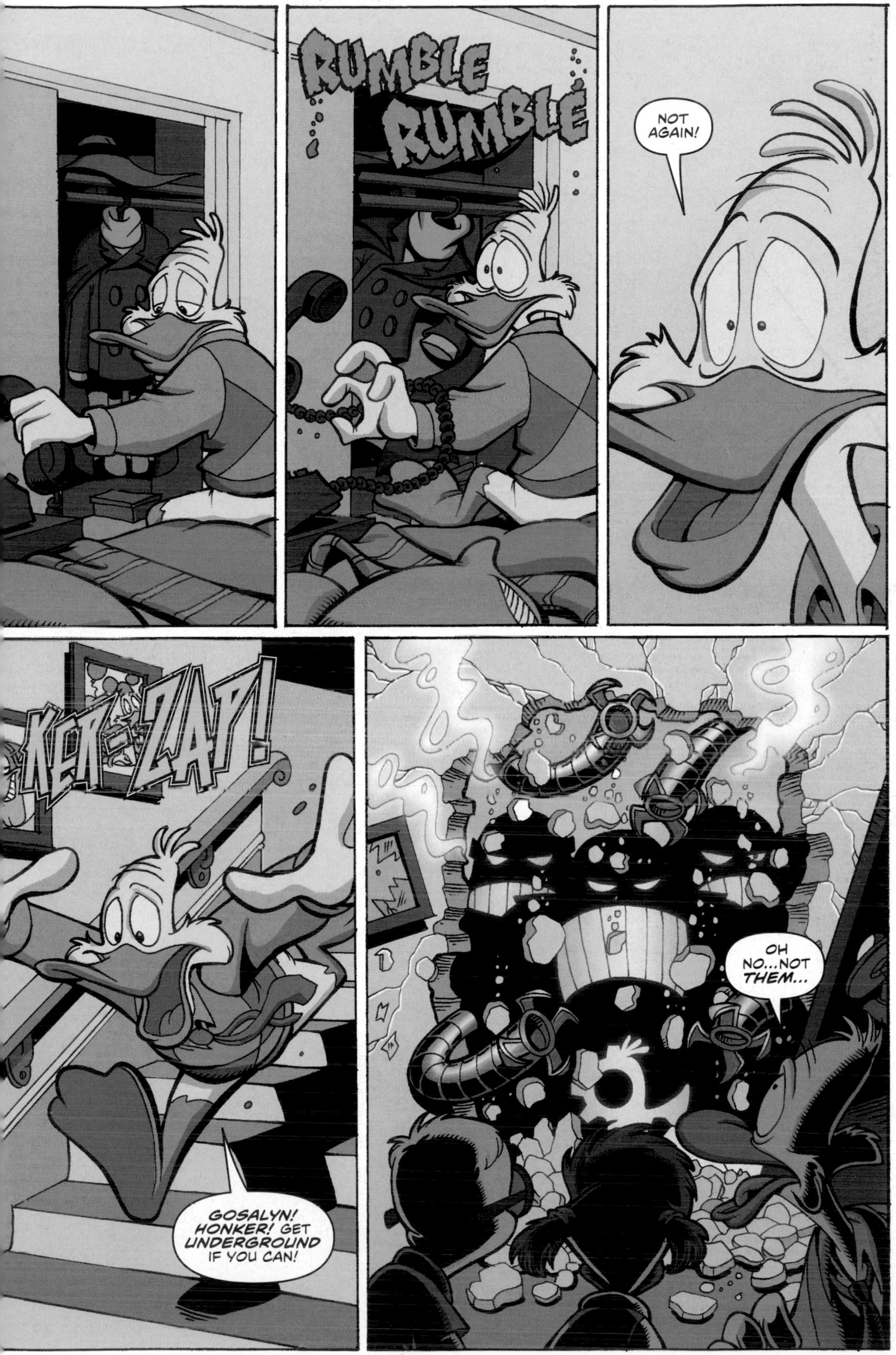
RUMBLE RUMBLE
NOT AGAIN!
KER-ZAP!
GOSALYN! HONKER! GET UNDERGROUND IF YOU CAN!
OH NO...NOT THEM...

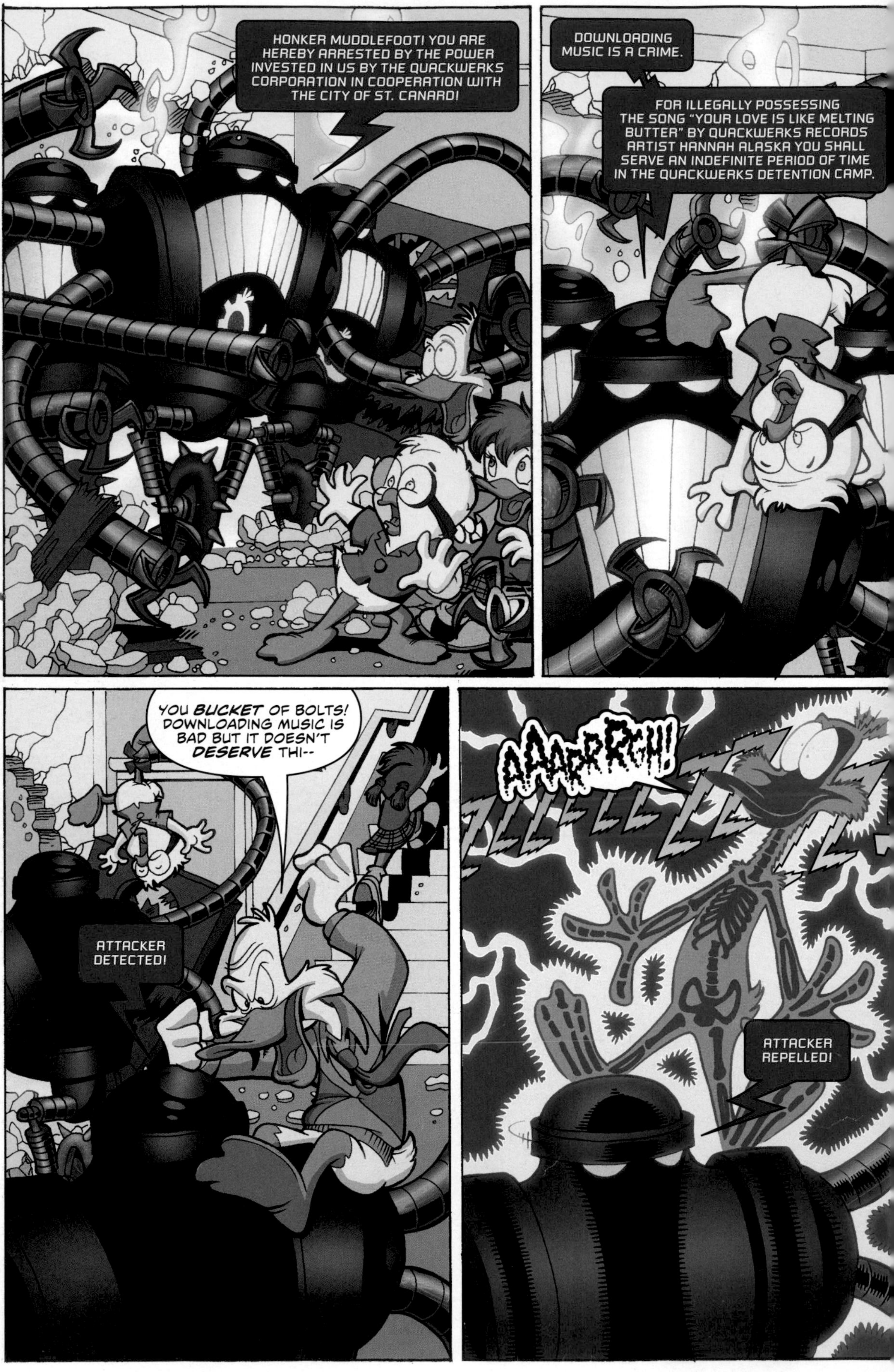
HONKER MUDDLEFOOT! YOU ARE HEREBY ARRESTED BY THE POWER INVESTED IN US BY THE QUACKWERKS CORPORATION IN COOPERATION WITH THE CITY OF ST. CANARD!
DOWNLOADING MUSIC IS A CRIME.
FOR ILLEGALLY POSSESSING THE SONG "YOUR LOVE IS LIKE MELTING BUTTER" BY QUACKWERKS RECORDS ARTIST HANNAH ALASKA YOU SHALL SERVE AN INDEFINITE PERIOD OF TIME IN THE QUACKWERKS DETENTION CAMP.
YOU BUCKET OF BOLTS! DOWNLOADING MUSIC IS BAD BUT IT DOESN'T DESERVE THI--
ATTACKER DETECTED!
AAAARRRGH!
ATTACKER REPELLED!

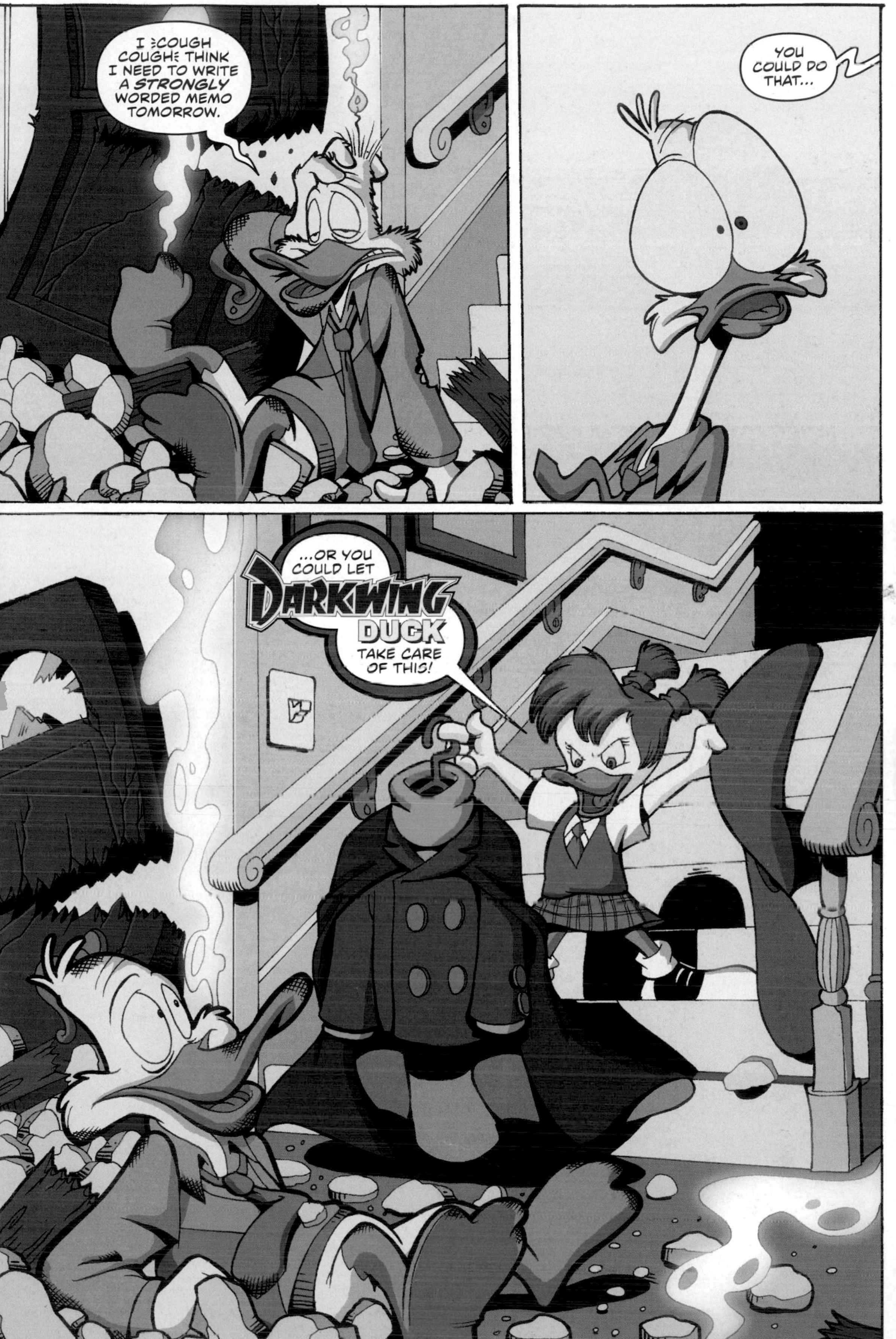
I *COUGH COUGH* THINK I NEED TO WRITE A STRONGLY WORDED MEMO TOMORROW.
YOU COULD DO THAT...
...OR YOU COULD LET DARKWING DUCK TAKE CARE OF THIS!

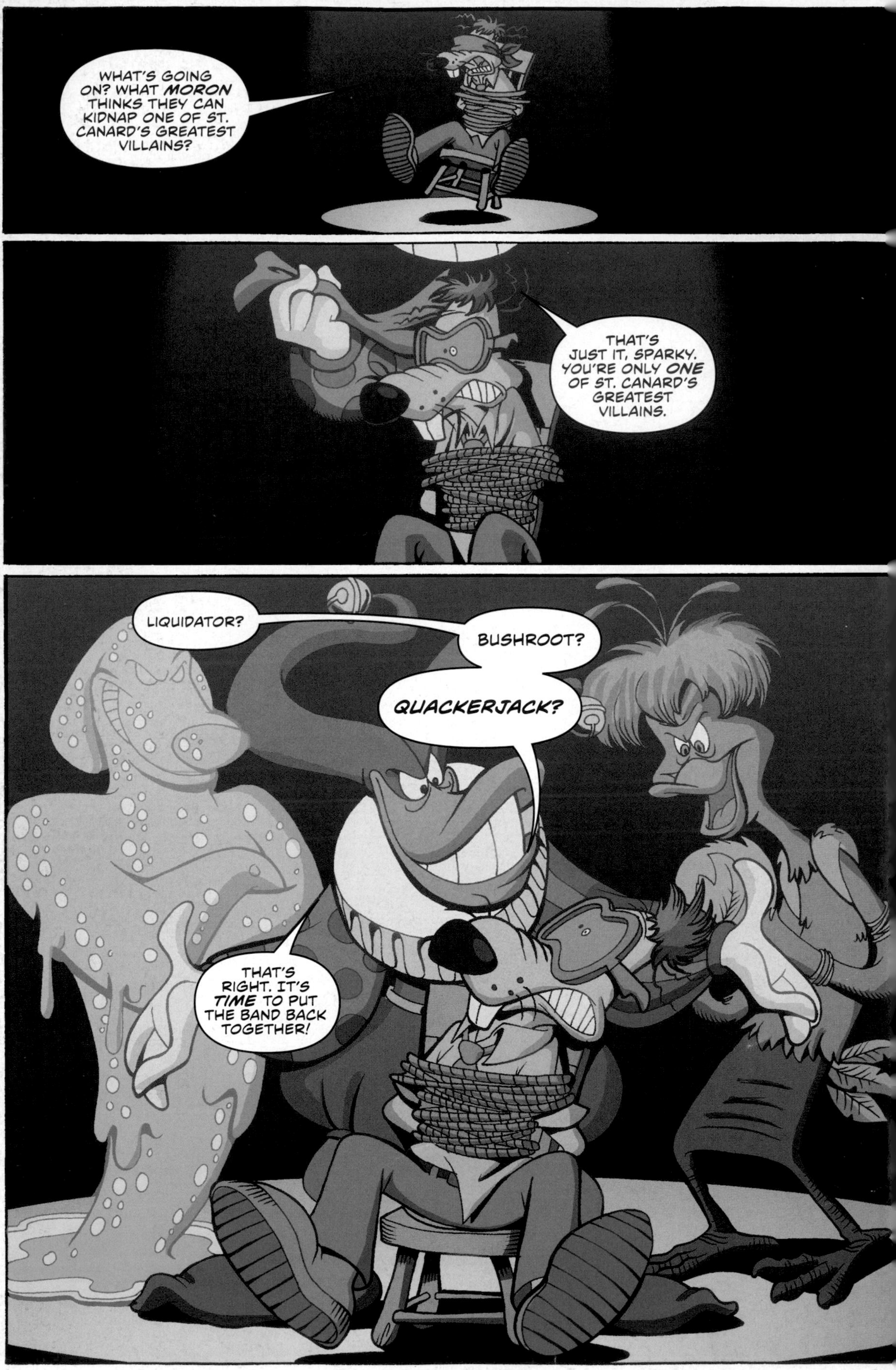
WHAT'S GOING ON? WHAT MORON THINKS THEY CAN KIDNAP ONE OF ST. CANARD'S GREATEST VILLAINS?
THAT'S JUST IT, SPARKY. YOU'RE ONLY ONE OF ST. CANARD'S GREATEST VILLAINS.
LIQUIDATOR?
BUSHROOT?
QUACKERJACK?
THAT'S RIGHT. IT'S TIME TO PUT THE BAND BACK TOGETHER!

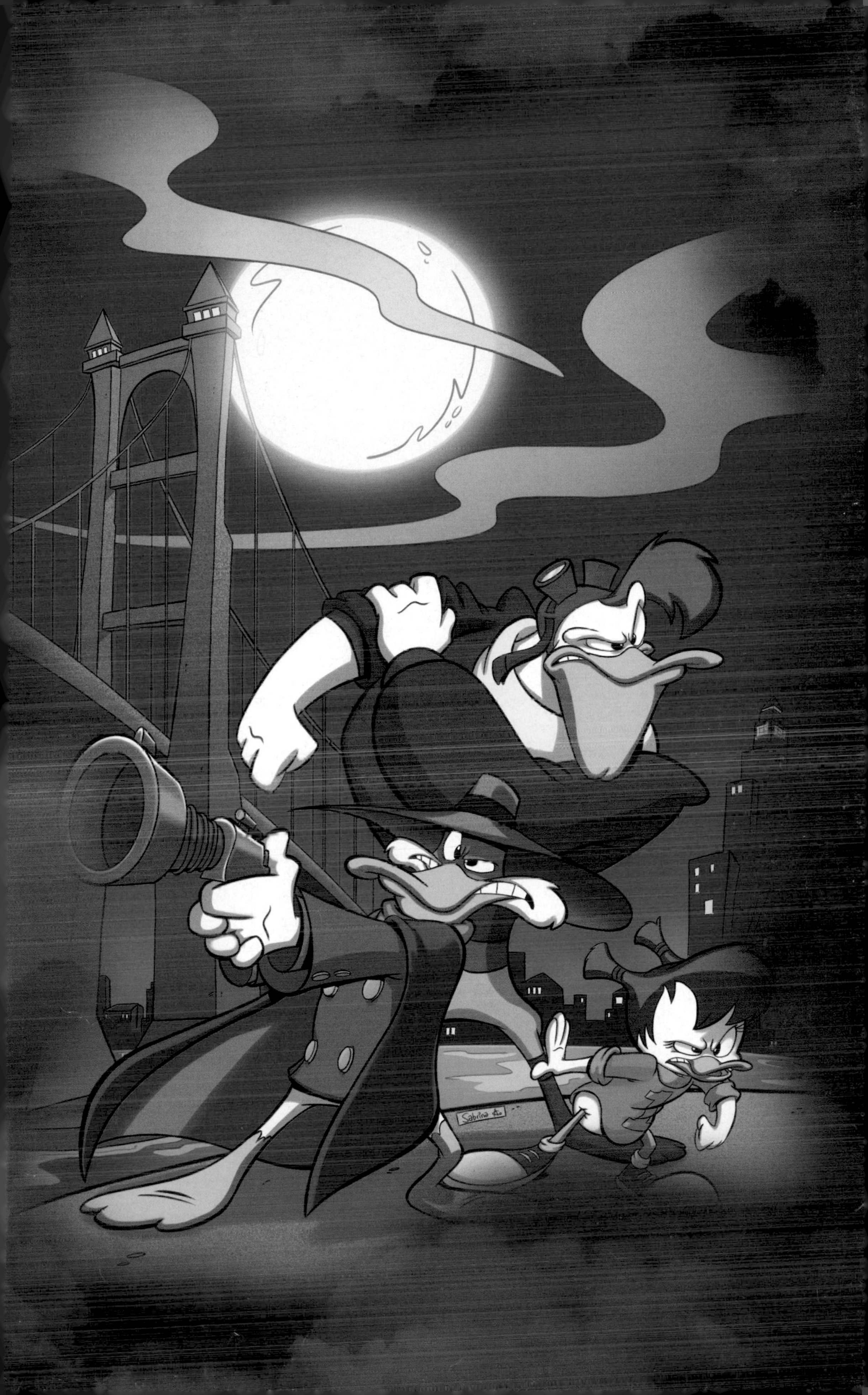
Sabrina

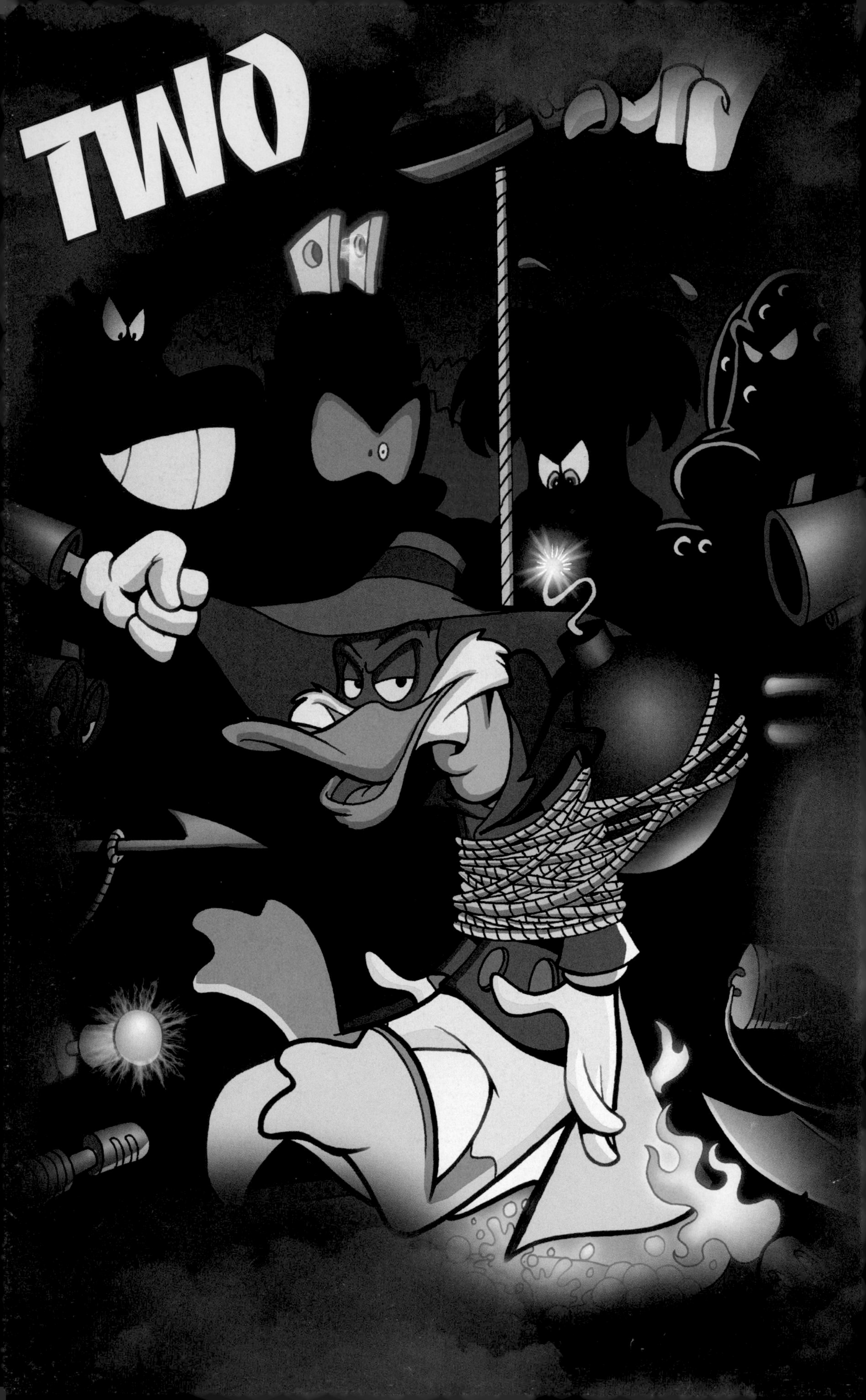
TWO

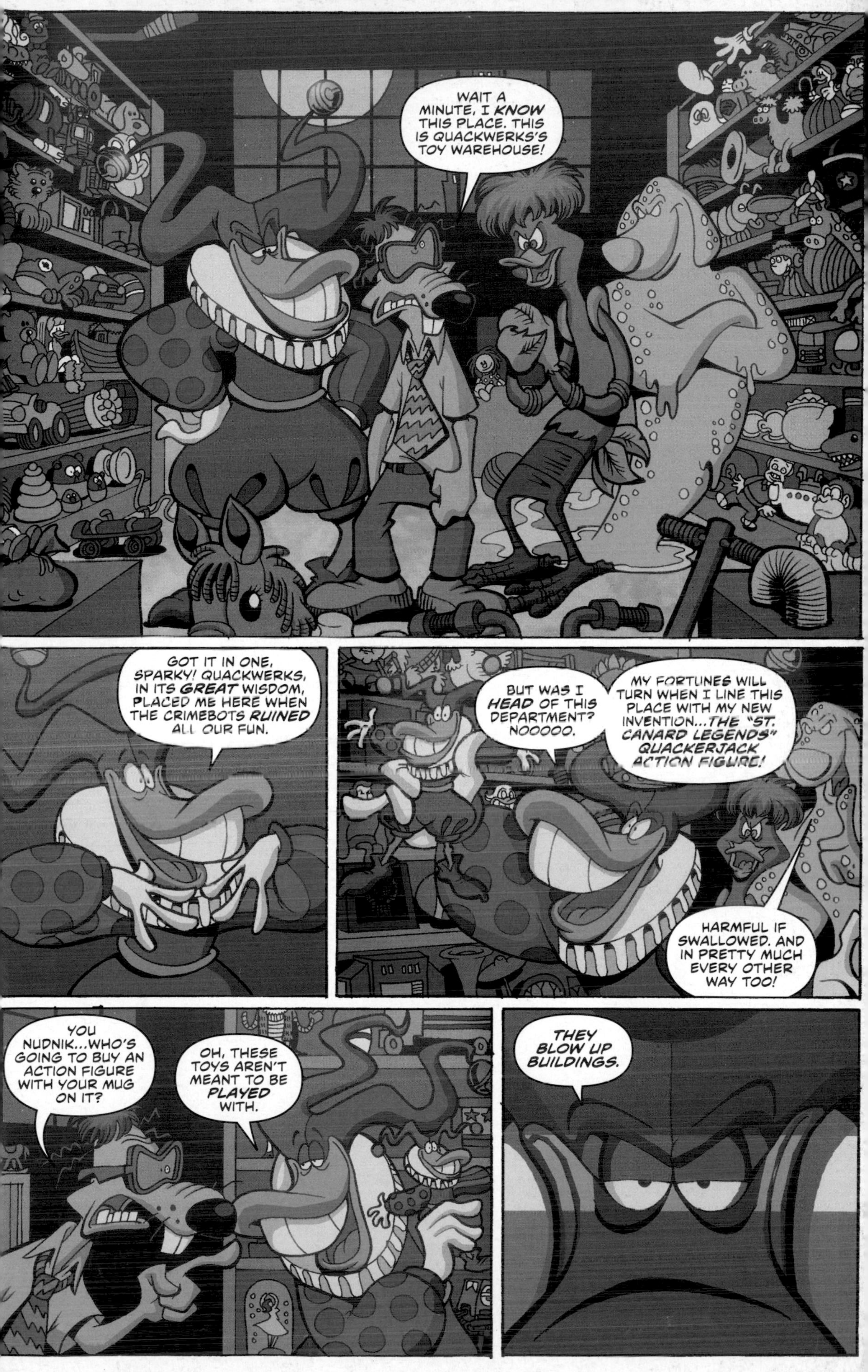
WAIT A MINUTE, I KNOW THIS PLACE. THIS IS QUACKWERKS'S TOY WAREHOUSE!
GOT IT IN ONE, SPARKY! QUACKWERKS, IN ITS GREAT WISDOM, PLACED ME HERE WHEN THE CRIMEBOTS RUINED ALL OUR FUN.
BUT WAS I HEAD OF THIS DEPARTMENT? NOOOOO.
MY FORTUNES WILL TURN WHEN I LINE THIS PLACE WITH MY NEW INVENTION...THE "ST. CANARD LEGENDS" QUACKERJACK ACTION FIGURE!
HARMFUL IF SWALLOWED. AND IN PRETTY MUCH EVERY OTHER WAY TOO!
YOU NUDNIK...WHO'S GOING TO BUY AN ACTION FIGURE WITH YOUR MUG ON IT?
OH, THESE TOYS AREN'T MEANT TO BE PLAYED WITH.
THEY BLOW UP BUILDINGS.

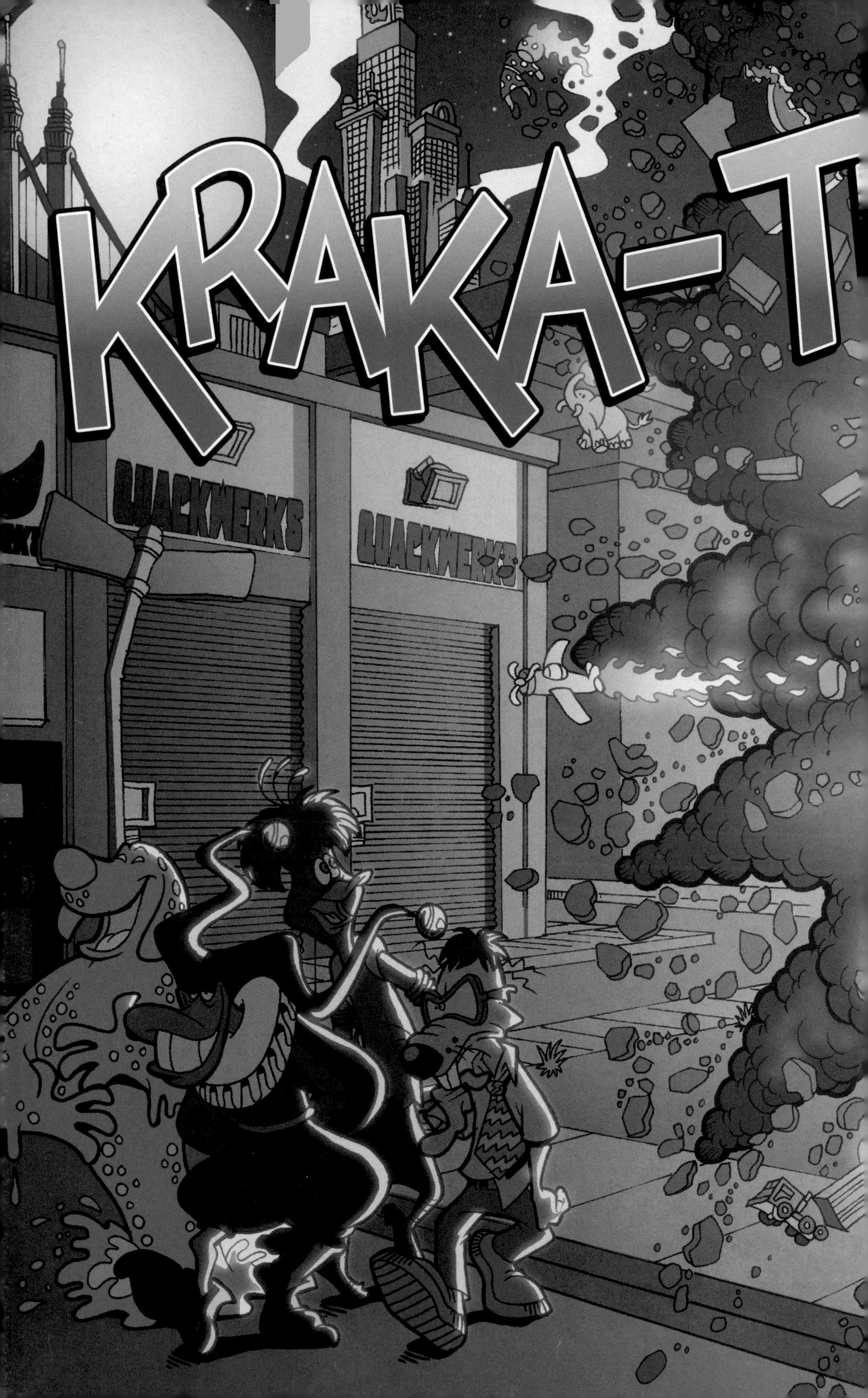
KRAKA-T
QUACKWERKS
QUACKWERKS

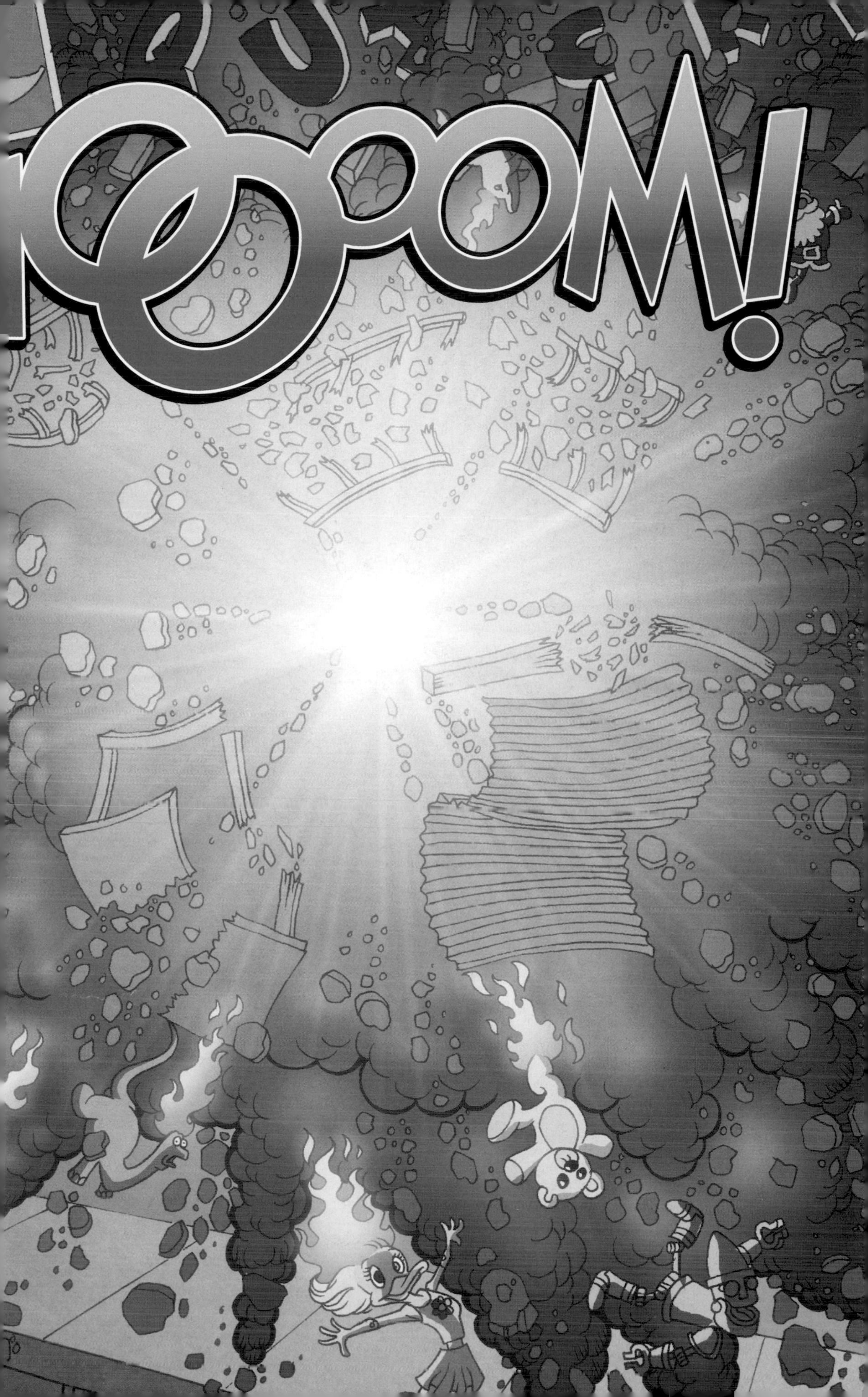
OOOM!

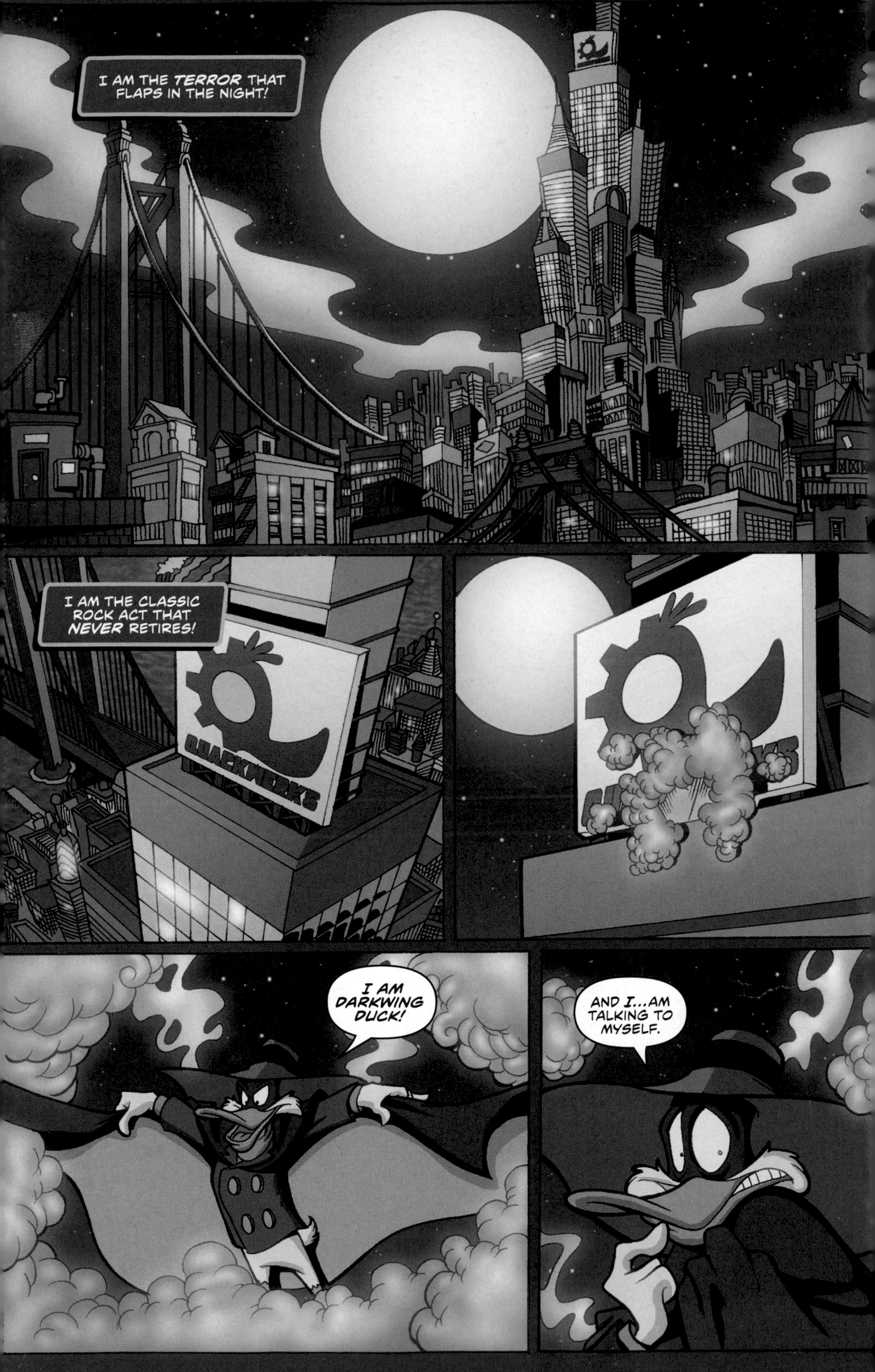
I AM THE *TERROR* THAT FLAPS IN THE NIGHT!
I AM THE CLASSIC ROCK ACT THAT *NEVER* RETIRES!
QUACKWERKS
I AM DARKWING DUCK!
AND *I*...AM TALKING TO MYSELF.

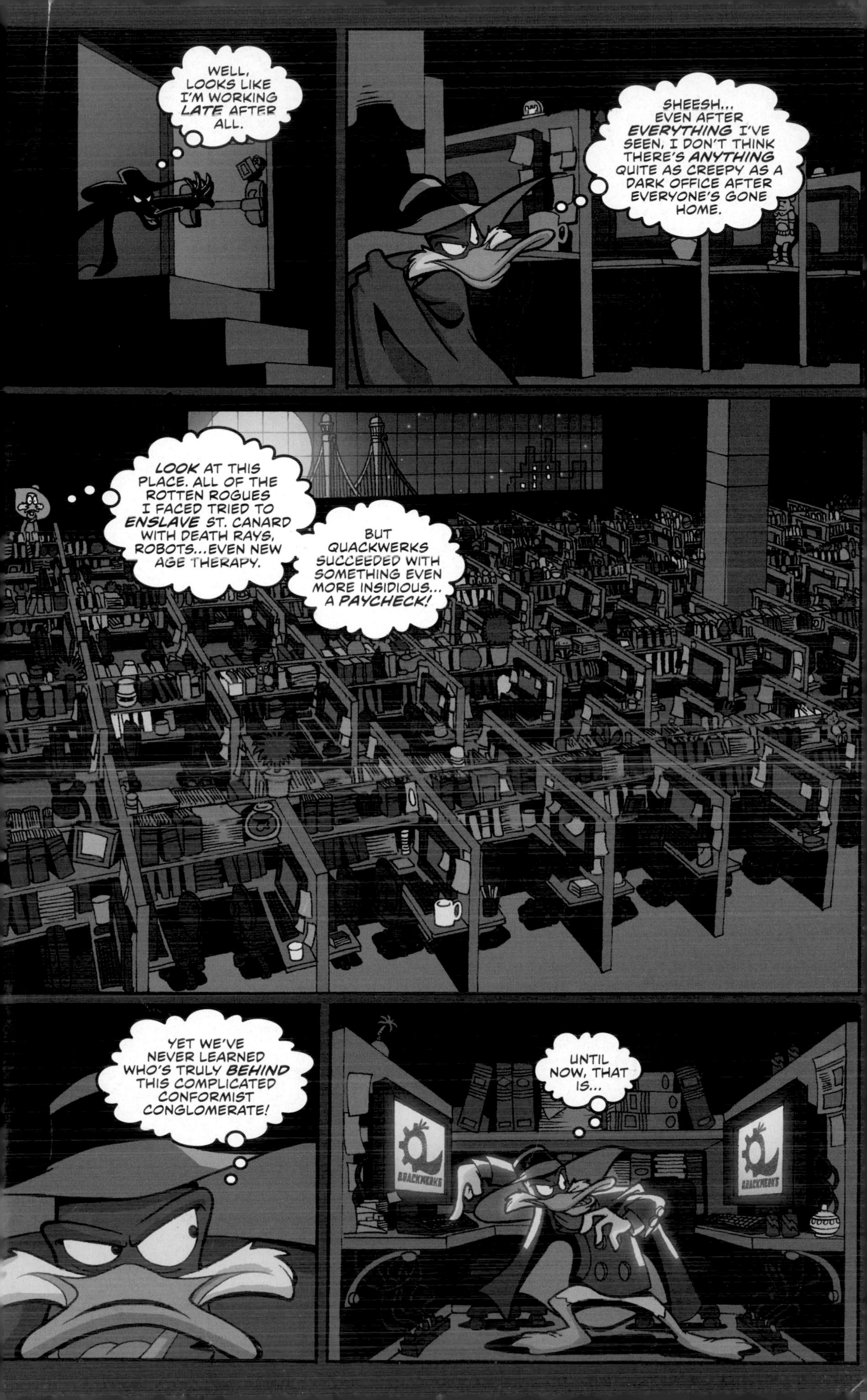
WELL, LOOKS LIKE I'M WORKING *LATE* AFTER ALL.
SHEESH... EVEN AFTER *EVERYTHING* I'VE SEEN, I DON'T THINK THERE'S *ANYTHING* QUITE AS CREEPY AS A DARK OFFICE AFTER EVERYONE'S GONE HOME.
LOOK AT THIS PLACE. ALL OF THE ROTTEN ROGUES I FACED TRIED TO *ENSLAVE* ST. CANARD WITH DEATH RAYS, ROBOTS...EVEN NEW AGE THERAPY.
BUT QUACKWERKS SUCCEEDED WITH SOMETHING EVEN MORE INSIDIOUS... A *PAYCHECK!*
YET WE'VE NEVER LEARNED WHO'S TRULY *BEHIND* THIS COMPLICATED CONFORMIST CONGLOMERATE!
UNTIL NOW, THAT IS...
QUACKWERKS
QUACKWERKS

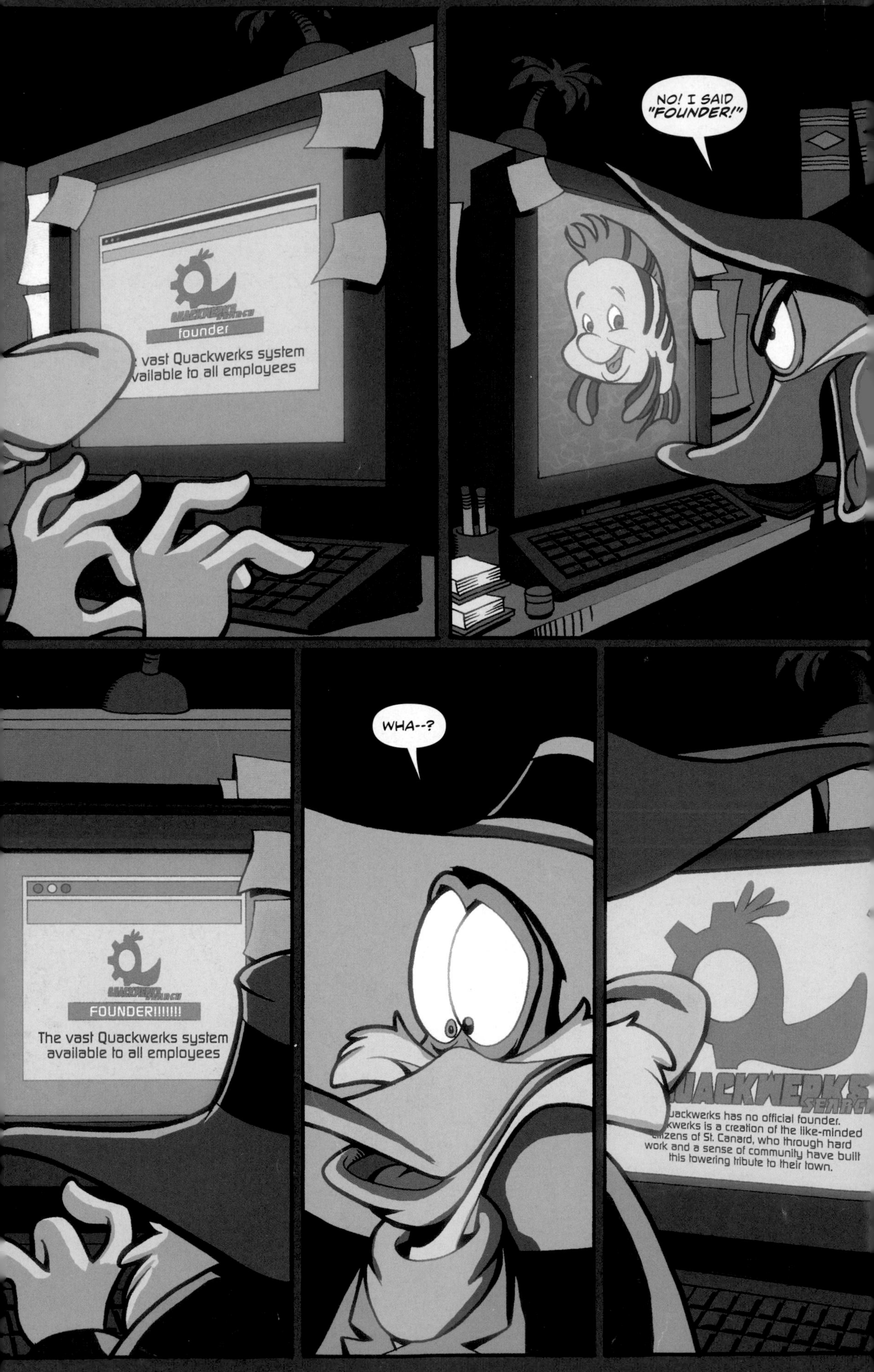
founder
vast Quackwerks system
vailable to all employees
NO! I SAID "FOUNDER!"
FOUNDER!!!!!!!
The vast Quackwerks system available to all employees
WHA--?
UACKWERKS
uackwerks has no official founder.
kwerks is a creation of the like-minded
izens of St. Canard, who through hard
work and a sense of community have built
this towering tribute to their town.

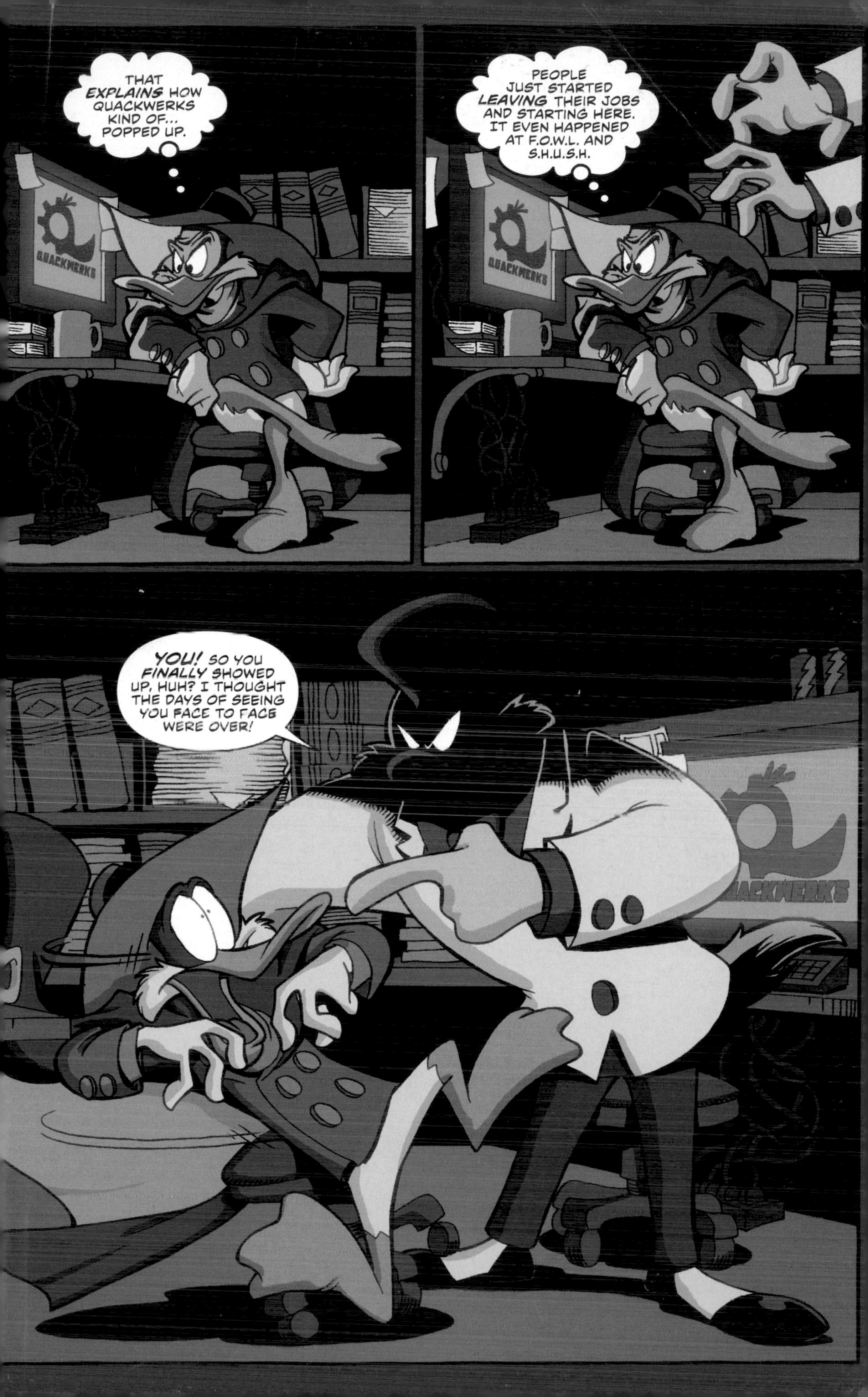

THAT EXPLAINS HOW QUACKWERKS KIND OF... POPPED UP.
QUACKWERKS
PEOPLE JUST STARTED LEAVING THEIR JOBS AND STARTING HERE. IT EVEN HAPPENED AT F.O.W.L. AND S.H.U.S.H.
QUACKWERKS
YOU! SO YOU FINALLY SHOWED UP, HUH? I THOUGHT THE DAYS OF SEEING YOU FACE TO FACE WERE OVER!

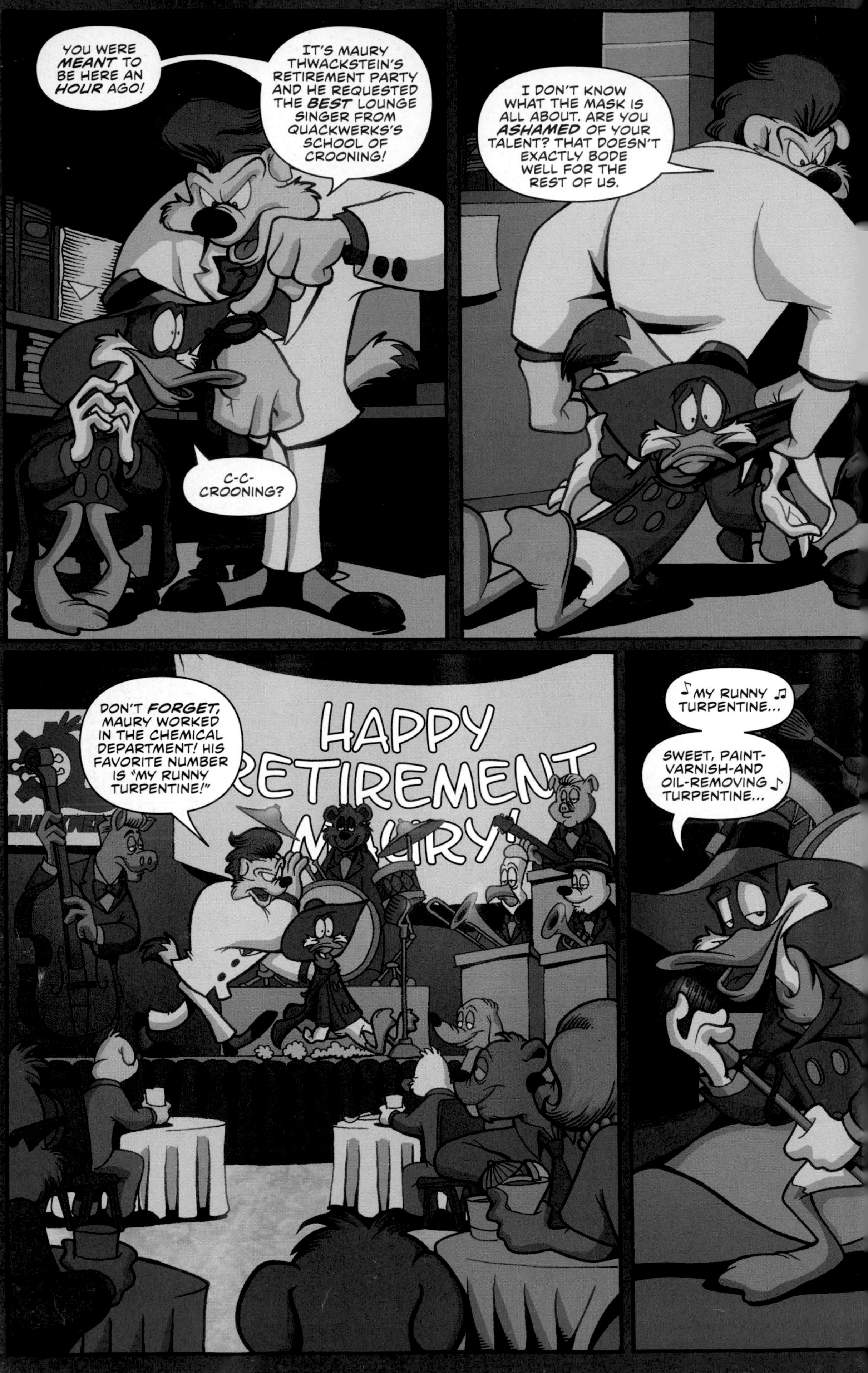
YOU WERE MEANT TO BE HERE AN HOUR AGO!
IT'S MAURY THWACKSTEIN'S RETIREMENT PARTY AND HE REQUESTED THE BEST LOUNGE SINGER FROM QUACKWERKS'S SCHOOL OF CROONING!
C-C-CROONING?
I DON'T KNOW WHAT THE MASK IS ALL ABOUT. ARE YOU ASHAMED OF YOUR TALENT? THAT DOESN'T EXACTLY BODE WELL FOR THE REST OF US.
DON'T FORGET, MAURY WORKED IN THE CHEMICAL DEPARTMENT! HIS FAVORITE NUMBER IS "MY RUNNY TURPENTINE!"
HAPPY RETIREMENT MAURY!
♪ MY RUNNY ♫ TURPENTINE...
SWEET, PAINT-VARNISH-AND OIL-REMOVING ♪ TURPENTINE...

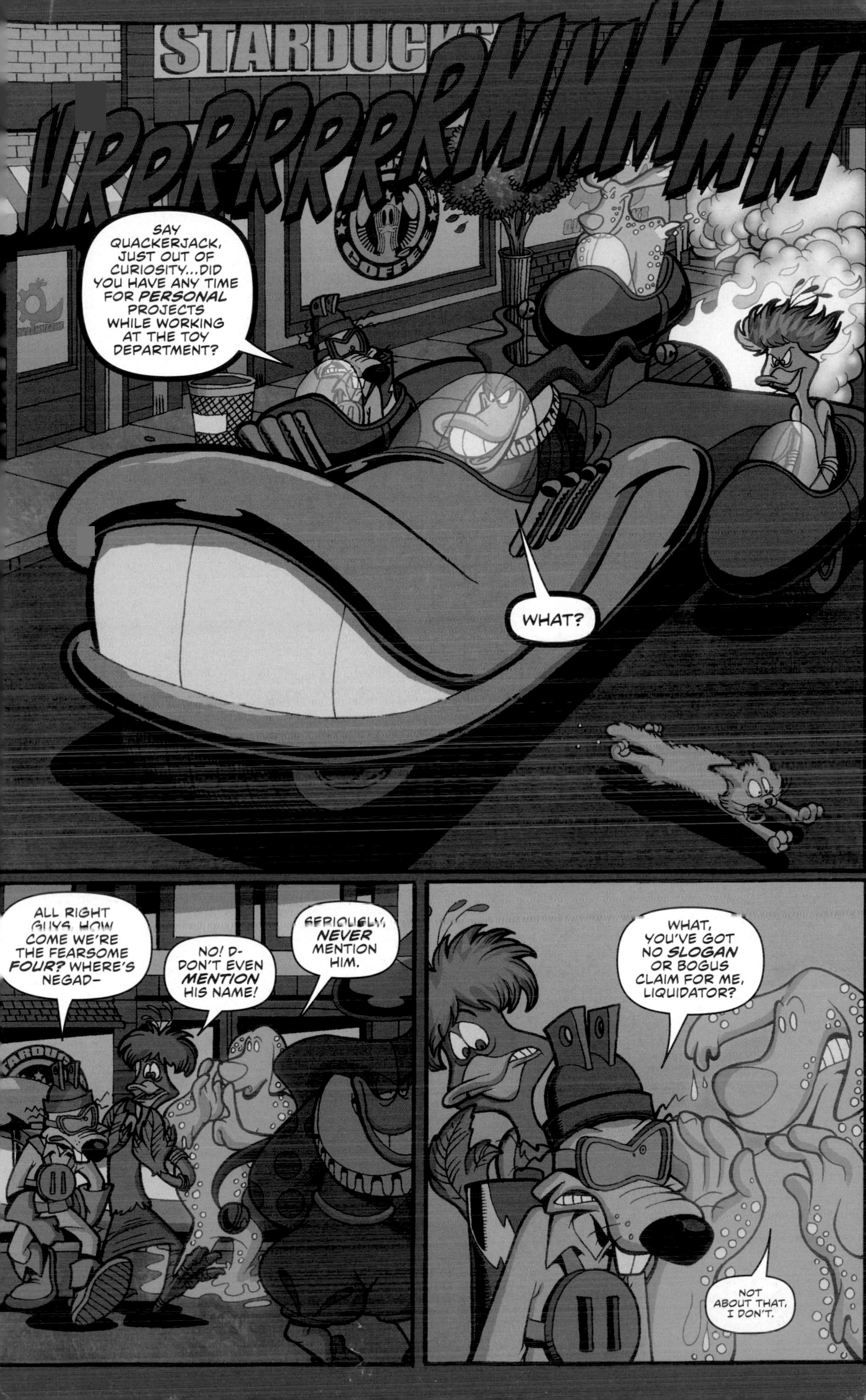
STARDUCKS
VRRRRRRRMMMMMM
SAY QUACKERJACK, JUST OUT OF CURIOSITY...DID YOU HAVE ANY TIME FOR PERSONAL PROJECTS WHILE WORKING AT THE TOY DEPARTMENT?
WHAT?
ALL RIGHT GUYS, HOW COME WE'RE THE FEARSOME FOUR? WHERE'S NEGAD–
NO! D-DON'T EVEN MENTION HIS NAME!
SERIOUSLY, NEVER MENTION HIM.
WHAT, YOU'VE GOT NO SLOGAN OR BOGUS CLAIM FOR ME, LIQUIDATOR?
NOT ABOUT THAT, I DON'T.

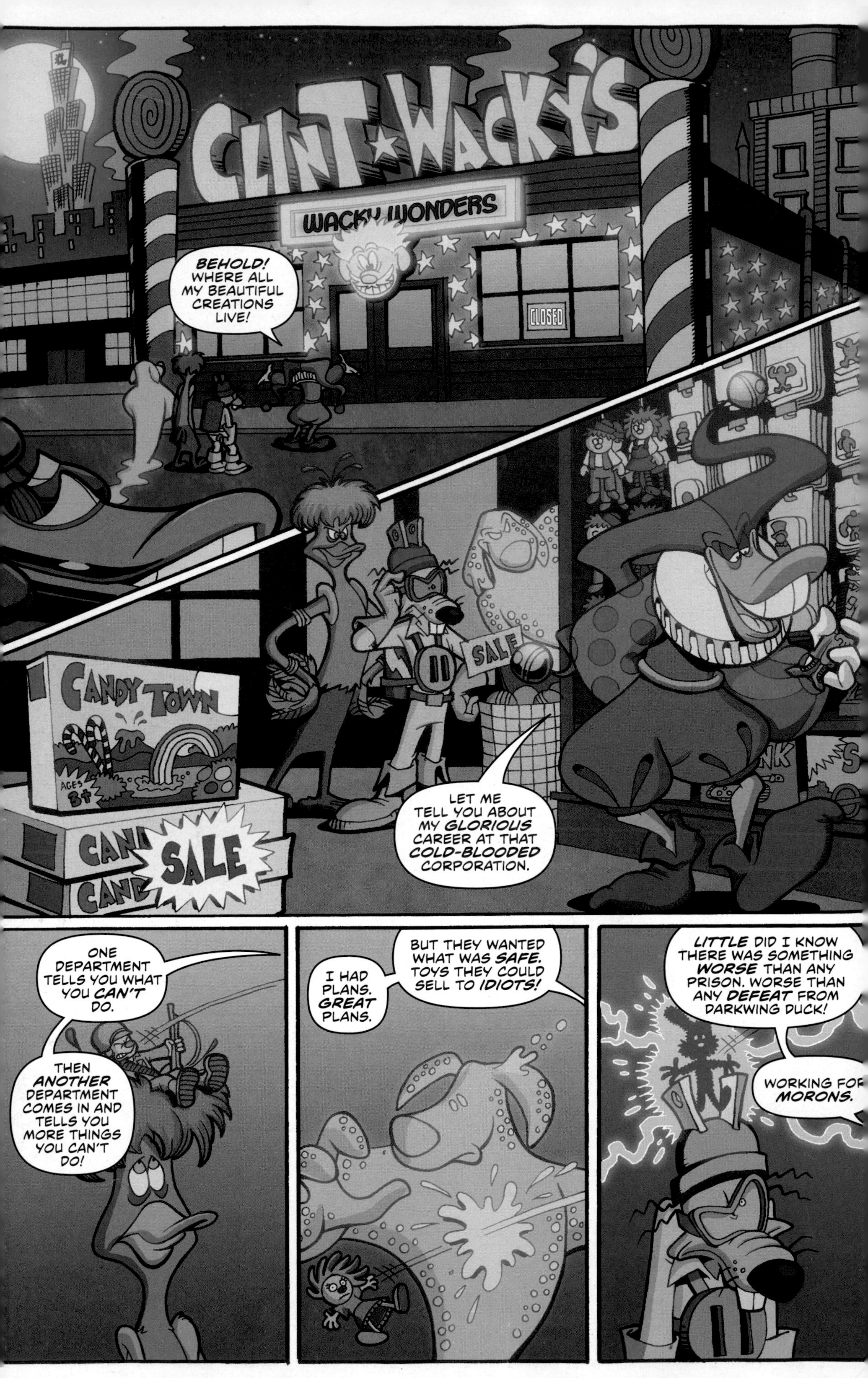

CLINT★WACKY'S
WACKY WONDERS
CLOSED
BEHOLD! WHERE ALL MY BEAUTIFUL CREATIONS LIVE!
CANDY TOWN
AGES 8+
SALE
SALE
LET ME TELL YOU ABOUT MY GLORIOUS CAREER AT THAT COLD-BLOODED CORPORATION.
ONE DEPARTMENT TELLS YOU WHAT YOU CAN'T DO.
THEN ANOTHER DEPARTMENT COMES IN AND TELLS YOU MORE THINGS YOU CAN'T DO!
I HAD PLANS. GREAT PLANS.
BUT THEY WANTED WHAT WAS SAFE. TOYS THEY COULD SELL TO IDIOTS!
LITTLE DID I KNOW THERE WAS SOMETHING WORSE THAN ANY PRISON. WORSE THAN ANY DEFEAT FROM DARKWING DUCK!
WORKING FOR MORONS.

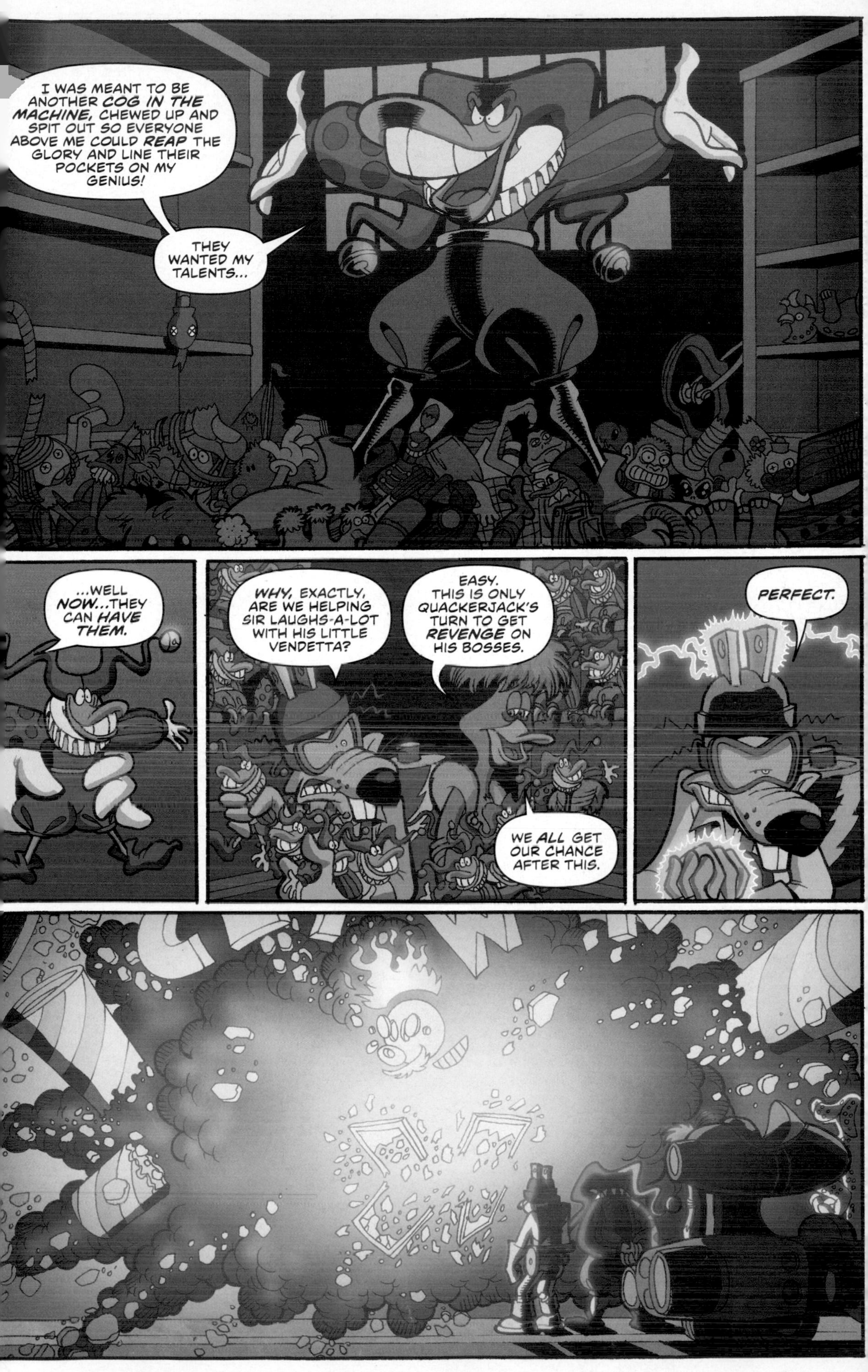

I WAS MEANT TO BE ANOTHER COG IN THE MACHINE, CHEWED UP AND SPIT OUT SO EVERYONE ABOVE ME COULD REAP THE GLORY AND LINE THEIR POCKETS ON MY GENIUS!
THEY WANTED MY TALENTS...
...WELL NOW...THEY CAN HAVE THEM.
WHY, EXACTLY, ARE WE HELPING SIR LAUGHS-A-LOT WITH HIS LITTLE VENDETTA?
EASY. THIS IS ONLY QUACKERJACK'S TURN TO GET REVENGE ON HIS BOSSES.
WE ALL GET OUR CHANCE AFTER THIS.
PERFECT.

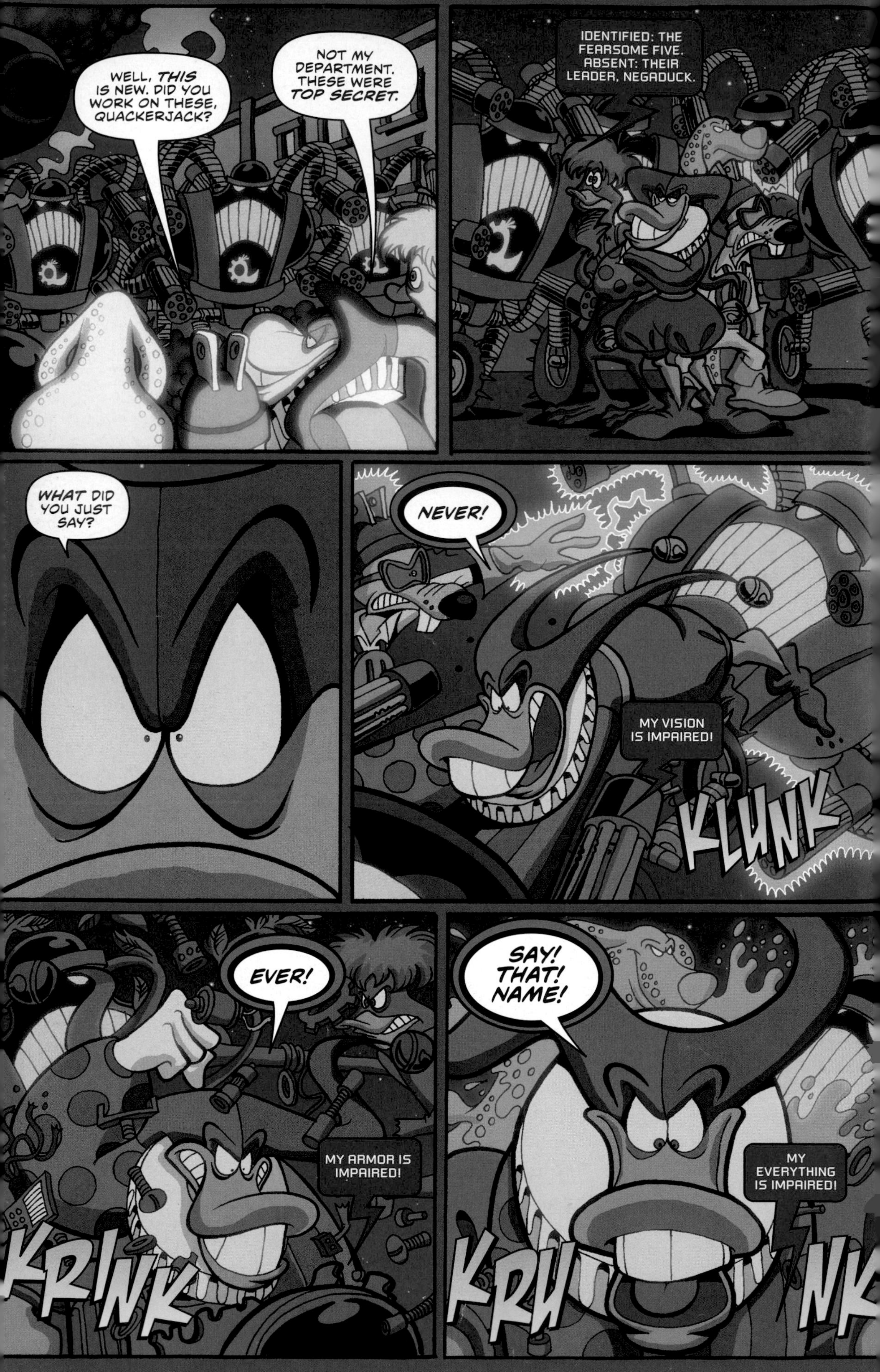
WELL, THIS IS NEW. DID YOU WORK ON THESE, QUACKERJACK?
NOT MY DEPARTMENT. THESE WERE TOP SECRET.
IDENTIFIED: THE FEARSOME FIVE. ABSENT: THEIR LEADER, NEGADUCK.
WHAT DID YOU JUST SAY?
NEVER!
MY VISION IS IMPAIRED!
KLUNK
EVER!
MY ARMOR IS IMPAIRED!
KRINK
SAY! THAT! NAME!
MY EVERYTHING IS IMPAIRED!
KRUNK

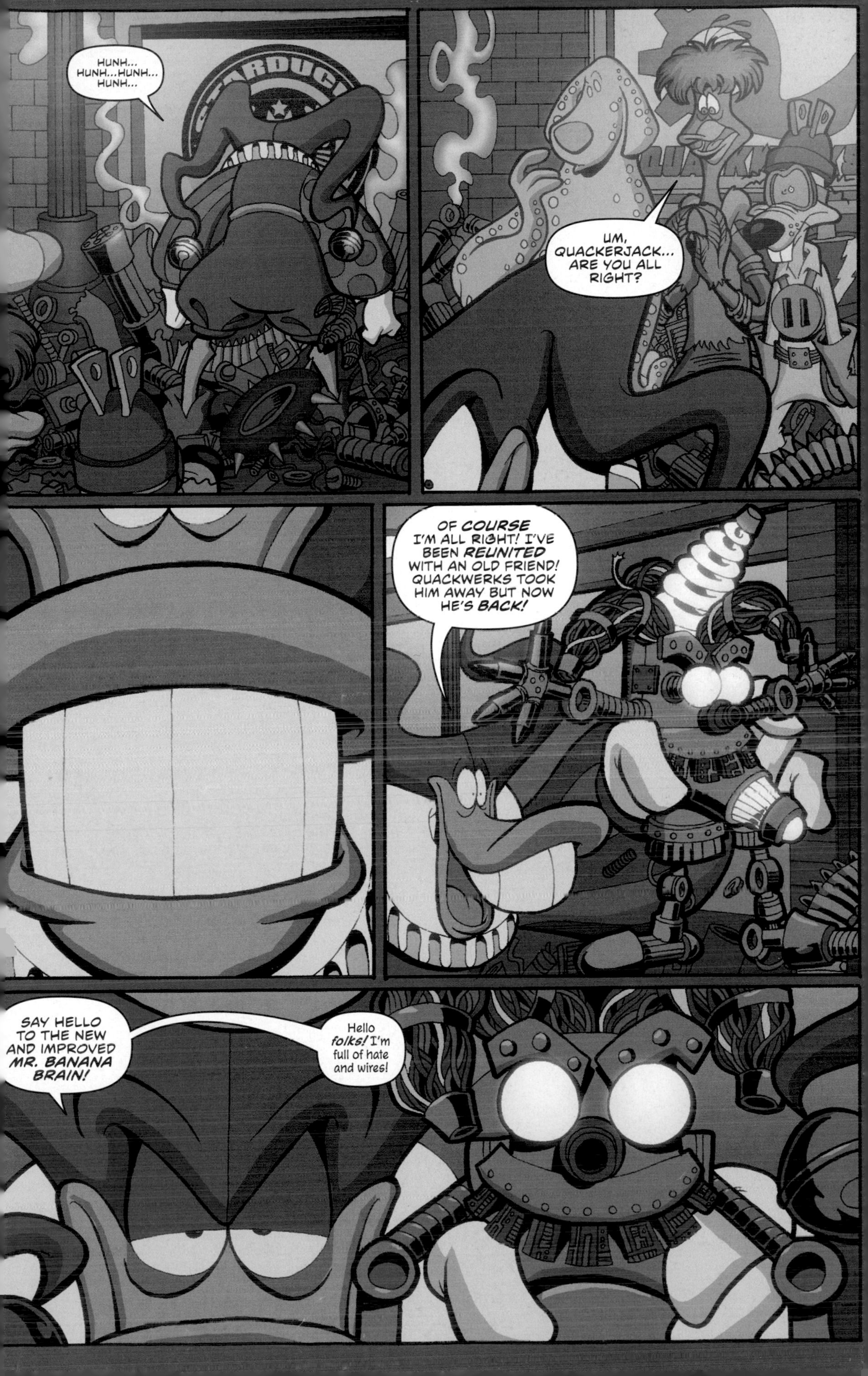
HUNH... HUNH...HUNH... HUNH...
UM, QUACKERJACK... ARE YOU ALL RIGHT?
OF COURSE I'M ALL RIGHT! I'VE BEEN REUNITED WITH AN OLD FRIEND! QUACKWERKS TOOK HIM AWAY BUT NOW HE'S BACK!
SAY HELLO TO THE NEW AND IMPROVED MR. BANANA BRAIN!
Hello folks! I'm full of hate and wires!

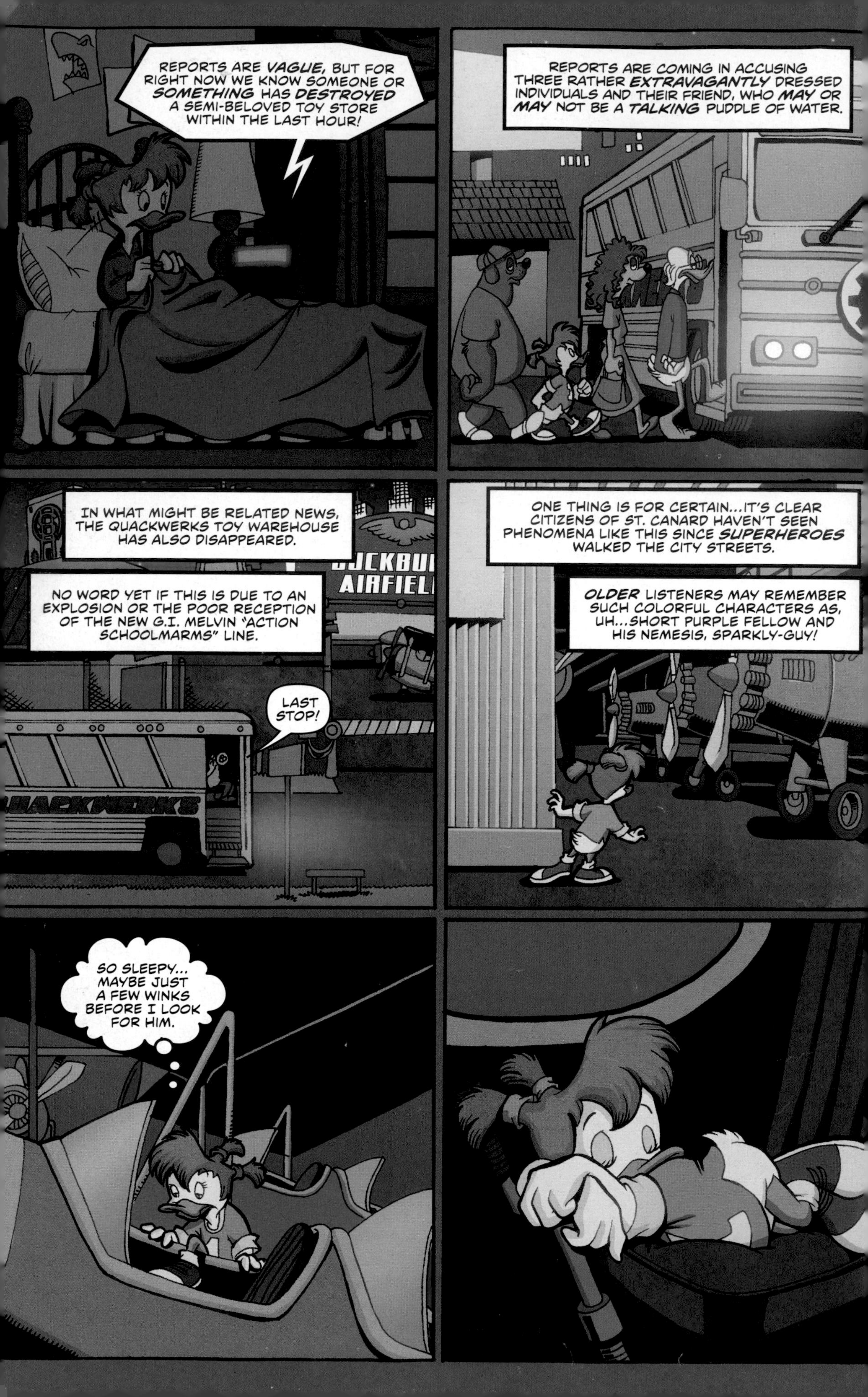

REPORTS ARE VAGUE, BUT FOR RIGHT NOW WE KNOW SOMEONE OR SOMETHING HAS DESTROYED A SEMI-BELOVED TOY STORE WITHIN THE LAST HOUR!
REPORTS ARE COMING IN ACCUSING THREE RATHER EXTRAVAGANTLY DRESSED INDIVIDUALS AND THEIR FRIEND, WHO MAY OR MAY NOT BE A TALKING PUDDLE OF WATER.
IN WHAT MIGHT BE RELATED NEWS, THE QUACKWERKS TOY WAREHOUSE HAS ALSO DISAPPEARED.
NO WORD YET IF THIS IS DUE TO AN EXPLOSION OR THE POOR RECEPTION OF THE NEW G.I. MELVIN "ACTION SCHOOLMARMS" LINE.
LAST STOP!
ONE THING IS FOR CERTAIN...IT'S CLEAR CITIZENS OF ST. CANARD HAVEN'T SEEN PHENOMENA LIKE THIS SINCE SUPERHEROES WALKED THE CITY STREETS.
OLDER LISTENERS MAY REMEMBER SUCH COLORFUL CHARACTERS AS, UH...SHORT PURPLE FELLOW AND HIS NEMESIS, SPARKLY-GUY!
SO SLEEPY... MAYBE JUST A FEW WINKS BEFORE I LOOK FOR HIM.

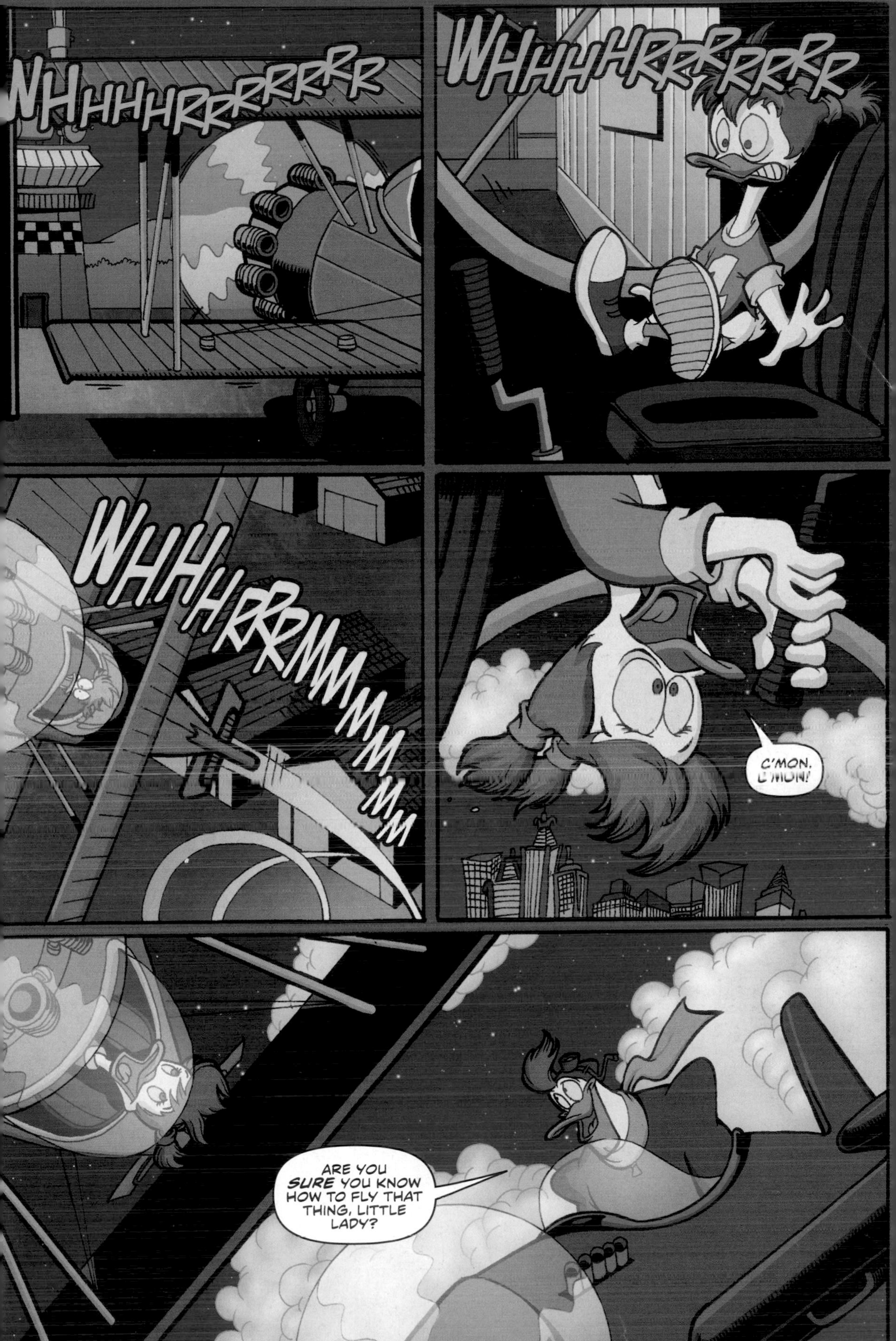
WHHHHRRRRRRR
WHHHHHRRRRRRRR
WHHHRRRMMMMMMMM
C'MON, C'MON!
ARE YOU *SURE* YOU KNOW HOW TO FLY THAT THING, LITTLE LADY?

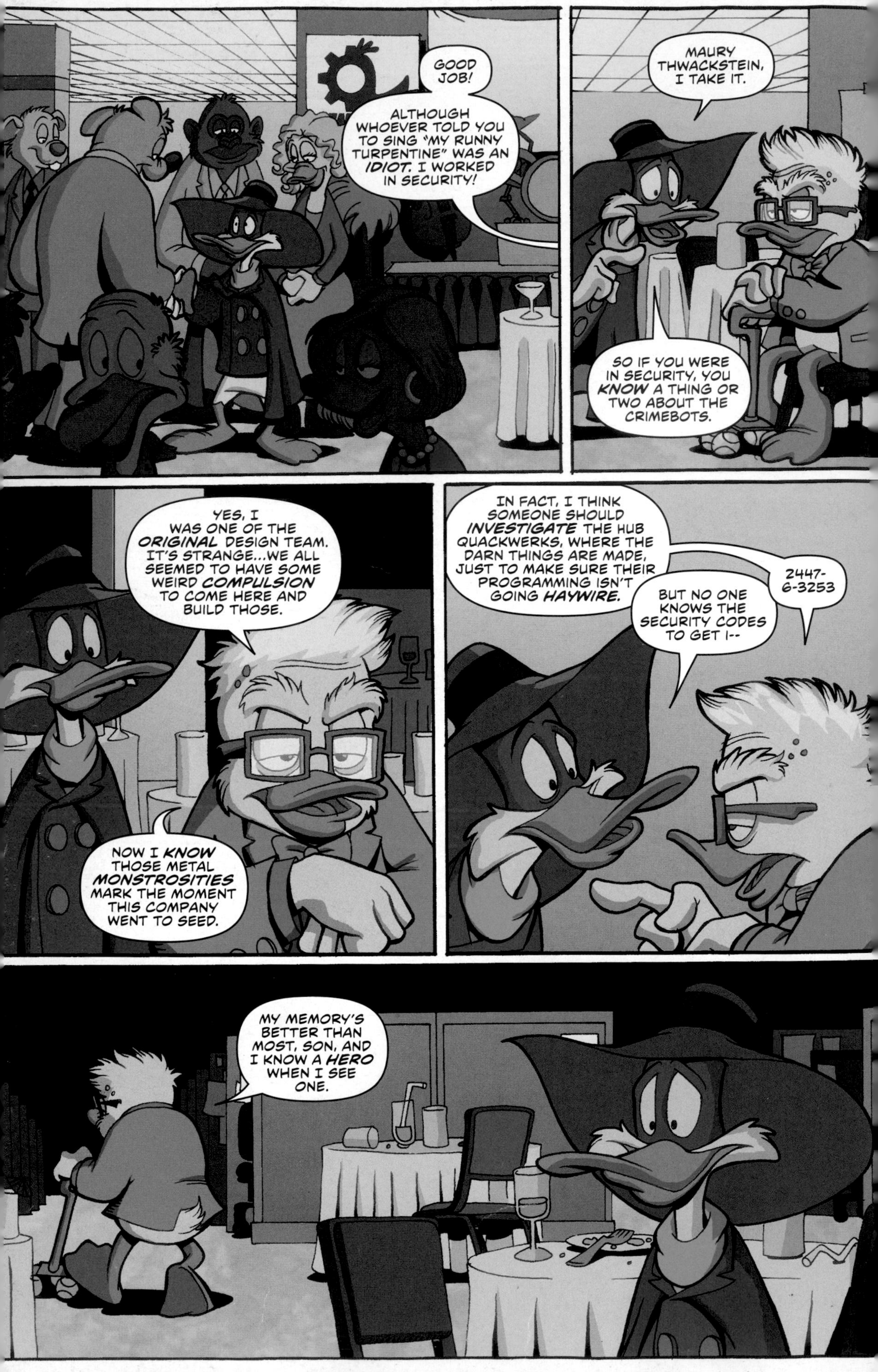
GOOD JOB!
ALTHOUGH WHOEVER TOLD YOU TO SING "MY RUNNY TURPENTINE" WAS AN IDIOT. I WORKED IN SECURITY!
MAURY THWACKSTEIN, I TAKE IT.
SO IF YOU WERE IN SECURITY, YOU KNOW A THING OR TWO ABOUT THE CRIMEBOTS.
YES, I WAS ONE OF THE ORIGINAL DESIGN TEAM. IT'S STRANGE...WE ALL SEEMED TO HAVE SOME WEIRD COMPULSION TO COME HERE AND BUILD THOSE.
NOW I KNOW THOSE METAL MONSTROSITIES MARK THE MOMENT THIS COMPANY WENT TO SEED.
IN FACT, I THINK SOMEONE SHOULD INVESTIGATE THE HUB QUACKWERKS, WHERE THE DARN THINGS ARE MADE, JUST TO MAKE SURE THEIR PROGRAMMING ISN'T GOING HAYWIRE.
BUT NO ONE KNOWS THE SECURITY CODES TO GET I--
2447-6-3253
MY MEMORY'S BETTER THAN MOST, SON, AND I KNOW A HERO WHEN I SEE ONE.

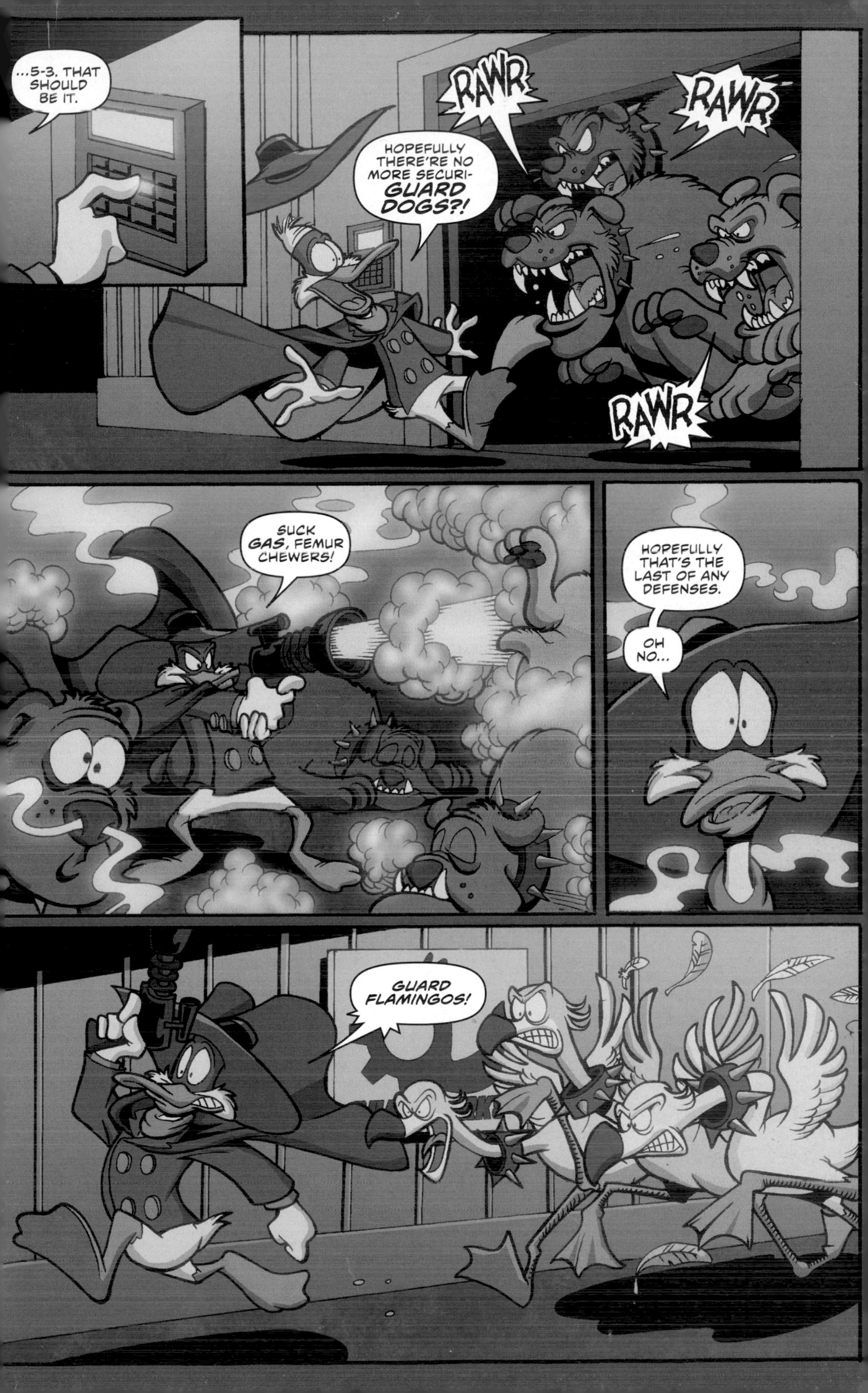
...5-3. THAT SHOULD BE IT.
RAWR
RAWR
HOPEFULLY THERE'RE NO MORE SECURI- GUARD DOGS?!
RAWR
SUCK GAS, FEMUR CHEWERS!
HOPEFULLY THAT'S THE LAST OF ANY DEFENSES.
OH NO...
GUARD FLAMINGOS!

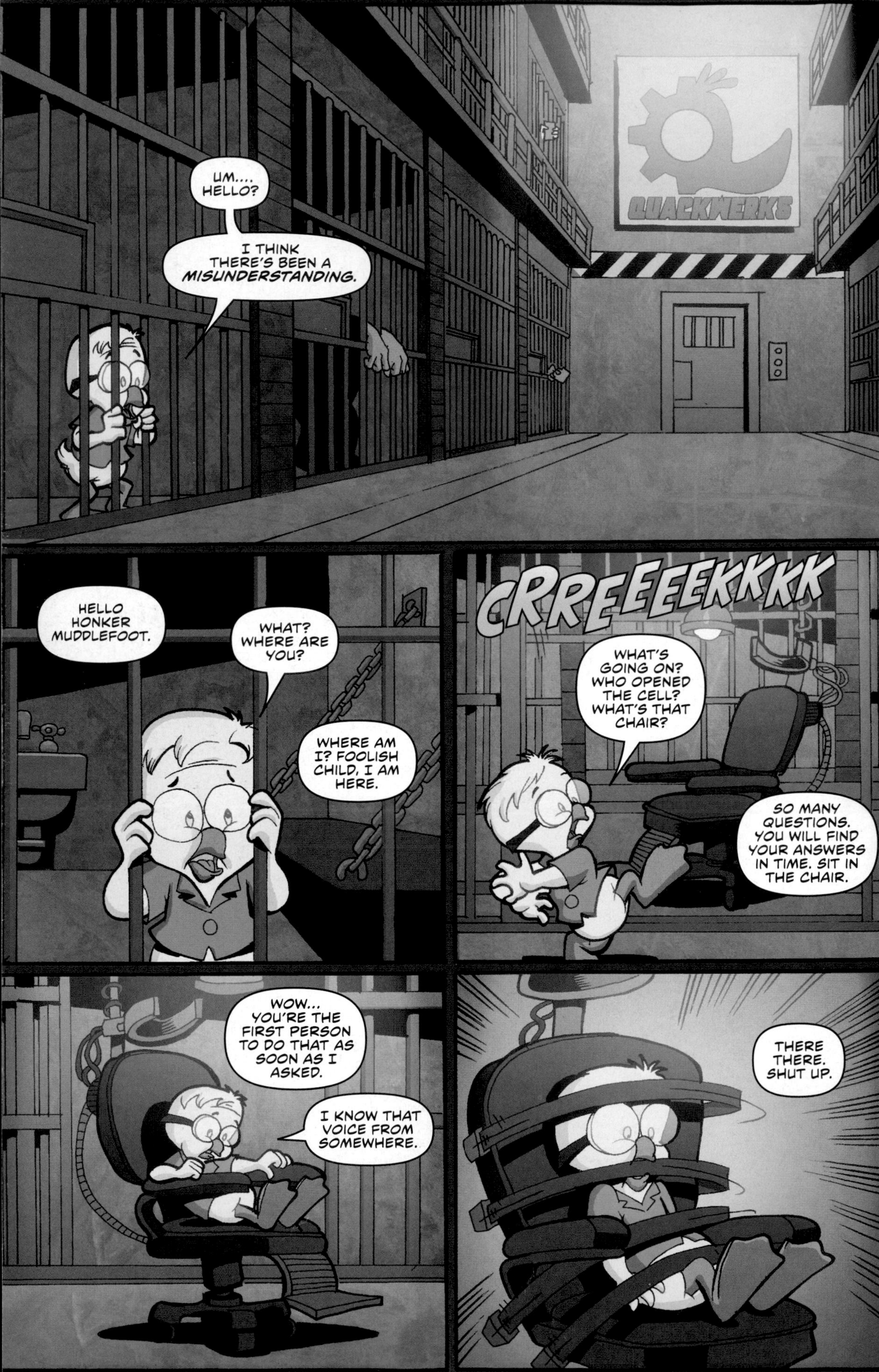
QUACKWERKS
UM.... HELLO?
I THINK THERE'S BEEN A MISUNDERSTANDING.
HELLO HONKER MUDDLEFOOT.
WHAT? WHERE ARE YOU?
WHERE AM I? FOOLISH CHILD, I AM HERE.
CRREEEEKKKK
WHAT'S GOING ON? WHO OPENED THE CELL? WHAT'S THAT CHAIR?
SO MANY QUESTIONS. YOU WILL FIND YOUR ANSWERS IN TIME. SIT IN THE CHAIR.
WOW... YOU'RE THE FIRST PERSON TO DO THAT AS SOON AS I ASKED.
I KNOW THAT VOICE FROM SOMEWHERE.
THERE THERE. SHUT UP.

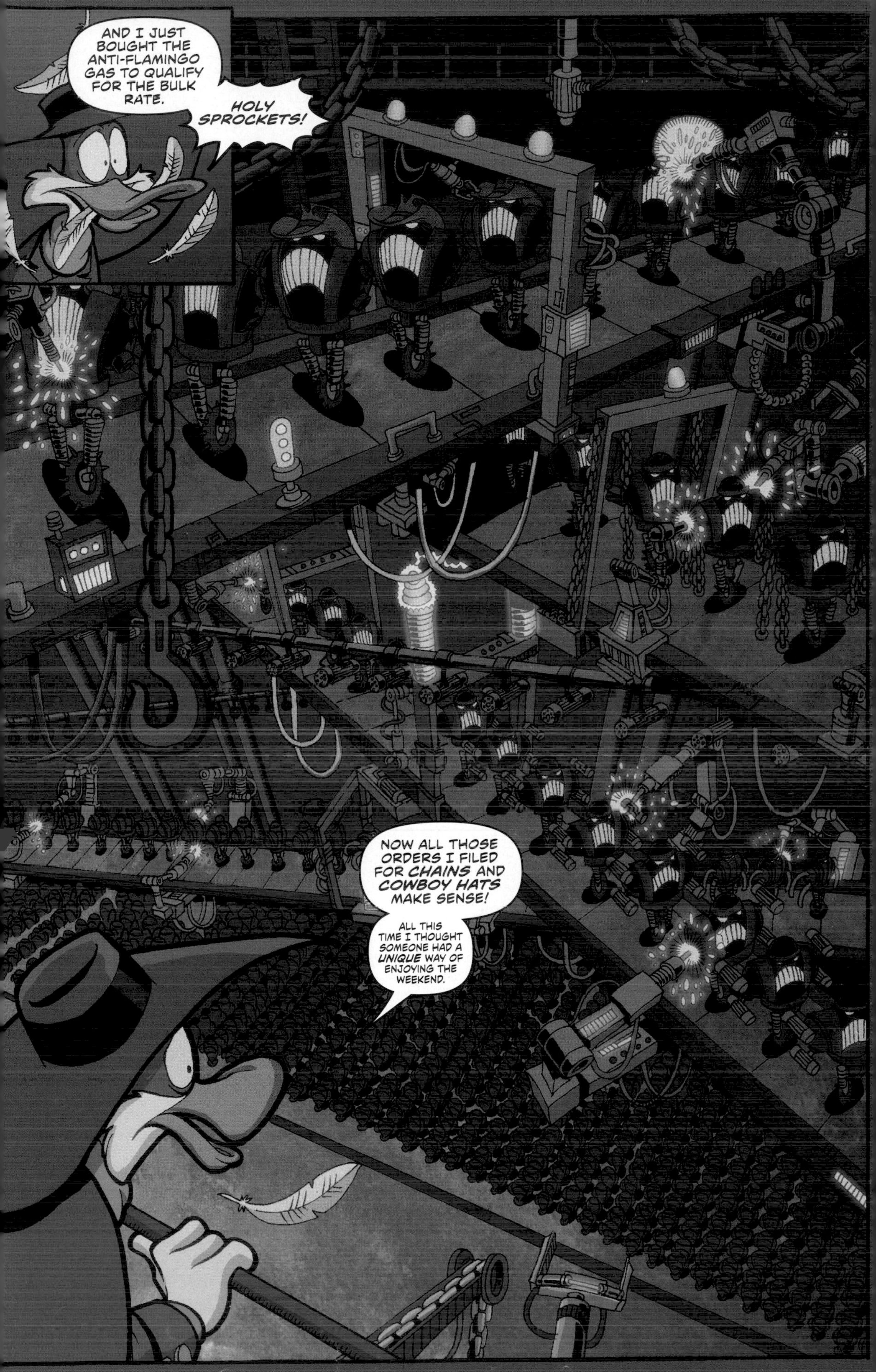

AND I JUST BOUGHT THE ANTI-FLAMINGO GAS TO QUALIFY FOR THE BULK RATE.
HOLY SPROCKETS!
NOW ALL THOSE ORDERS I FILED FOR CHAINS AND COWBOY HATS MAKE SENSE!
ALL THIS TIME I THOUGHT SOMEONE HAD A UNIQUE WAY OF ENJOYING THE WEEKEND.

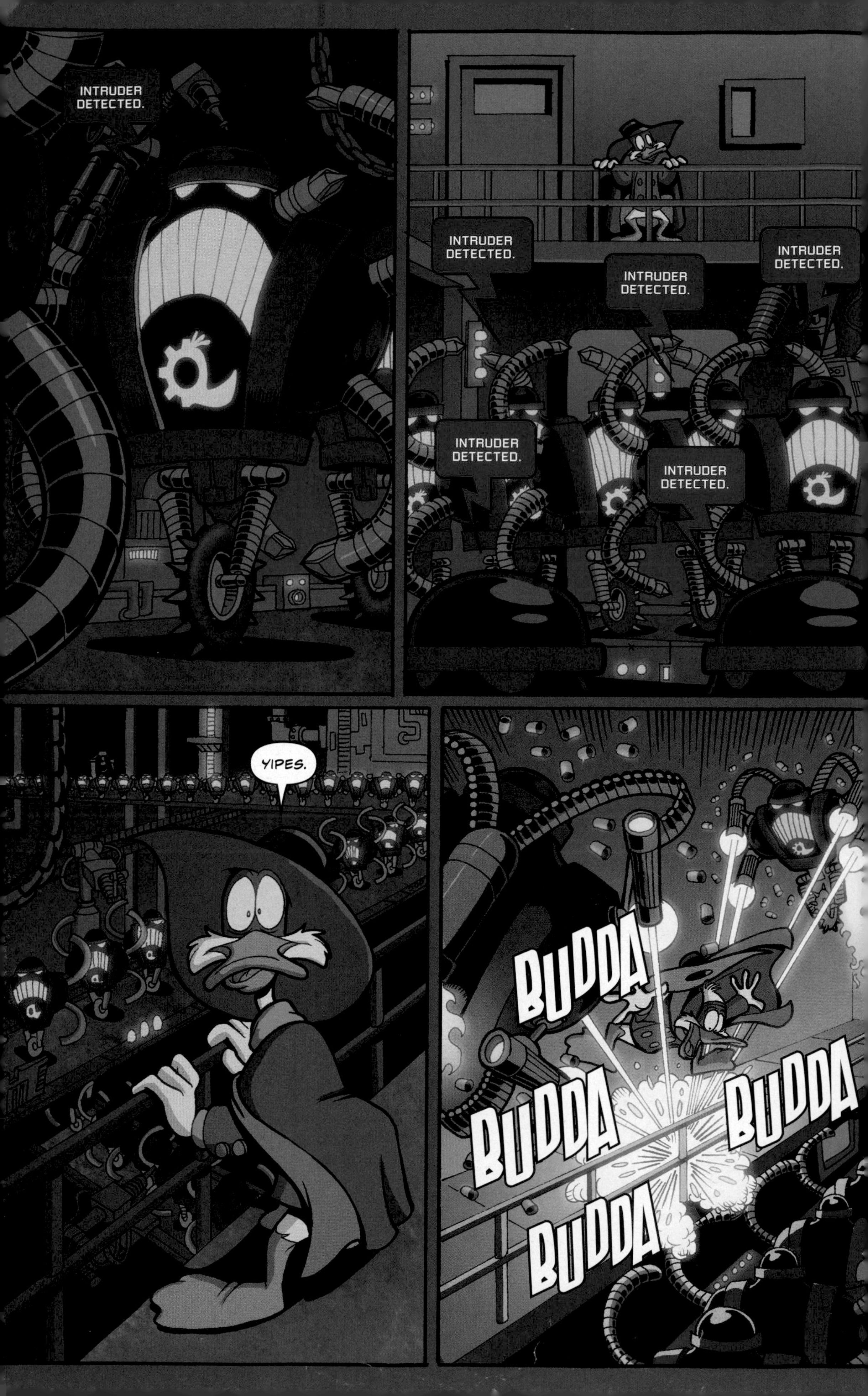
INTRUDER DETECTED.
INTRUDER DETECTED.
INTRUDER DETECTED.
INTRUDER DETECTED.
INTRUDER DETECTED.
INTRUDER DETECTED.
YIPES.
BUDDA
BUDDA
BUDDA
BUDDA

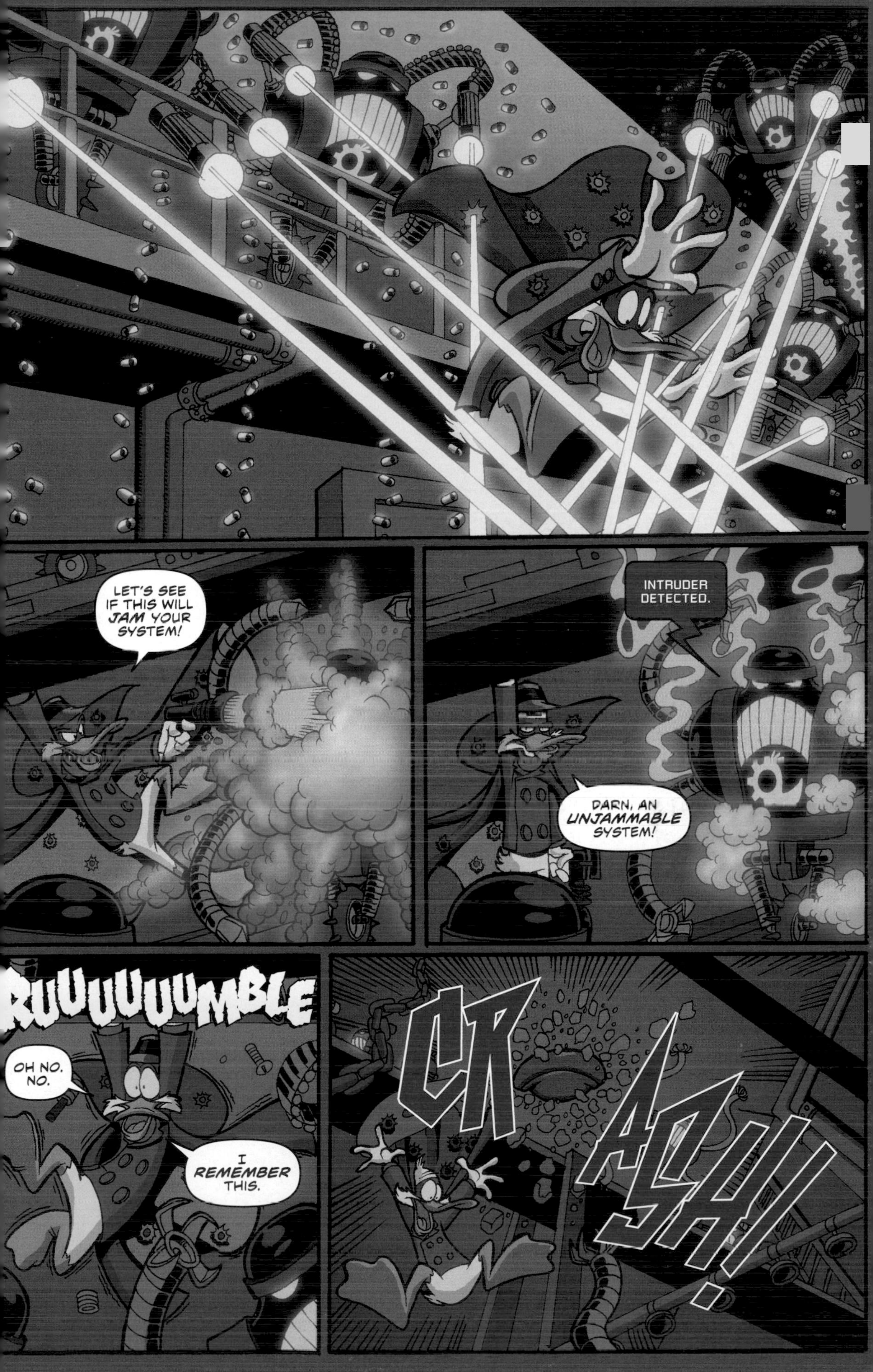
LET'S SEE IF THIS WILL JAM YOUR SYSTEM!
INTRUDER DETECTED.
DARN, AN UNJAMMABLE SYSTEM!
RUUUUUUMBLE
OH NO. NO.
I REMEMBER THIS.
CRASH!!

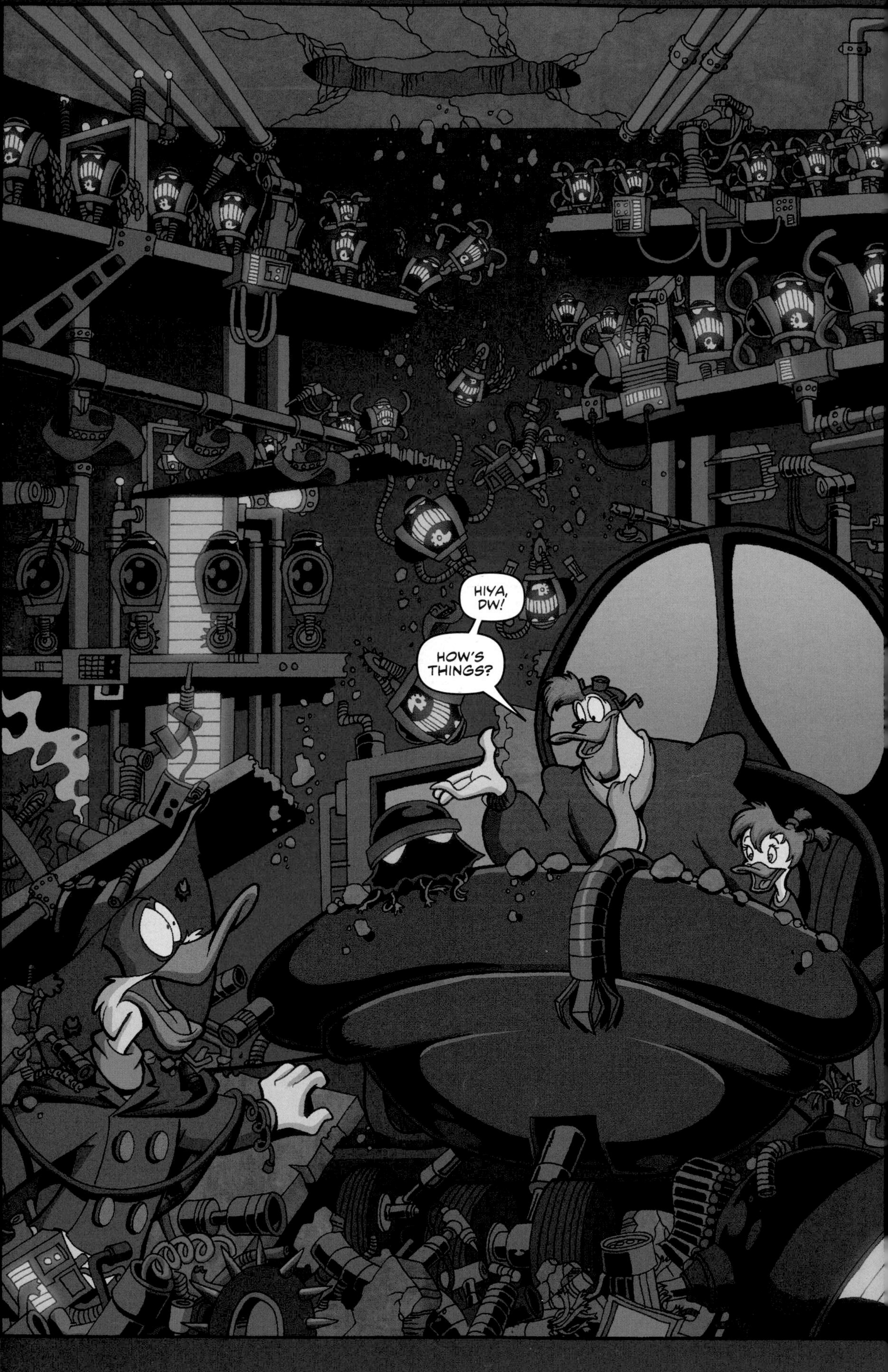
HIYA, DW!
HOW'S THINGS?

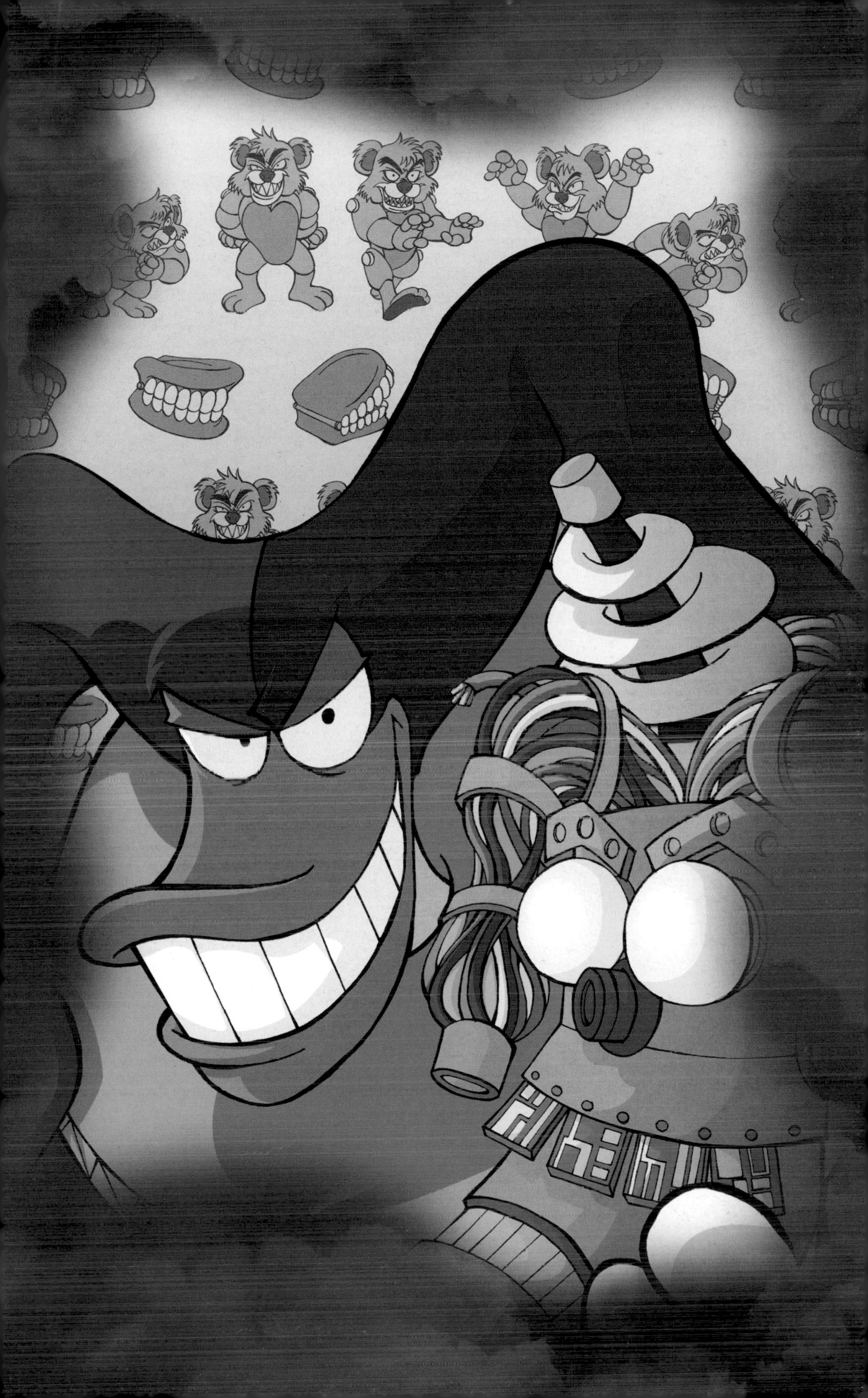

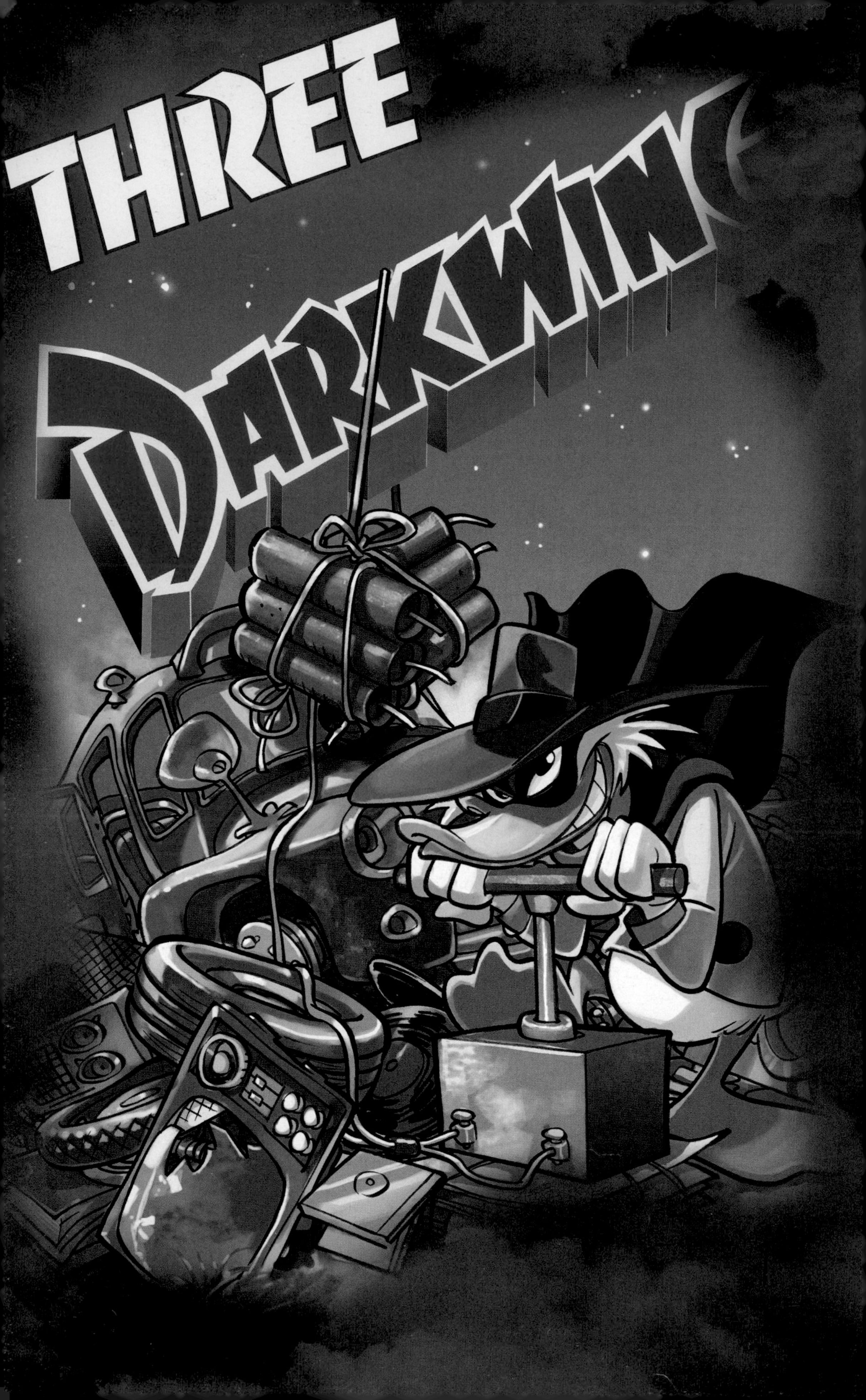
THREE
DARKWING

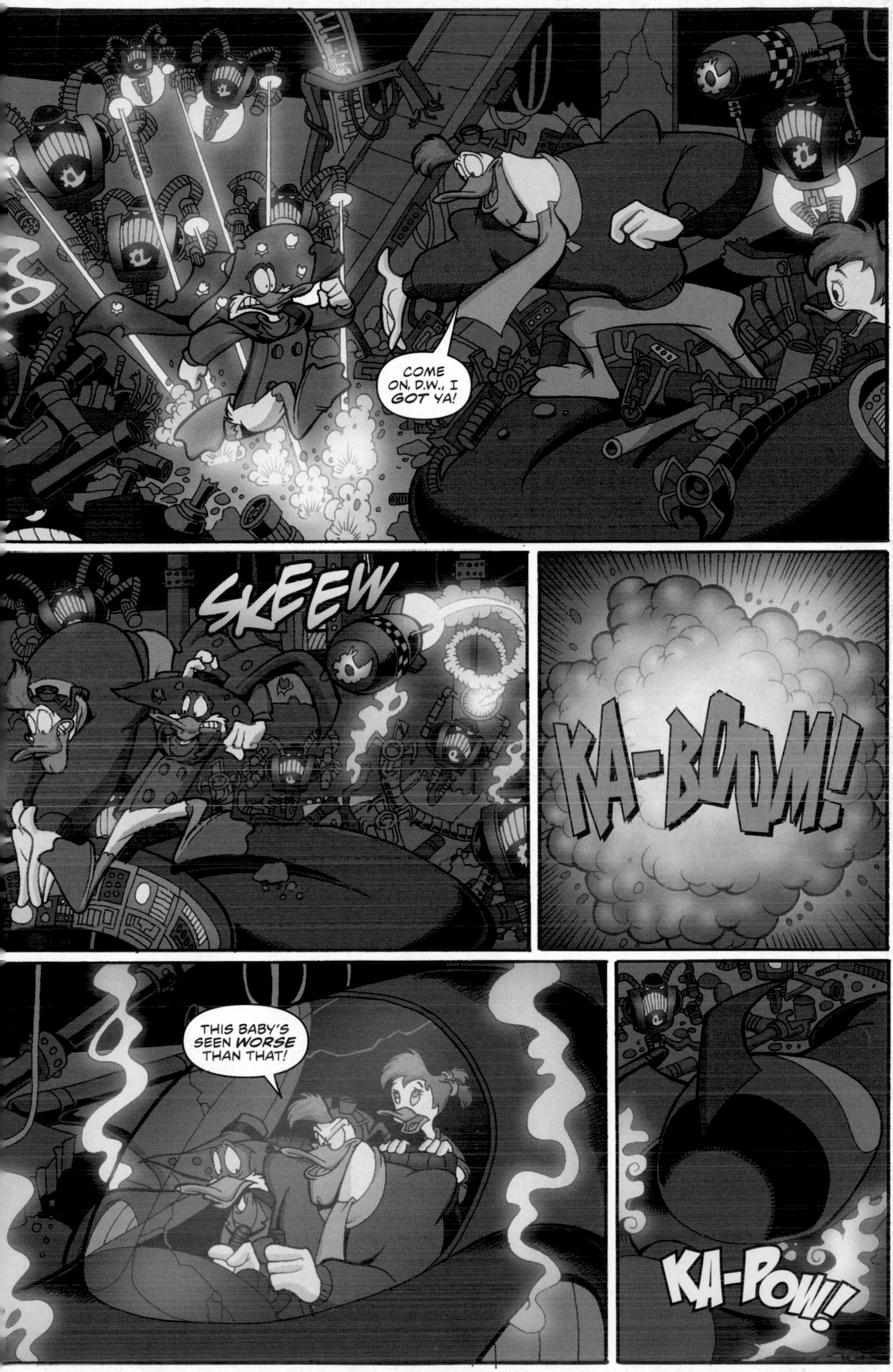
COME ON, D.W., I GOT YA!
SKEEW
KA-BOOM!!
THIS BABY'S SEEN WORSE THAN THAT!
KA-POW!!

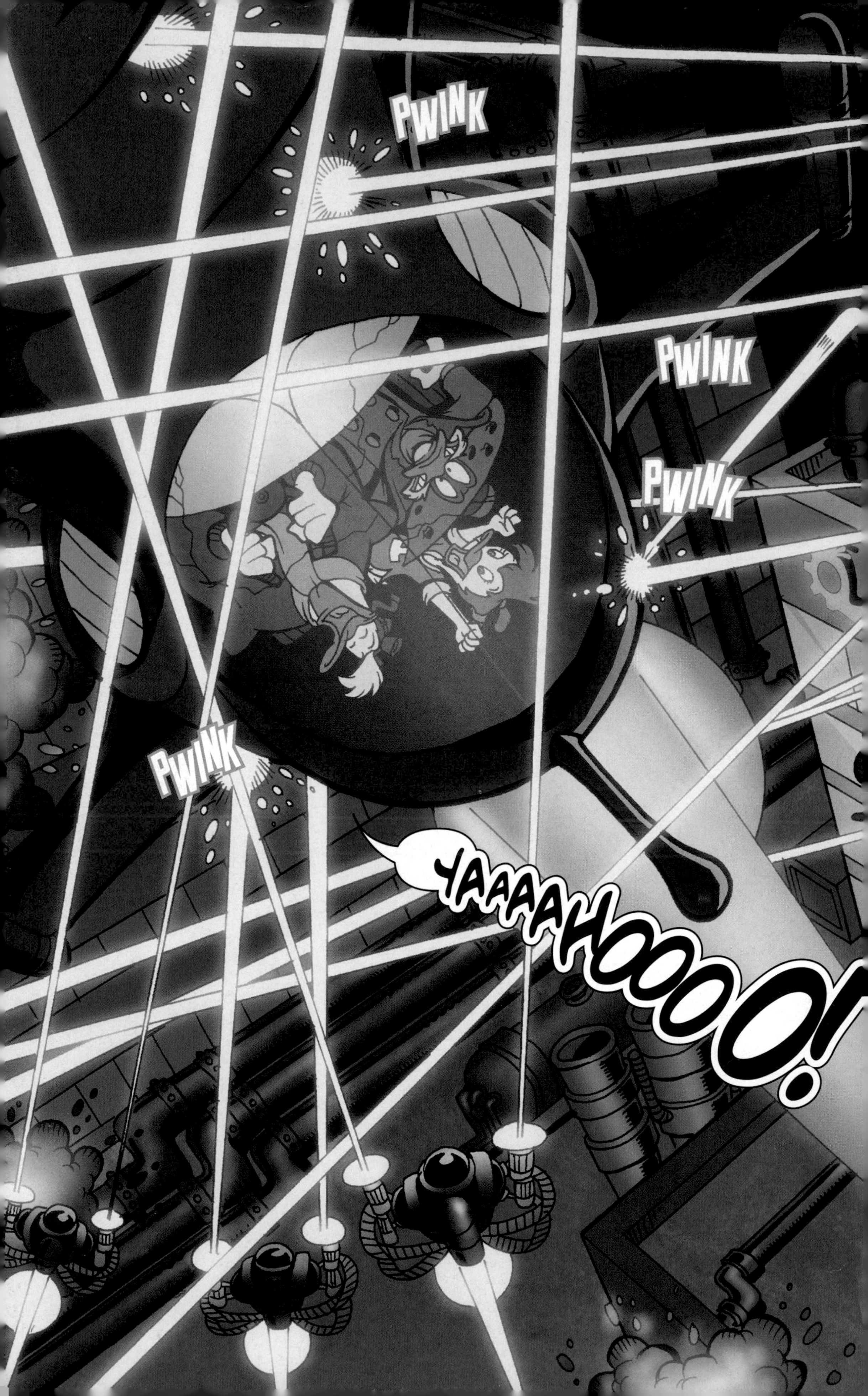
PWINK
PWINK
PWINK
PWINK
YAAAAHOOOOO!

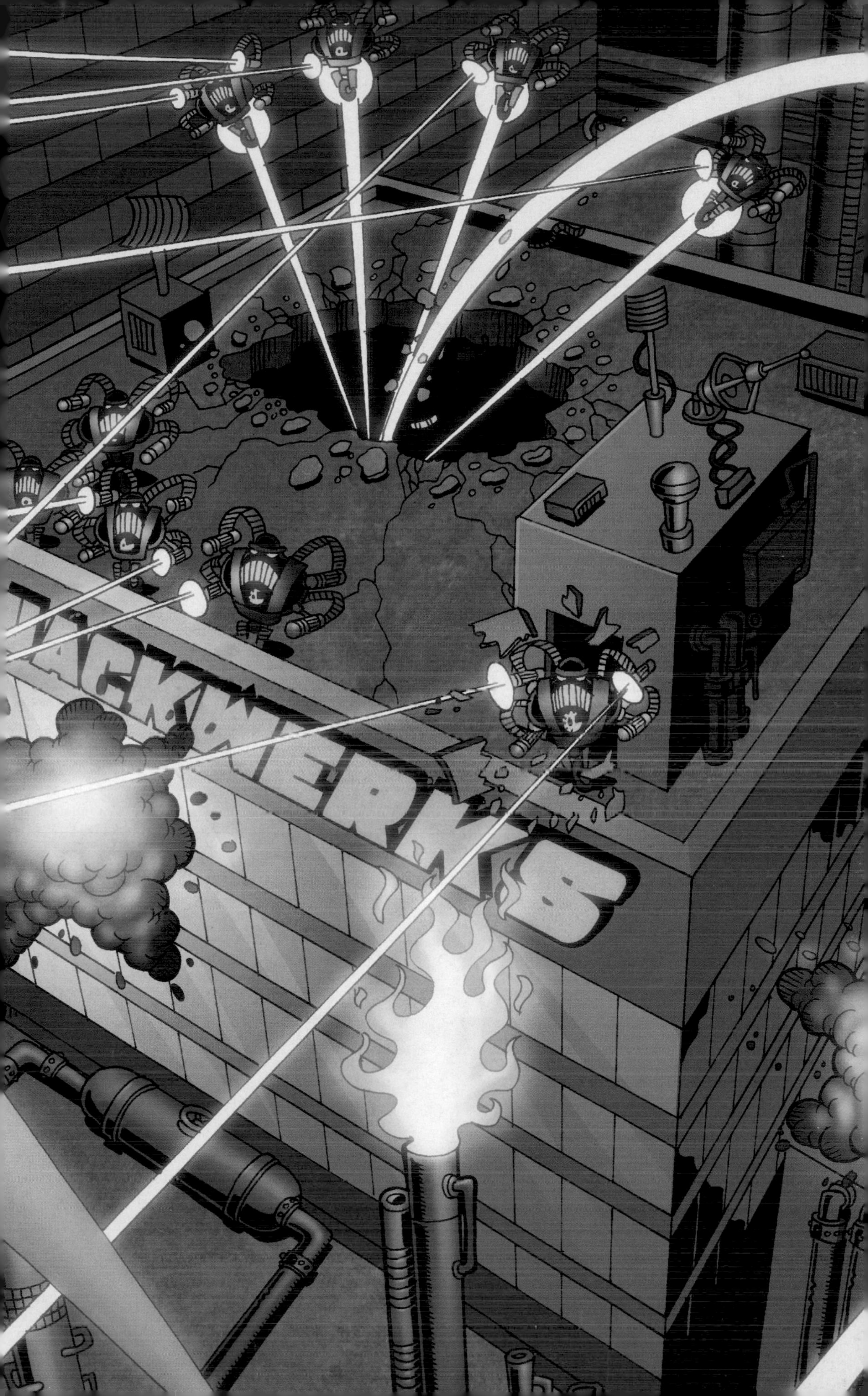
ACKWERKS

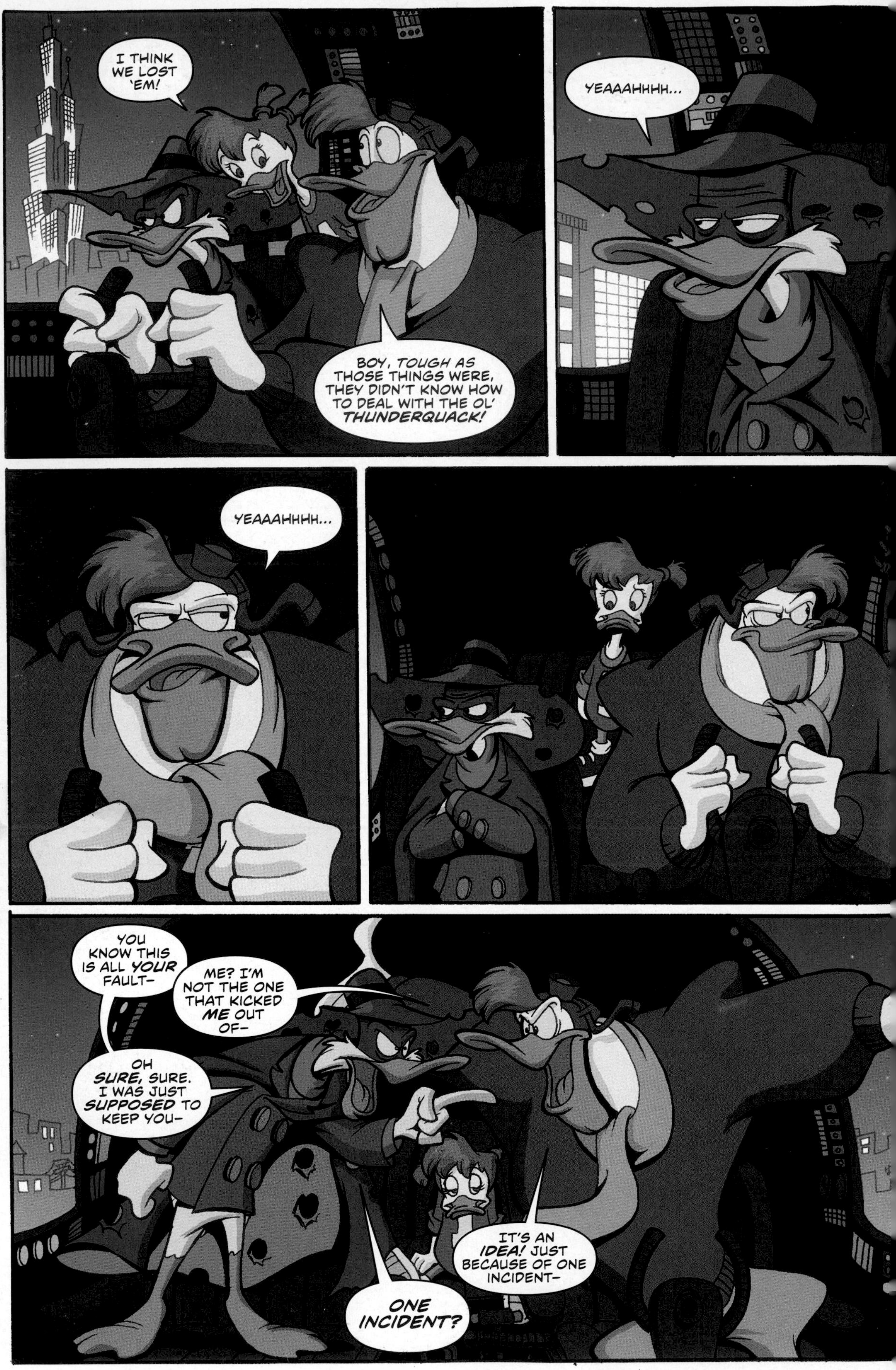
I THINK WE LOST 'EM!
BOY, TOUGH AS THOSE THINGS WERE, THEY DIDN'T KNOW HOW TO DEAL WITH THE OL' THUNDERQUACK!
YEAAAHHHH...
YEAAAHHHH...
YOU KNOW THIS IS ALL YOUR FAULT-
ME? I'M NOT THE ONE THAT KICKED ME OUT OF-
OH SURE, SURE. I WAS JUST SUPPOSED TO KEEP YOU-
IT'S AN IDEA! JUST BECAUSE OF ONE INCIDENT-
ONE INCIDENT?

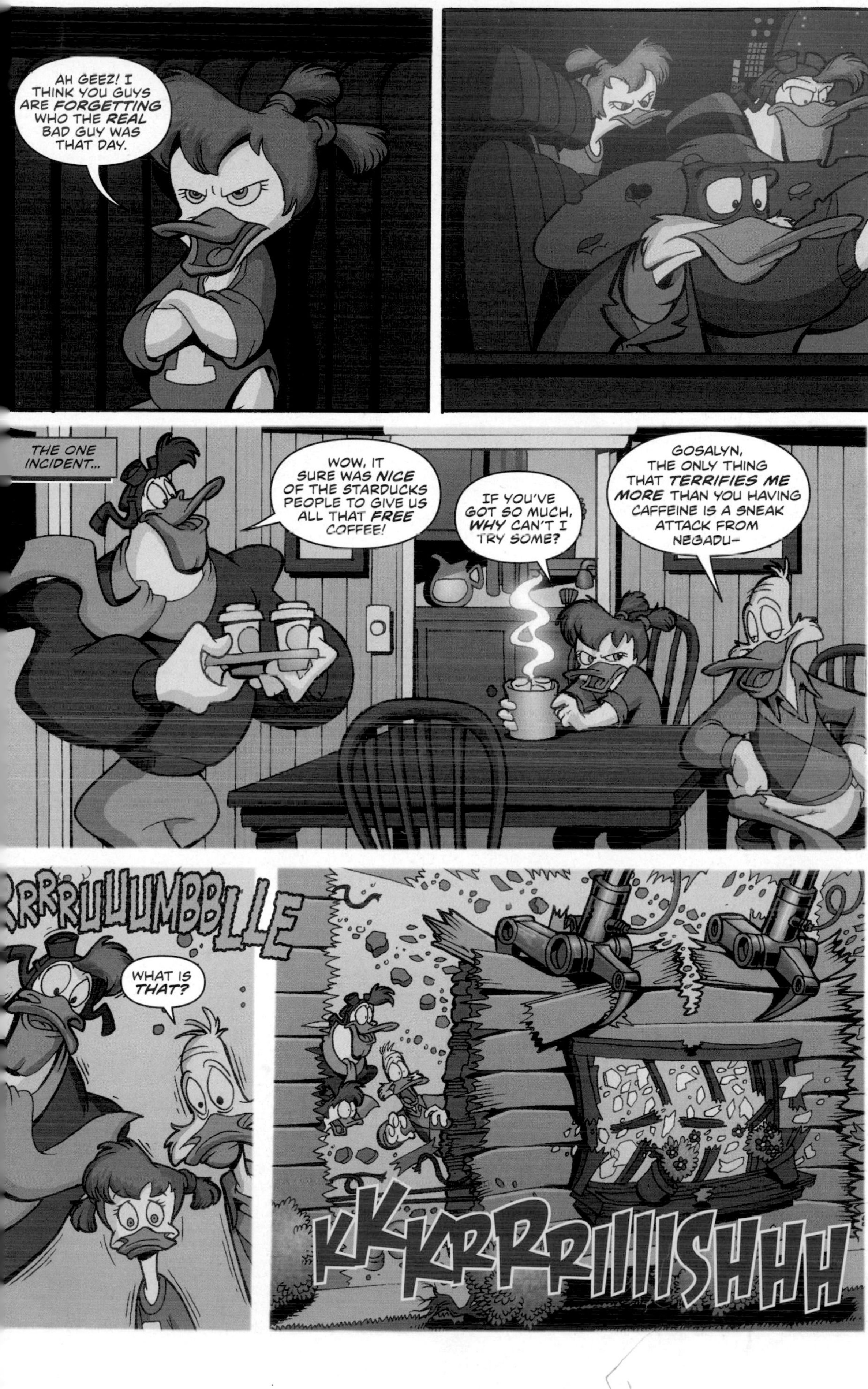

AH GEEZ! I THINK YOU GUYS ARE FORGETTING WHO THE REAL BAD GUY WAS THAT DAY.
THE ONE INCIDENT...
WOW, IT SURE WAS NICE OF THE STARDUCKS PEOPLE TO GIVE US ALL THAT FREE COFFEE!
IF YOU'VE GOT SO MUCH, WHY CAN'T I TRY SOME?
GOSALYN, THE ONLY THING THAT TERRIFIES ME MORE THAN YOU HAVING CAFFEINE IS A SNEAK ATTACK FROM NEGADU–
RRRUUUMBBLLE
WHAT IS THAT?
KKKRRRIIIISHHH

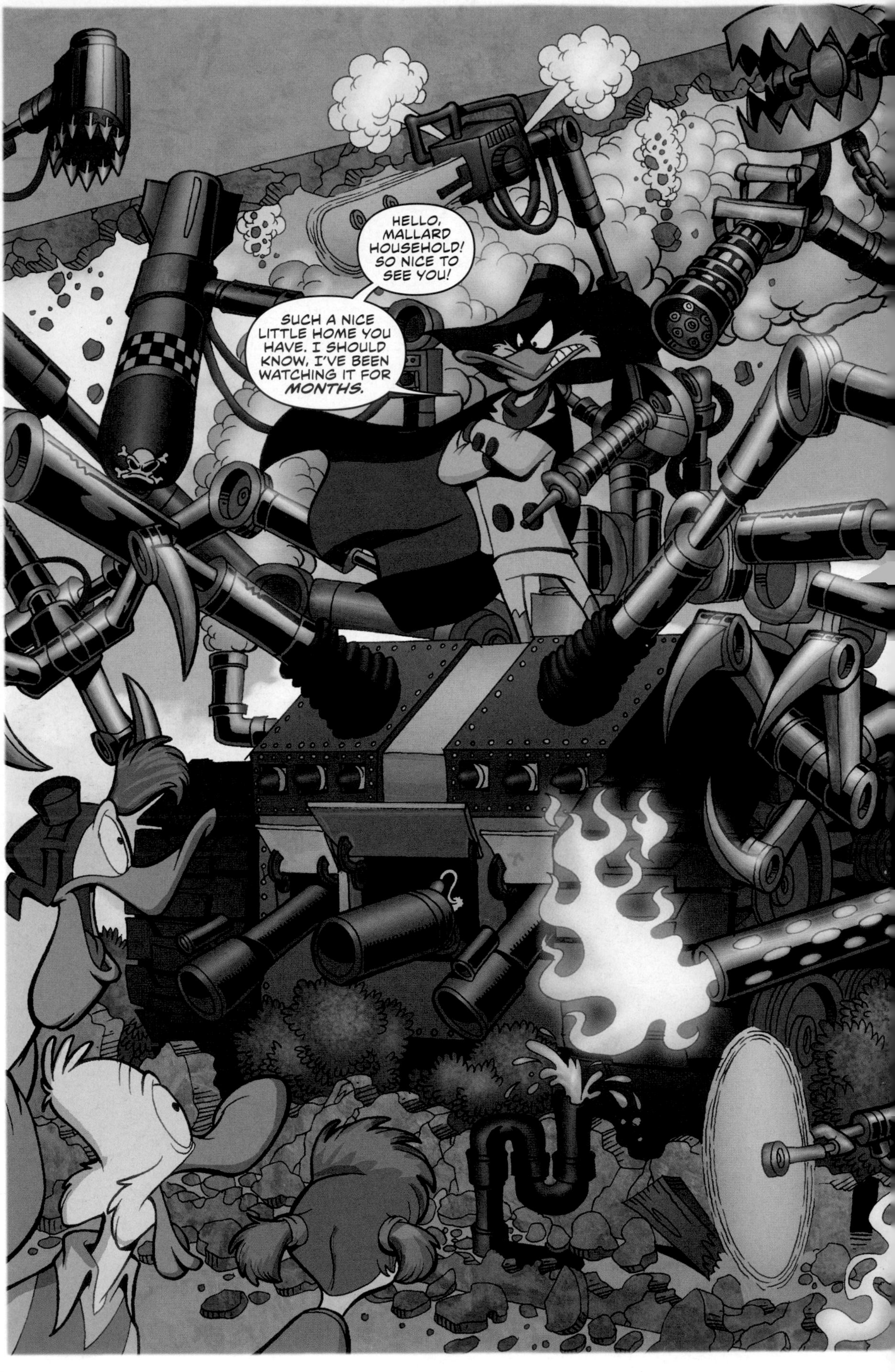
HELLO, MALLARD HOUSEHOLD! SO NICE TO SEE YOU!
SUCH A NICE LITTLE HOME YOU HAVE. I SHOULD KNOW, I'VE BEEN WATCHING IT FOR *MONTHS*.

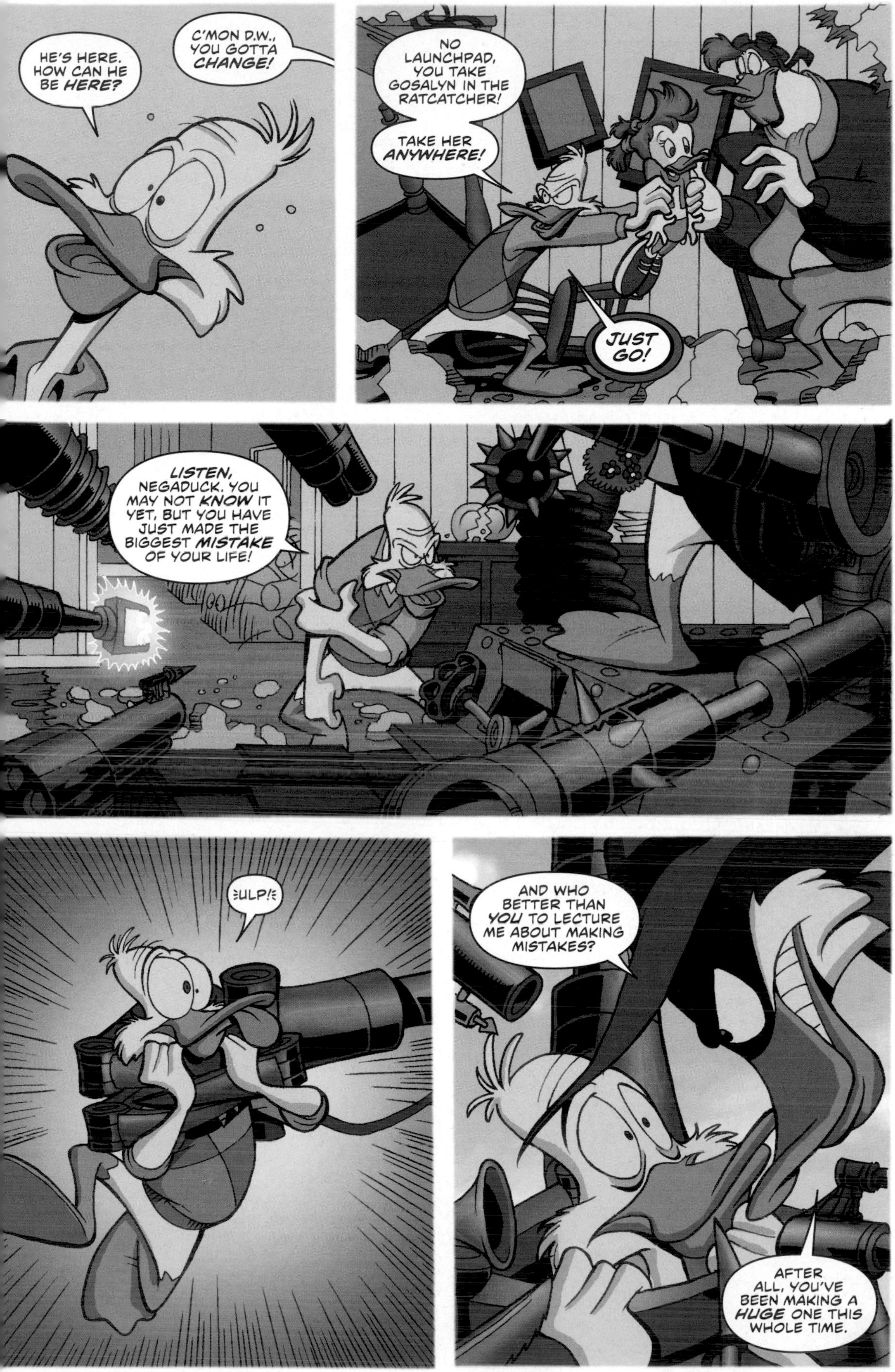

HE'S HERE. HOW CAN HE BE *HERE?*
C'MON D.W., YOU GOTTA *CHANGE!*
NO LAUNCHPAD, YOU TAKE GOSALYN IN THE RATCATCHER!
TAKE HER *ANYWHERE!*
JUST GO!
LISTEN, NEGADUCK. YOU MAY NOT *KNOW* IT YET, BUT YOU HAVE JUST MADE THE BIGGEST *MISTAKE* OF YOUR LIFE!
ULP!
AND WHO BETTER THAN *YOU* TO LECTURE ME ABOUT MAKING MISTAKES?
AFTER ALL, YOU'VE BEEN MAKING A *HUGE* ONE THIS WHOLE TIME.

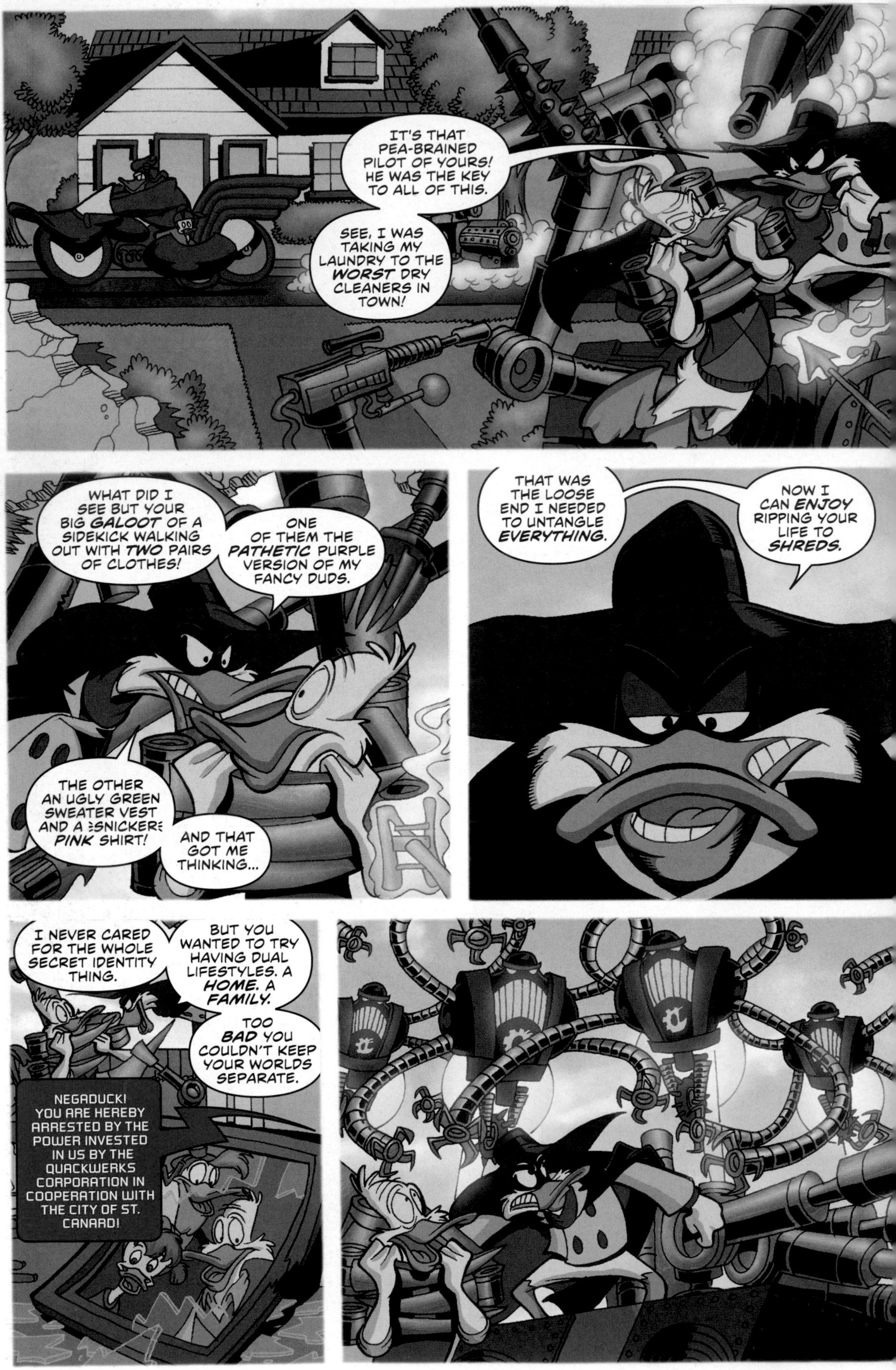
IT'S THAT PEA-BRAINED PILOT OF YOURS! HE WAS THE KEY TO ALL OF THIS.
SEE, I WAS TAKING MY LAUNDRY TO THE WORST DRY CLEANERS IN TOWN!
WHAT DID I SEE BUT YOUR BIG GALOOT OF A SIDEKICK WALKING OUT WITH TWO PAIRS OF CLOTHES!
ONE OF THEM THE PATHETIC PURPLE VERSION OF MY FANCY DUDS.
THE OTHER AN UGLY GREEN SWEATER VEST AND A ≥SNICKER≤ PINK SHIRT!
AND THAT GOT ME THINKING...
THAT WAS THE LOOSE END I NEEDED TO UNTANGLE EVERYTHING.
NOW I CAN ENJOY RIPPING YOUR LIFE TO SHREDS.
I NEVER CARED FOR THE WHOLE SECRET IDENTITY THING.
BUT YOU WANTED TO TRY HAVING DUAL LIFESTYLES. A HOME. A FAMILY.
TOO BAD YOU COULDN'T KEEP YOUR WORLDS SEPARATE.
NEGADUCK! YOU ARE HEREBY ARRESTED BY THE POWER INVESTED IN US BY THE QUACKWERKS CORPORATION IN COOPERATION WITH THE CITY OF ST. CANARD!

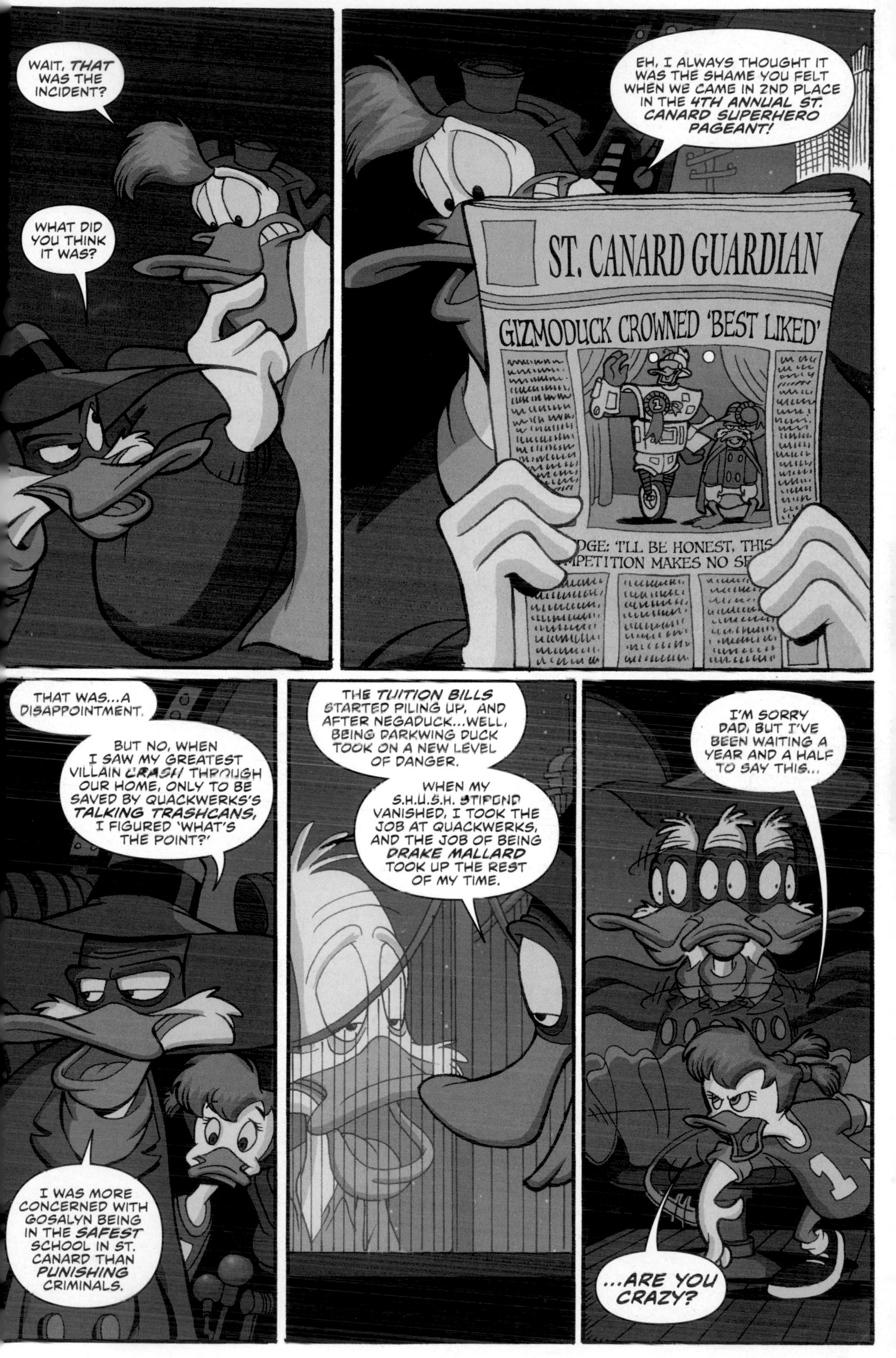
WAIT, THAT WAS THE INCIDENT?
WHAT DID YOU THINK IT WAS?
EH, I ALWAYS THOUGHT IT WAS THE SHAME YOU FELT WHEN WE CAME IN 2ND PLACE IN THE 4TH ANNUAL ST. CANARD SUPERHERO PAGEANT!
ST. CANARD GUARDIAN
GIZMODUCK CROWNED 'BEST LIKED'
THAT WAS...A DISAPPOINTMENT.
BUT NO, WHEN I SAW MY GREATEST VILLAIN CRASH THROUGH OUR HOME, ONLY TO BE SAVED BY QUACKWERKS'S TALKING TRASHCANS, I FIGURED 'WHAT'S THE POINT?'
I WAS MORE CONCERNED WITH GOSALYN BEING IN THE SAFEST SCHOOL IN ST. CANARD THAN PUNISHING CRIMINALS.
THE TUITION BILLS STARTED PILING UP, AND AFTER NEGADUCK...WELL, BEING DARKWING DUCK TOOK ON A NEW LEVEL OF DANGER.
WHEN MY S.H.U.S.H. STIPEND VANISHED, I TOOK THE JOB AT QUACKWERKS, AND THE JOB OF BEING DRAKE MALLARD TOOK UP THE REST OF MY TIME.
I'M SORRY DAD, BUT I'VE BEEN WAITING A YEAR AND A HALF TO SAY THIS...
...ARE YOU CRAZY?

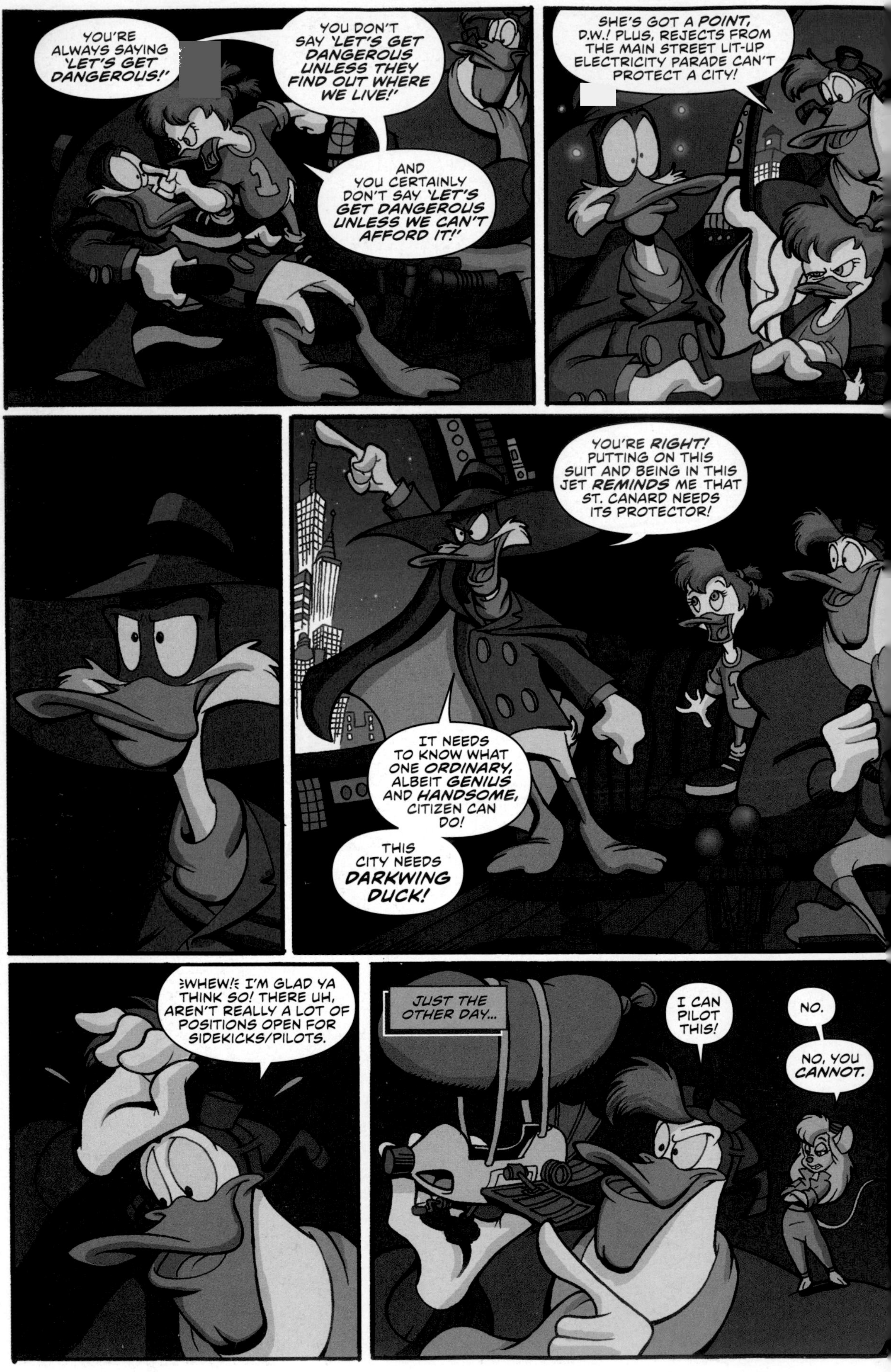
YOU'RE ALWAYS SAYING 'LET'S GET DANGEROUS!'
YOU DON'T SAY 'LET'S GET DANGEROUS UNLESS THEY FIND OUT WHERE WE LIVE!'
AND YOU CERTAINLY DON'T SAY 'LET'S GET DANGEROUS UNLESS WE CAN'T AFFORD IT!'
SHE'S GOT A POINT, D.W.! PLUS, REJECTS FROM THE MAIN STREET LIT-UP ELECTRICITY PARADE CAN'T PROTECT A CITY!
YOU'RE RIGHT! PUTTING ON THIS SUIT AND BEING IN THIS JET REMINDS ME THAT ST. CANARD NEEDS ITS PROTECTOR!
IT NEEDS TO KNOW WHAT ONE ORDINARY, ALBEIT GENIUS AND HANDSOME, CITIZEN CAN DO!
THIS CITY NEEDS DARKWING DUCK!
WHEW! I'M GLAD YA THINK SO! THERE UH, AREN'T REALLY A LOT OF POSITIONS OPEN FOR SIDEKICKS/PILOTS.
JUST THE OTHER DAY...
I CAN PILOT THIS!
NO.
NO, YOU CANNOT.

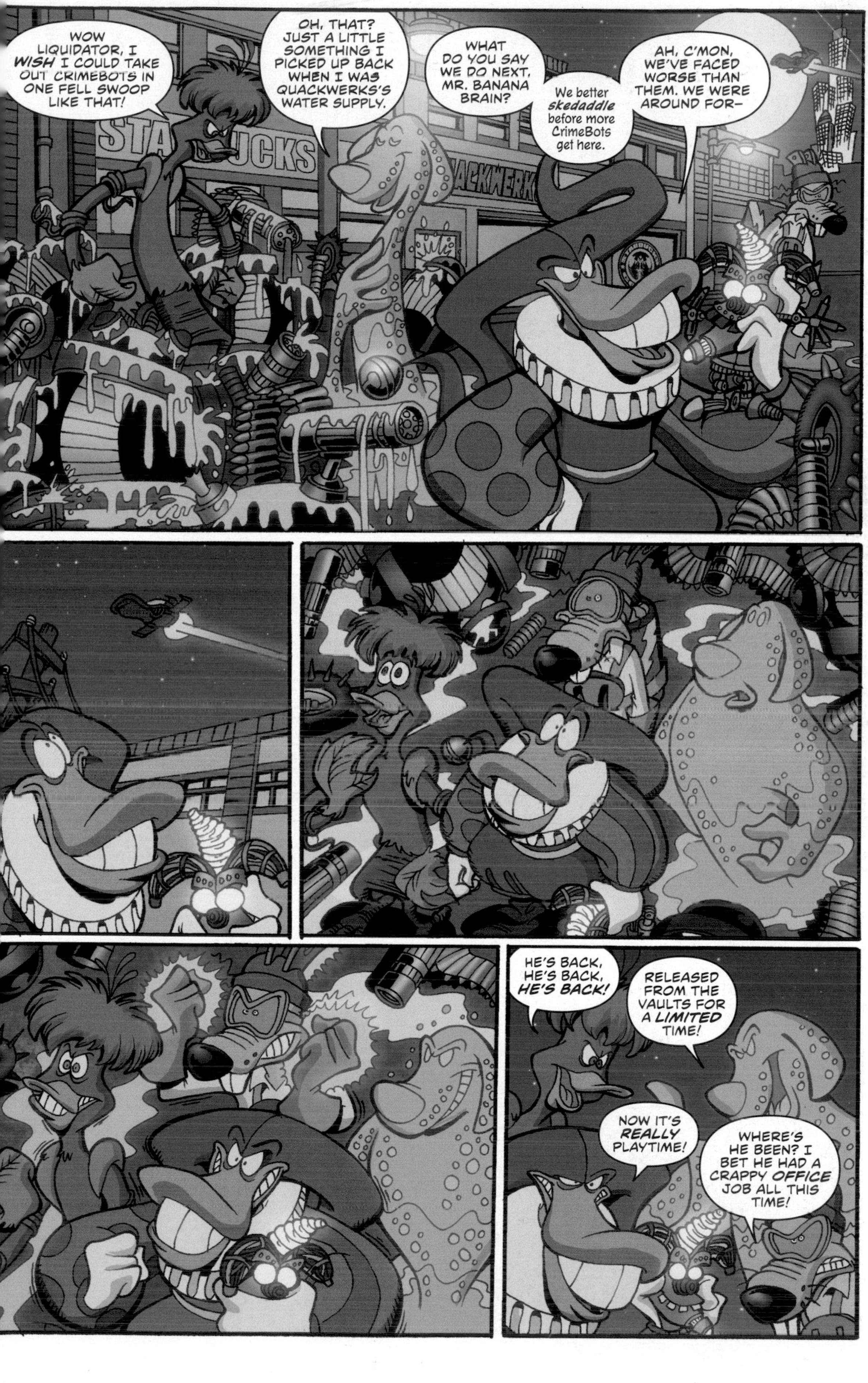
WOW LIQUIDATOR, I WISH I COULD TAKE OUT CRIMEBOTS IN ONE FELL SWOOP LIKE THAT!
OH, THAT? JUST A LITTLE SOMETHING I PICKED UP BACK WHEN I WAS QUACKWERKS'S WATER SUPPLY.
WHAT DO YOU SAY WE DO NEXT, MR. BANANA BRAIN?
We better skedaddle before more CrimeBots get here.
AH, C'MON, WE'VE FACED WORSE THAN THEM. WE WERE AROUND FOR—
HE'S BACK, HE'S BACK, HE'S BACK!
RELEASED FROM THE VAULTS FOR A LIMITED TIME!
NOW IT'S REALLY PLAYTIME!
WHERE'S HE BEEN? I BET HE HAD A CRAPPY OFFICE JOB ALL THIS TIME!

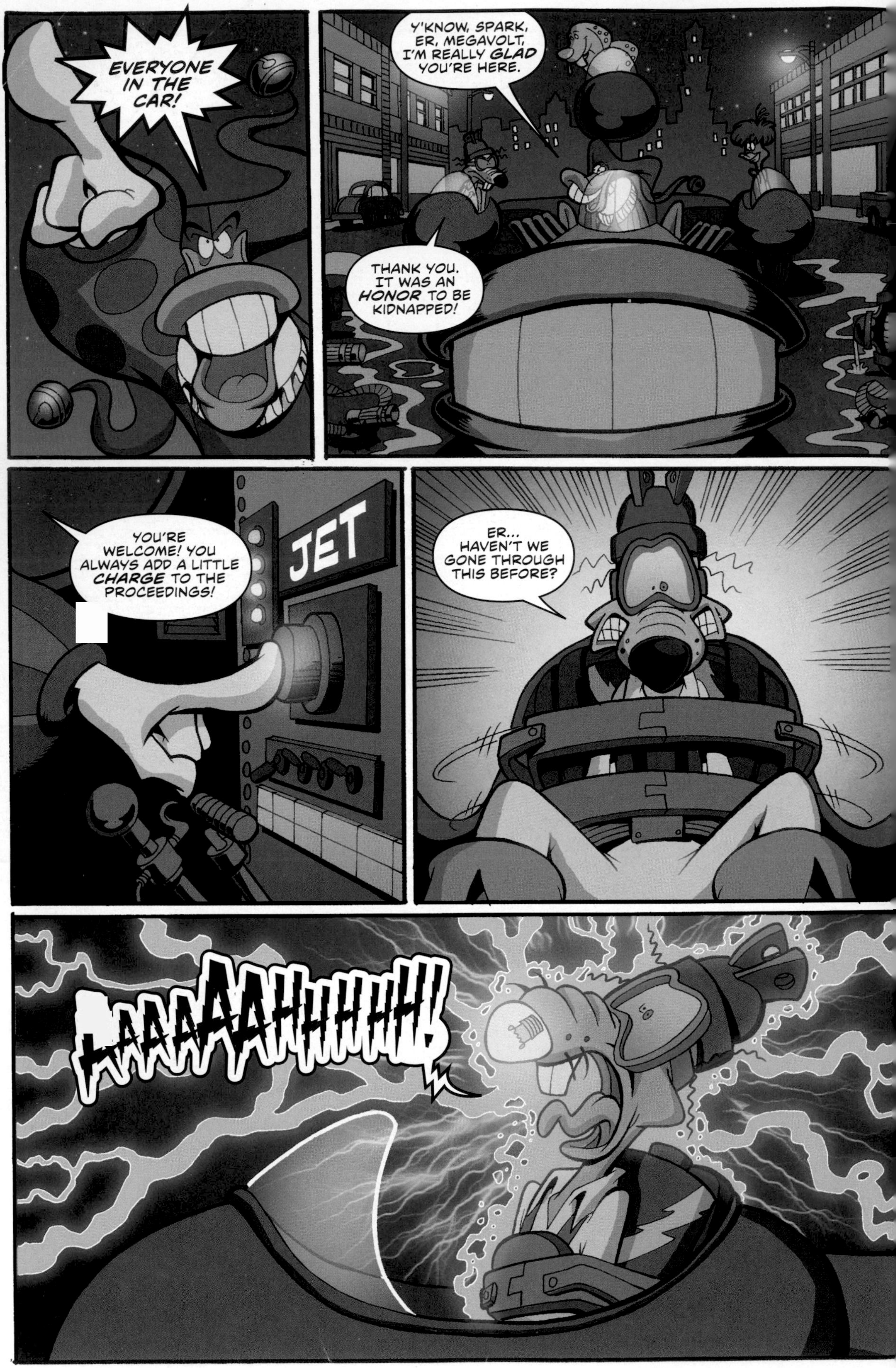
EVERYONE IN THE CAR!
Y'KNOW, SPARK, ER, MEGAVOLT, I'M REALLY GLAD YOU'RE HERE.
THANK YOU. IT WAS AN HONOR TO BE KIDNAPPED!
YOU'RE WELCOME! YOU ALWAYS ADD A LITTLE CHARGE TO THE PROCEEDINGS!
JET
ER... HAVEN'T WE GONE THROUGH THIS BEFORE?
AAAAAAHHHHHH!

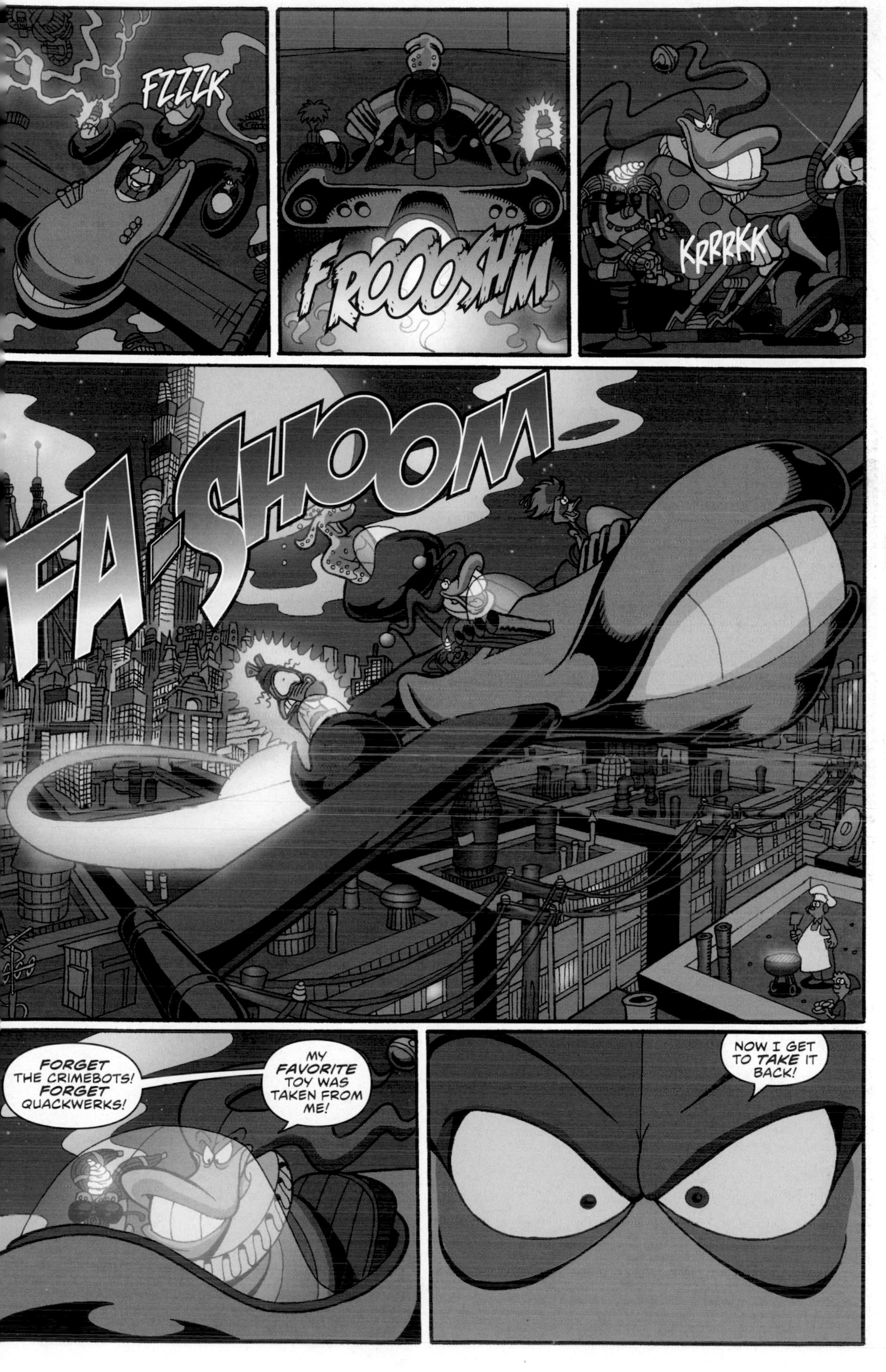
FZZZK
FROOOSHM
KRRRKK
FA-SHOOM
FORGET THE CRIMEBOTS! FORGET QUACKWERKS!
MY FAVORITE TOY WAS TAKEN FROM ME!
NOW I GET TO TAKE IT BACK!

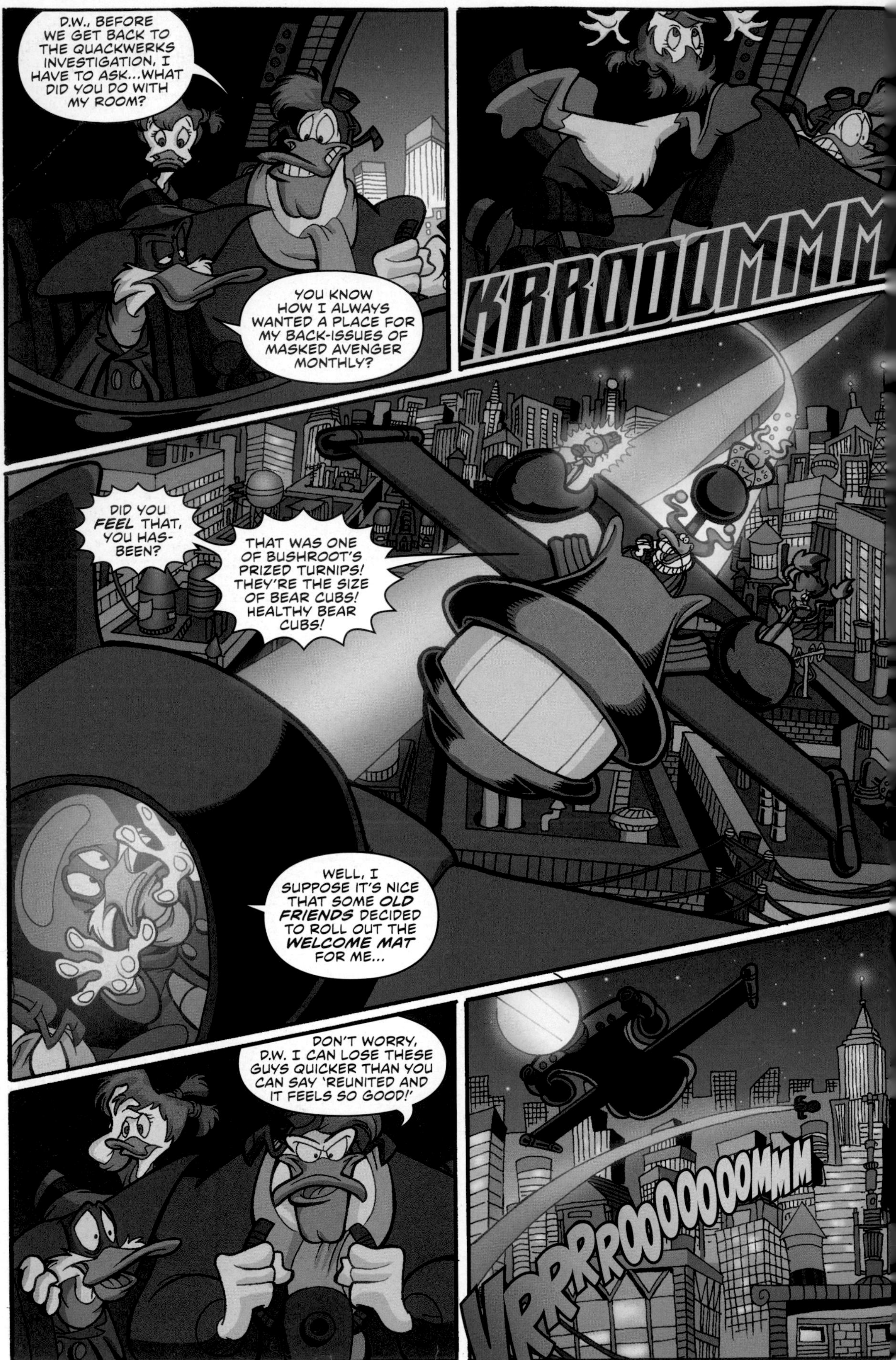
D.W., BEFORE WE GET BACK TO THE QUACKWERKS INVESTIGATION, I HAVE TO ASK...WHAT DID YOU DO WITH MY ROOM?
YOU KNOW HOW I ALWAYS WANTED A PLACE FOR MY BACK-ISSUES OF MASKED AVENGER MONTHLY?
KRROOOMMM
DID YOU *FEEL* THAT, YOU HAS-BEEN?
THAT WAS ONE OF BUSHROOT'S PRIZED TURNIPS! THEY'RE THE SIZE OF BEAR CUBS! HEALTHY BEAR CUBS!
WELL, I SUPPOSE IT'S NICE THAT SOME *OLD FRIENDS* DECIDED TO ROLL OUT THE *WELCOME MAT* FOR ME...
DON'T WORRY, D.W. I CAN LOSE THESE GUYS QUICKER THAN YOU CAN SAY 'REUNITED AND IT FEELS SO GOOD!'
VRRRROOOOOOOMMM

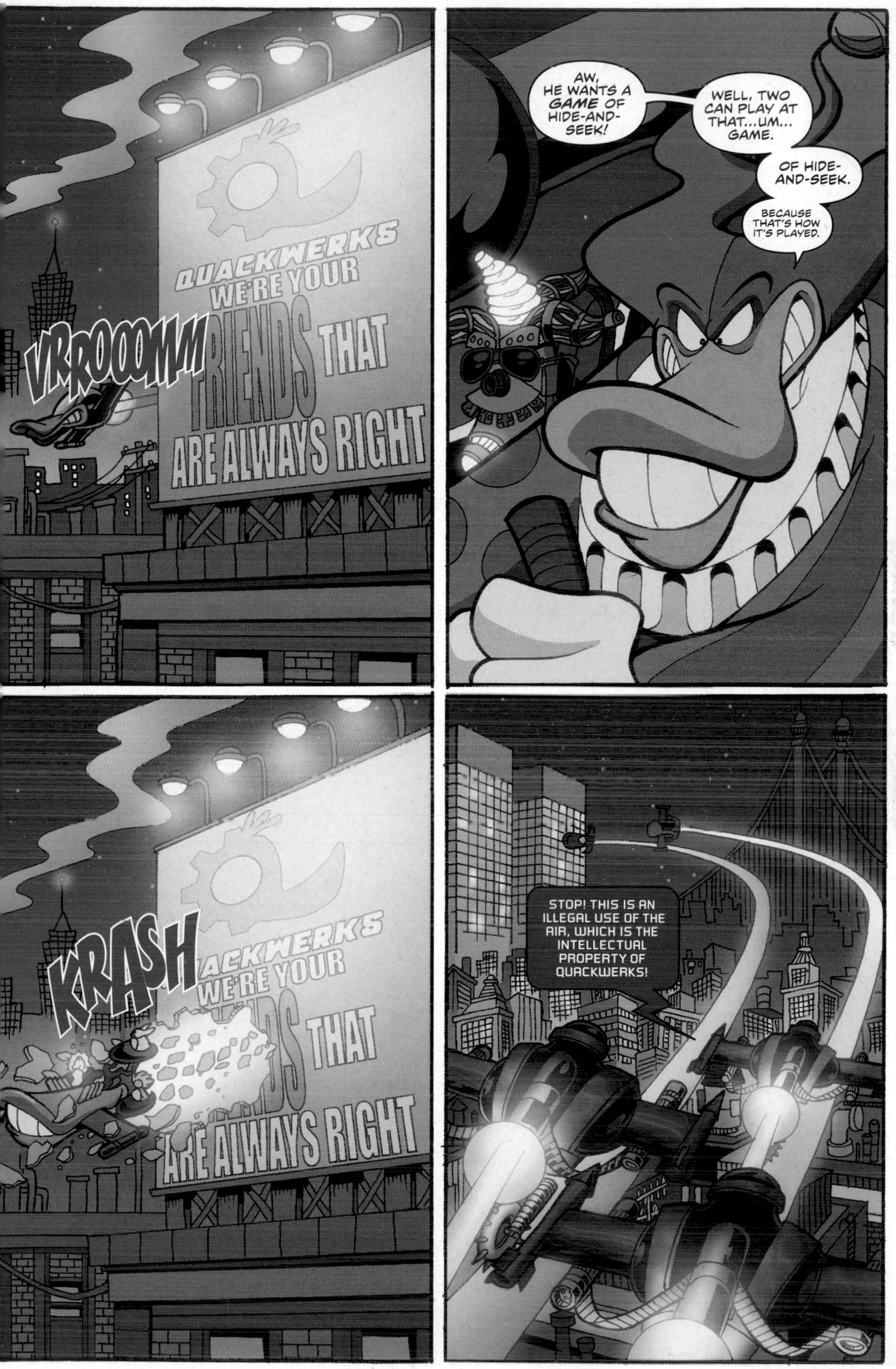
QUACKWERKS
WE'RE YOUR
FRIENDS THAT
ARE ALWAYS RIGHT
VRROOOMM
AW, HE WANTS A GAME OF HIDE-AND-SEEK!
WELL, TWO CAN PLAY AT THAT...UM... GAME.
OF HIDE-AND-SEEK.
BECAUSE THAT'S HOW IT'S PLAYED.
KRASH
ACKWERKS
WE'RE YOUR
DS THAT
ARE ALWAYS RIGHT
STOP! THIS IS AN ILLEGAL USE OF THE AIR, WHICH IS THE INTELLECTUAL PROPERTY OF QUACKWERKS!

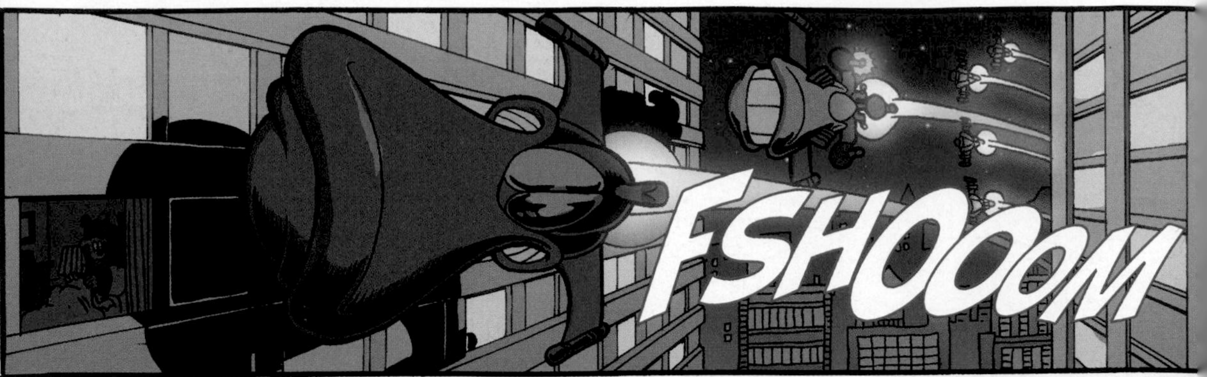
FSHOOOM

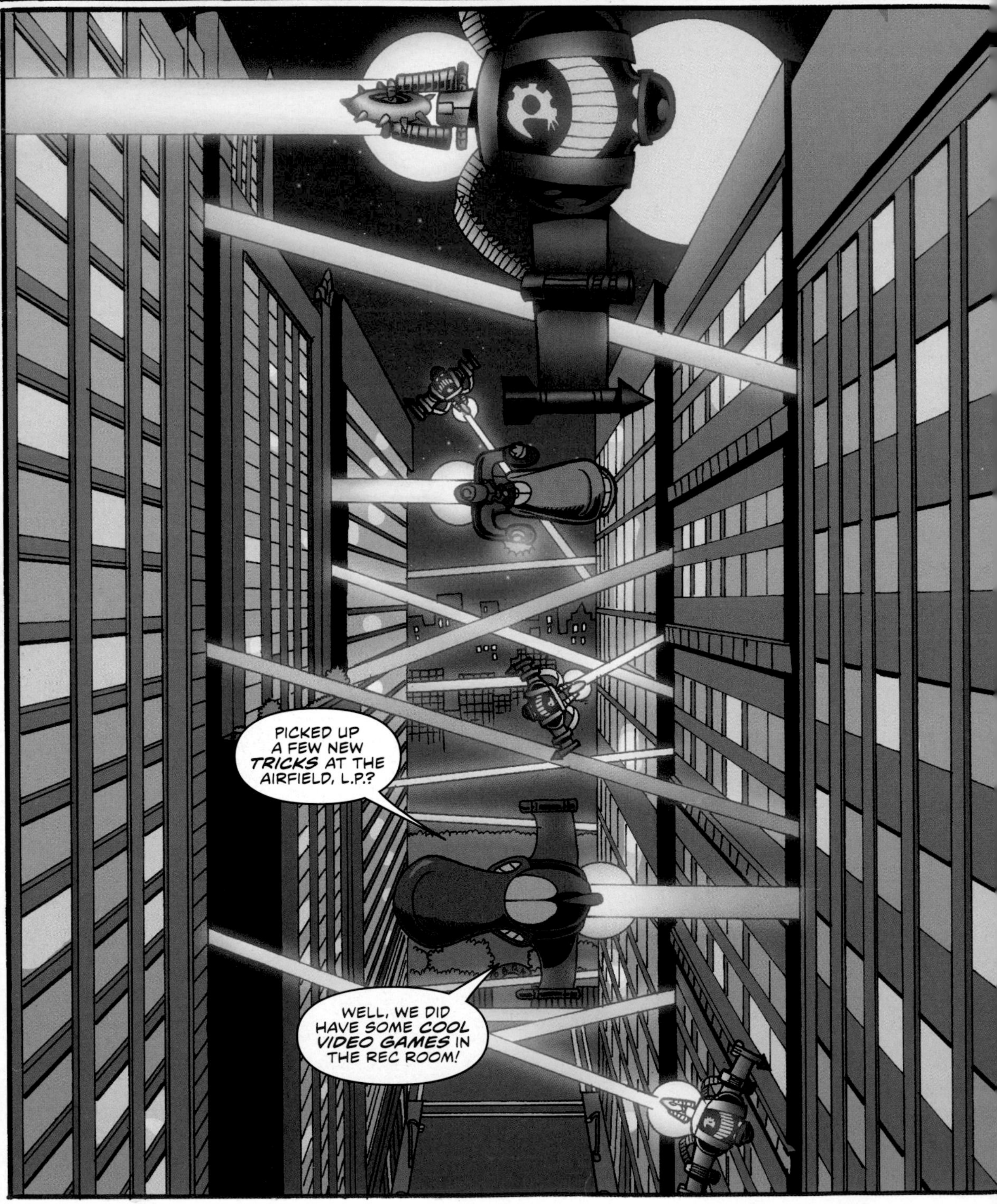
PICKED UP A FEW NEW TRICKS AT THE AIRFIELD, L.P.?
WELL, WE DID HAVE SOME COOL VIDEO GAMES IN THE REC ROOM!

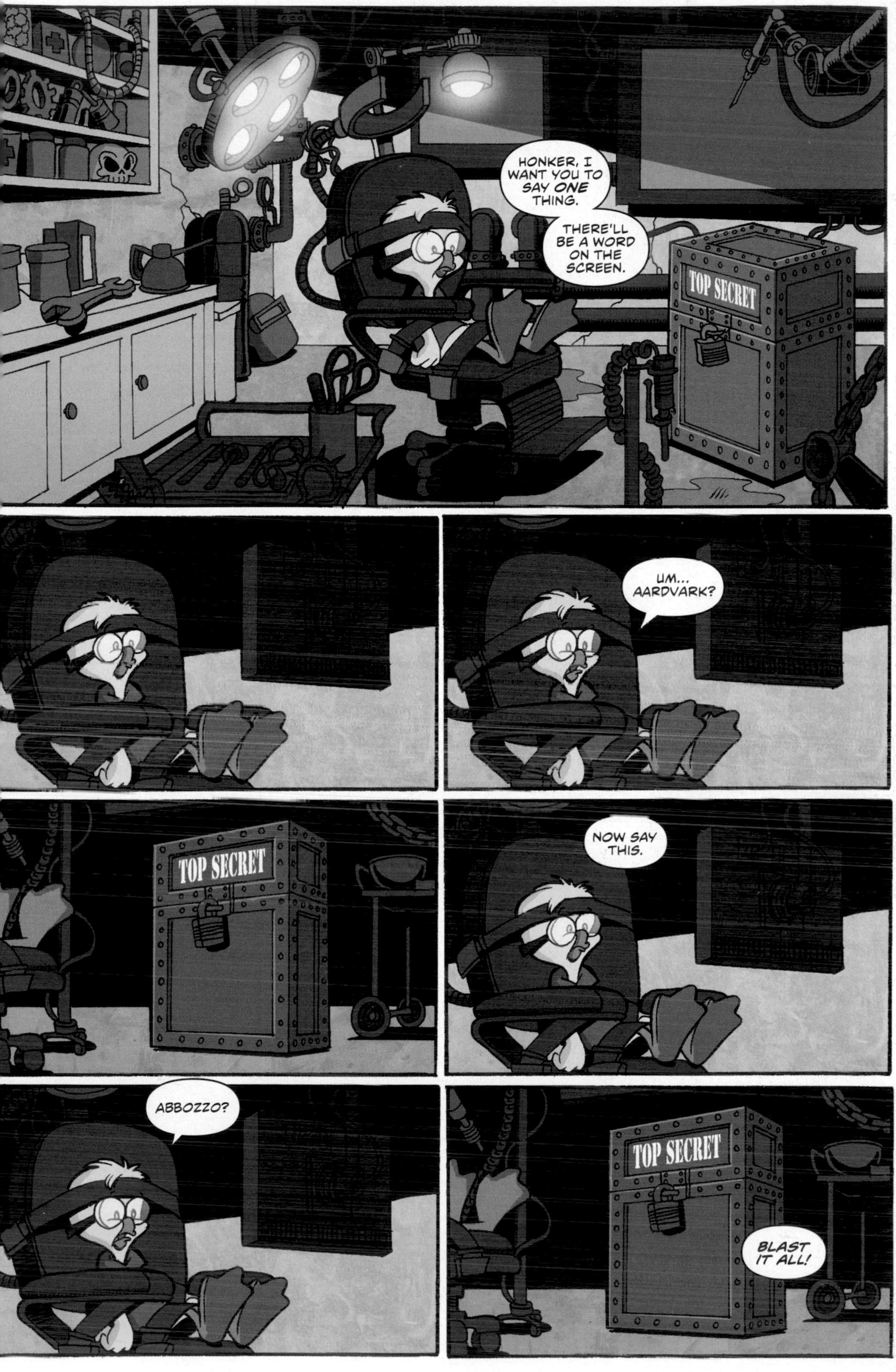
HONKER, I WANT YOU TO SAY ONE THING.
THERE'LL BE A WORD ON THE SCREEN.
TOP SECRET
UM... AARDVARK?
TOP SECRET
NOW SAY THIS.
ABBOZZO?
TOP SECRET
BLAST IT ALL!

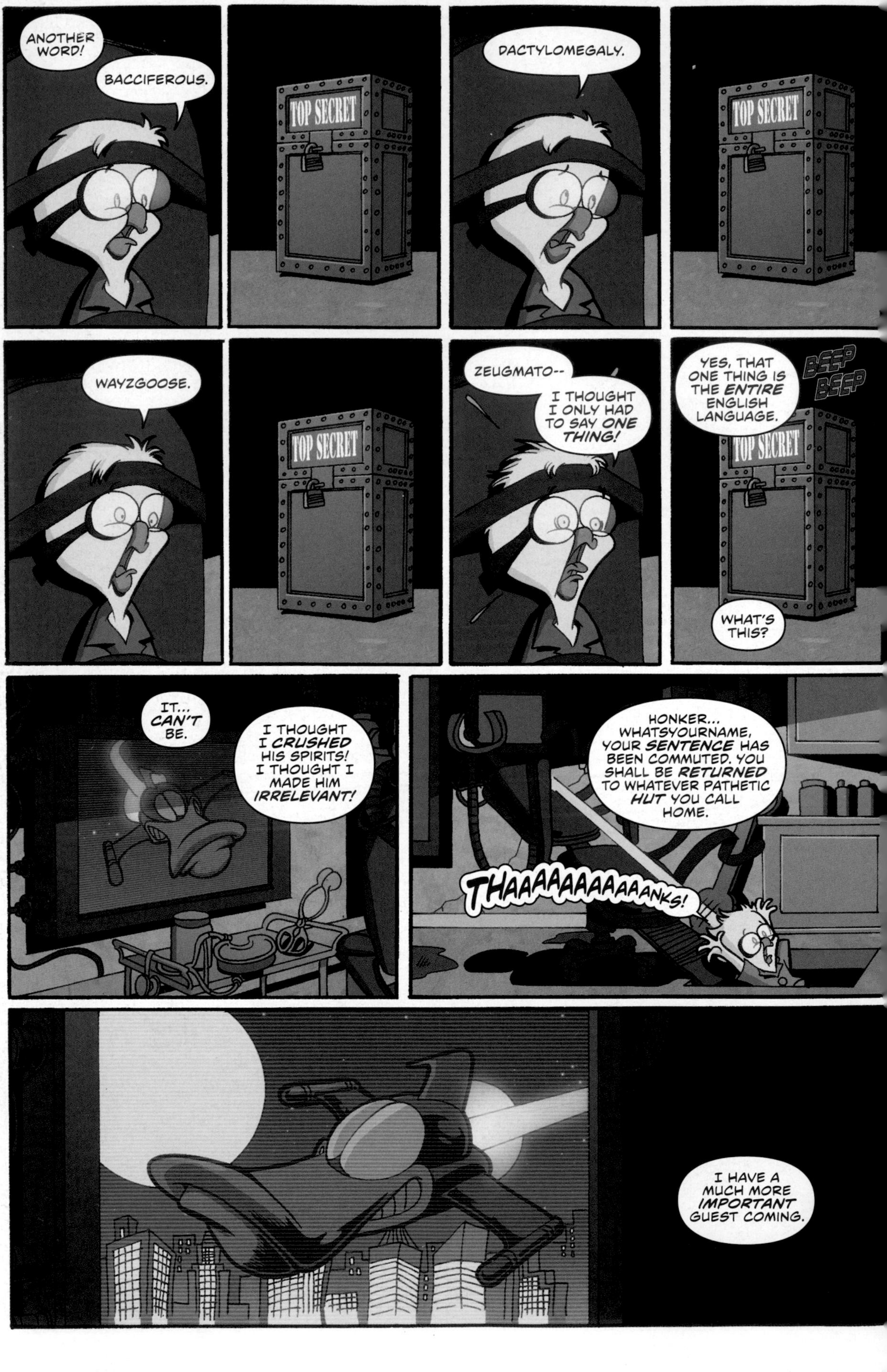
ANOTHER WORD!
BACCIFEROUS.
TOP SECRET
DACTYLOMEGALY.
TOP SECRET
WAYZGOOSE.
TOP SECRET
ZEUGMATO--
I THOUGHT I ONLY HAD TO SAY ONE THING!
YES, THAT ONE THING IS THE ENTIRE ENGLISH LANGUAGE.
BEEP BEEP
TOP SECRET
WHAT'S THIS?
IT... CAN'T BE.
I THOUGHT I CRUSHED HIS SPIRITS! I THOUGHT I MADE HIM IRRELEVANT!
HONKER... WHATSYOURNAME, YOUR SENTENCE HAS BEEN COMMUTED. YOU SHALL BE RETURNED TO WHATEVER PATHETIC HUT YOU CALL HOME.
THAAAAAAAAAAANKS!
I HAVE A MUCH MORE IMPORTANT GUEST COMING.

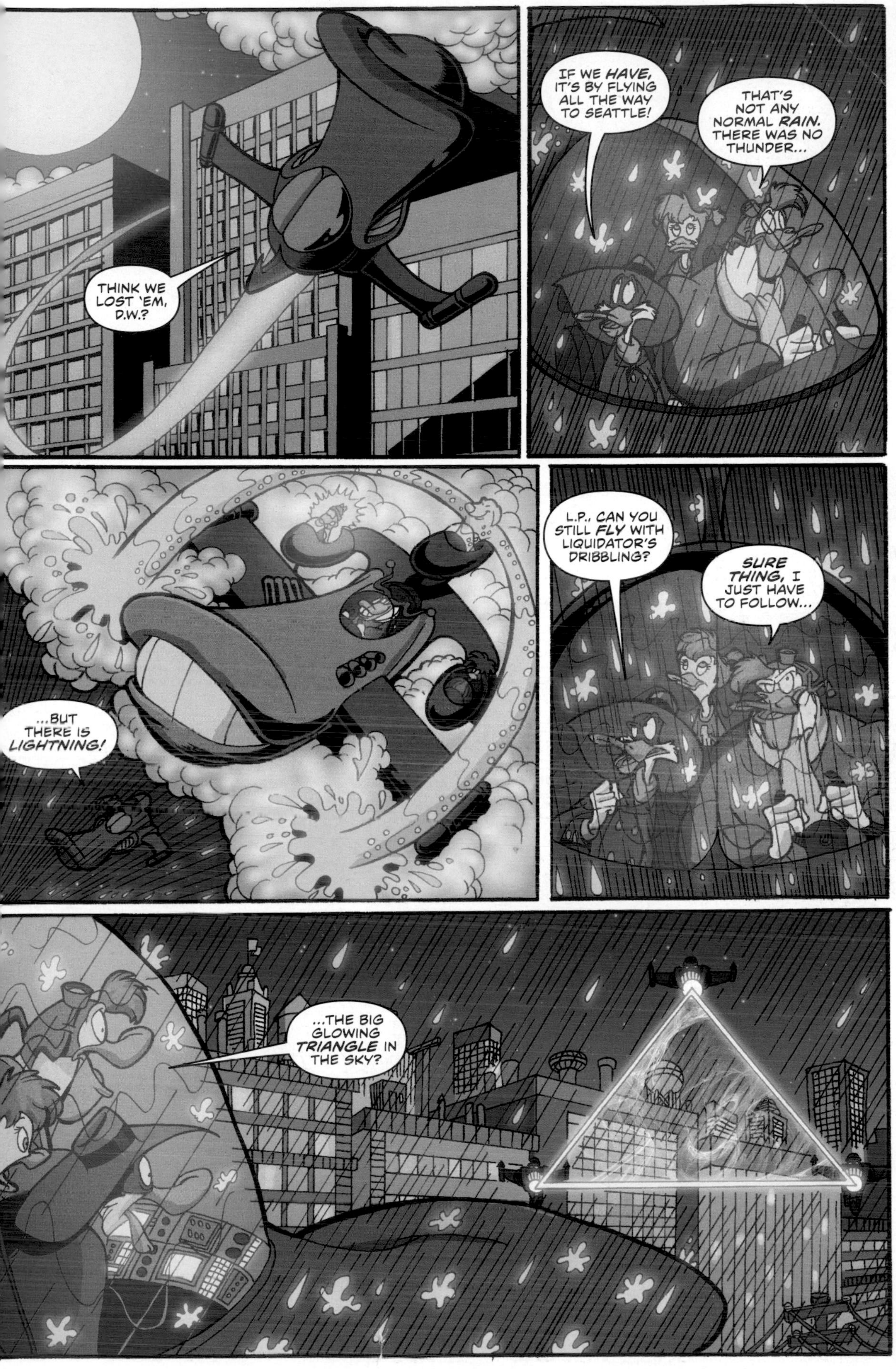
THINK WE LOST 'EM, D.W.?
IF WE HAVE, IT'S BY FLYING ALL THE WAY TO SEATTLE!
THAT'S NOT ANY NORMAL RAIN. THERE WAS NO THUNDER...
...BUT THERE IS LIGHTNING!
L.P., CAN YOU STILL FLY WITH LIQUIDATOR'S DRIBBLING?
SURE THING, I JUST HAVE TO FOLLOW...
...THE BIG GLOWING TRIANGLE IN THE SKY?

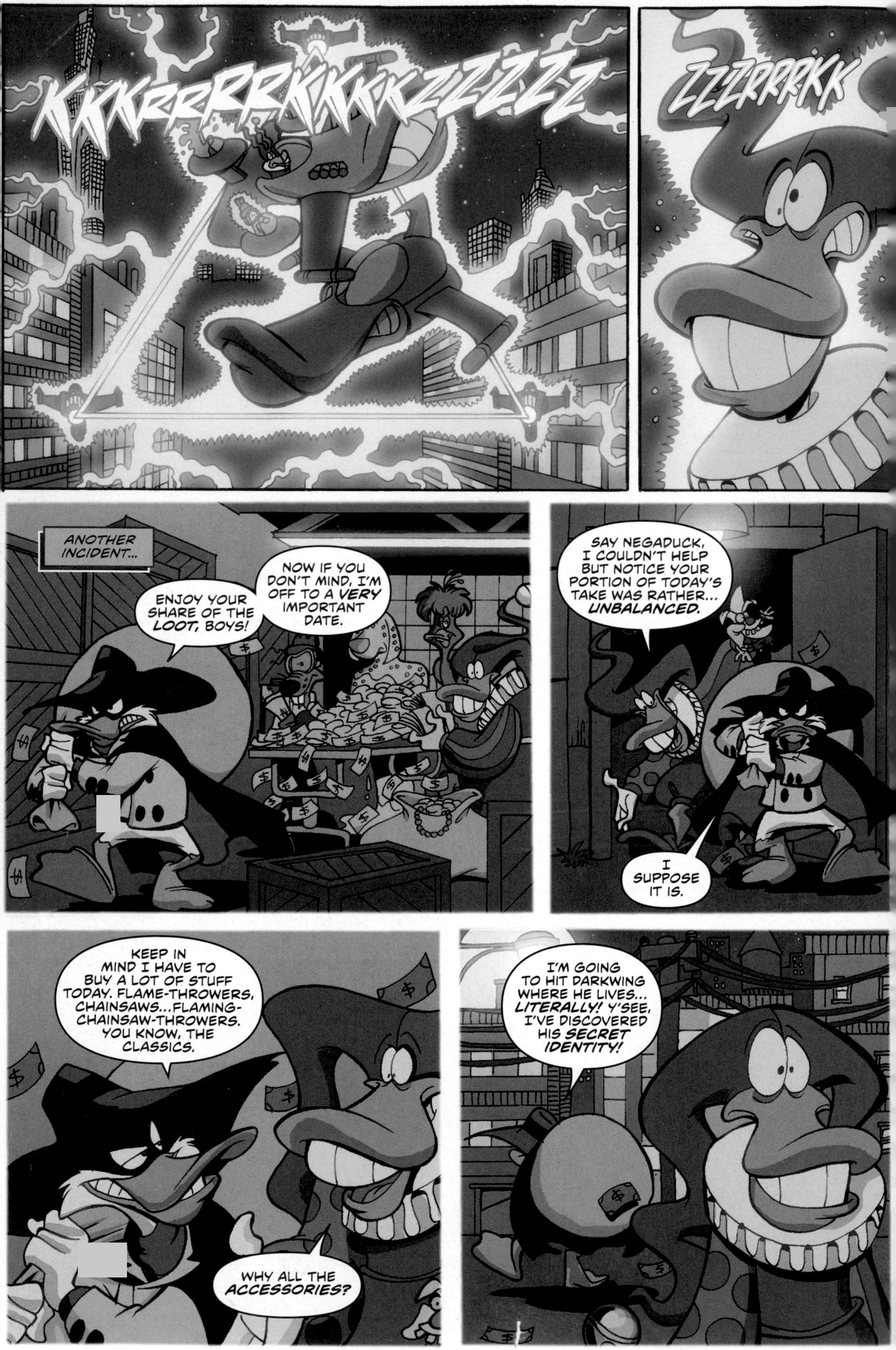

KKKRRRRKKKKKZZZZZZZ
ZZZRRRKK
ANOTHER INCIDENT...
ENJOY YOUR SHARE OF THE *LOOT*, BOYS!
NOW IF YOU DON'T MIND, I'M OFF TO A *VERY* IMPORTANT DATE.
SAY NEGADUCK, I COULDN'T HELP BUT NOTICE YOUR PORTION OF TODAY'S TAKE WAS RATHER... *UNBALANCED.*
I SUPPOSE IT IS.
WHY ALL THE *ACCESSORIES?*
KEEP IN MIND I HAVE TO BUY A LOT OF STUFF TODAY. FLAME-THROWERS, CHAINSAWS...FLAMING-CHAINSAW-THROWERS. YOU KNOW, THE CLASSICS.
I'M GOING TO HIT DARKWING WHERE HE LIVES... *LITERALLY!* Y'SEE, I'VE DISCOVERED HIS *SECRET IDENTITY!*

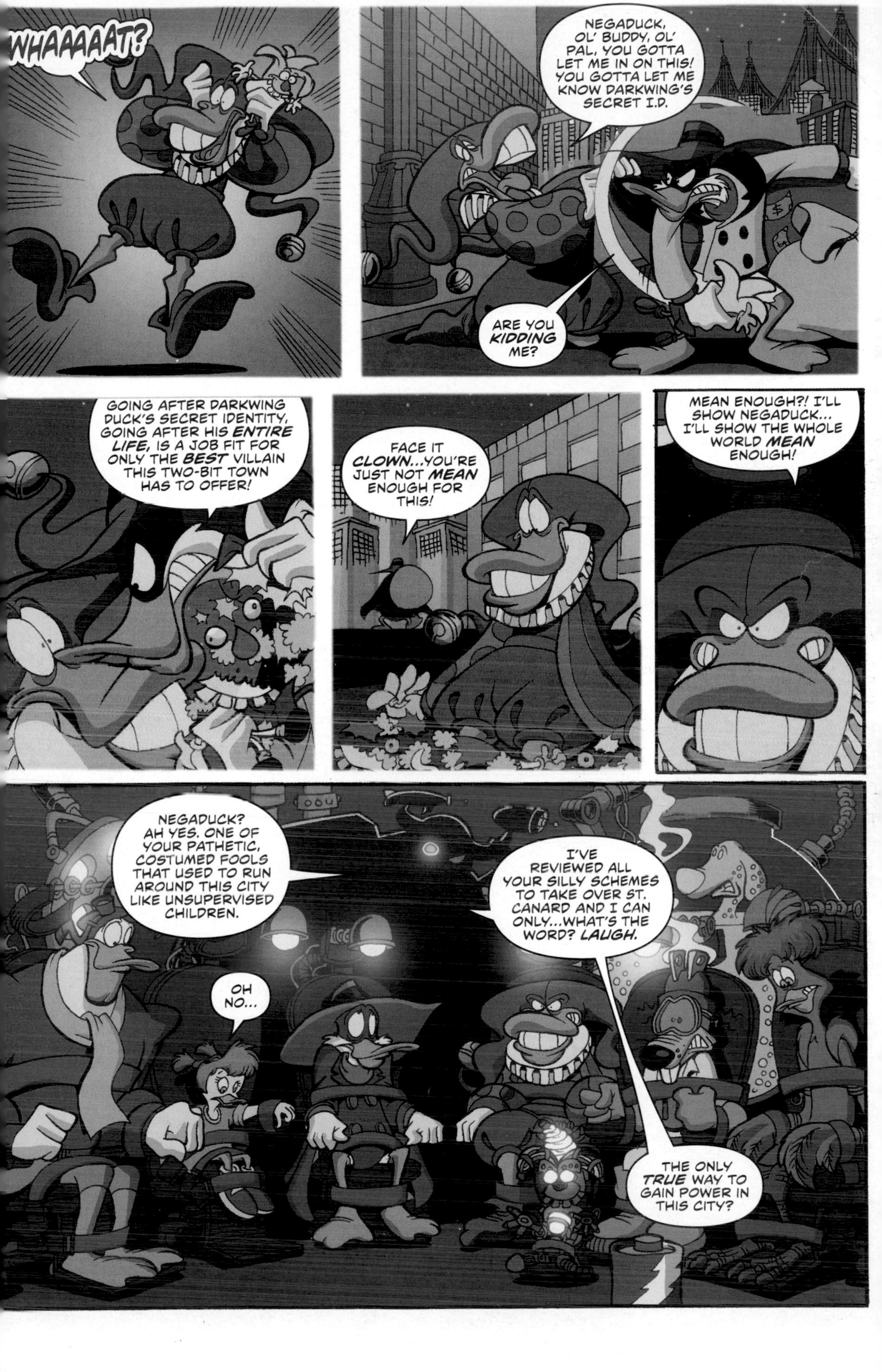
WHAAAAAT?
NEGADUCK, OL' BUDDY, OL' PAL, YOU GOTTA LET ME IN ON THIS! YOU GOTTA LET ME KNOW DARKWING'S SECRET I.D.
ARE YOU KIDDING ME?
GOING AFTER DARKWING DUCK'S SECRET IDENTITY, GOING AFTER HIS ENTIRE LIFE, IS A JOB FIT FOR ONLY THE BEST VILLAIN THIS TWO-BIT TOWN HAS TO OFFER!
FACE IT CLOWN...YOU'RE JUST NOT MEAN ENOUGH FOR THIS!
MEAN ENOUGH?! I'LL SHOW NEGADUCK... I'LL SHOW THE WHOLE WORLD MEAN ENOUGH!
NEGADUCK? AH YES. ONE OF YOUR PATHETIC, COSTUMED FOOLS THAT USED TO RUN AROUND THIS CITY LIKE UNSUPERVISED CHILDREN.
OH NO...
I'VE REVIEWED ALL YOUR SILLY SCHEMES TO TAKE OVER ST. CANARD AND I CAN ONLY...WHAT'S THE WORD? LAUGH.
THE ONLY TRUE WAY TO GAIN POWER IN THIS CITY?

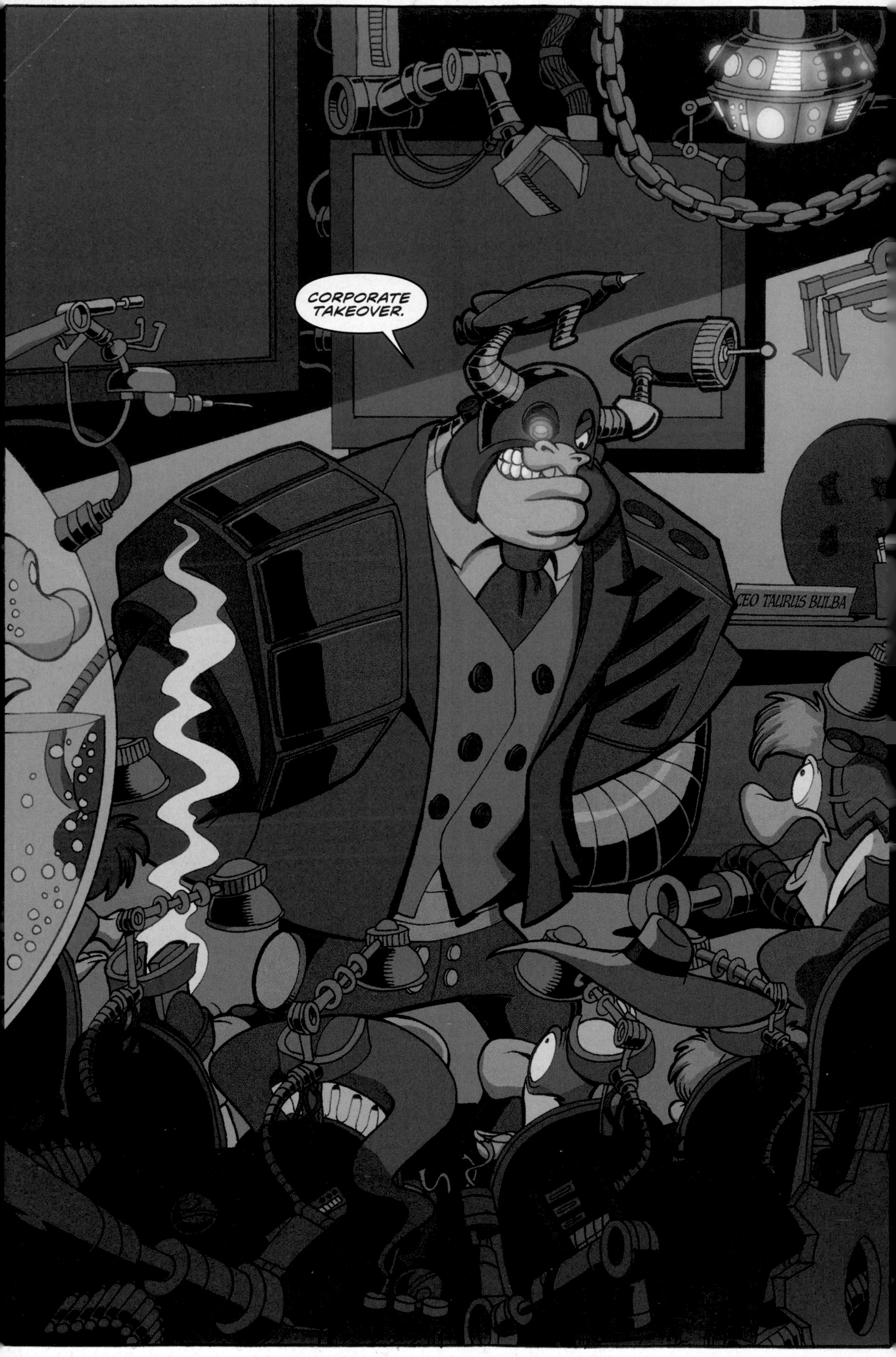
CORPORATE TAKEOVER.
CEO TAURUS BULBA

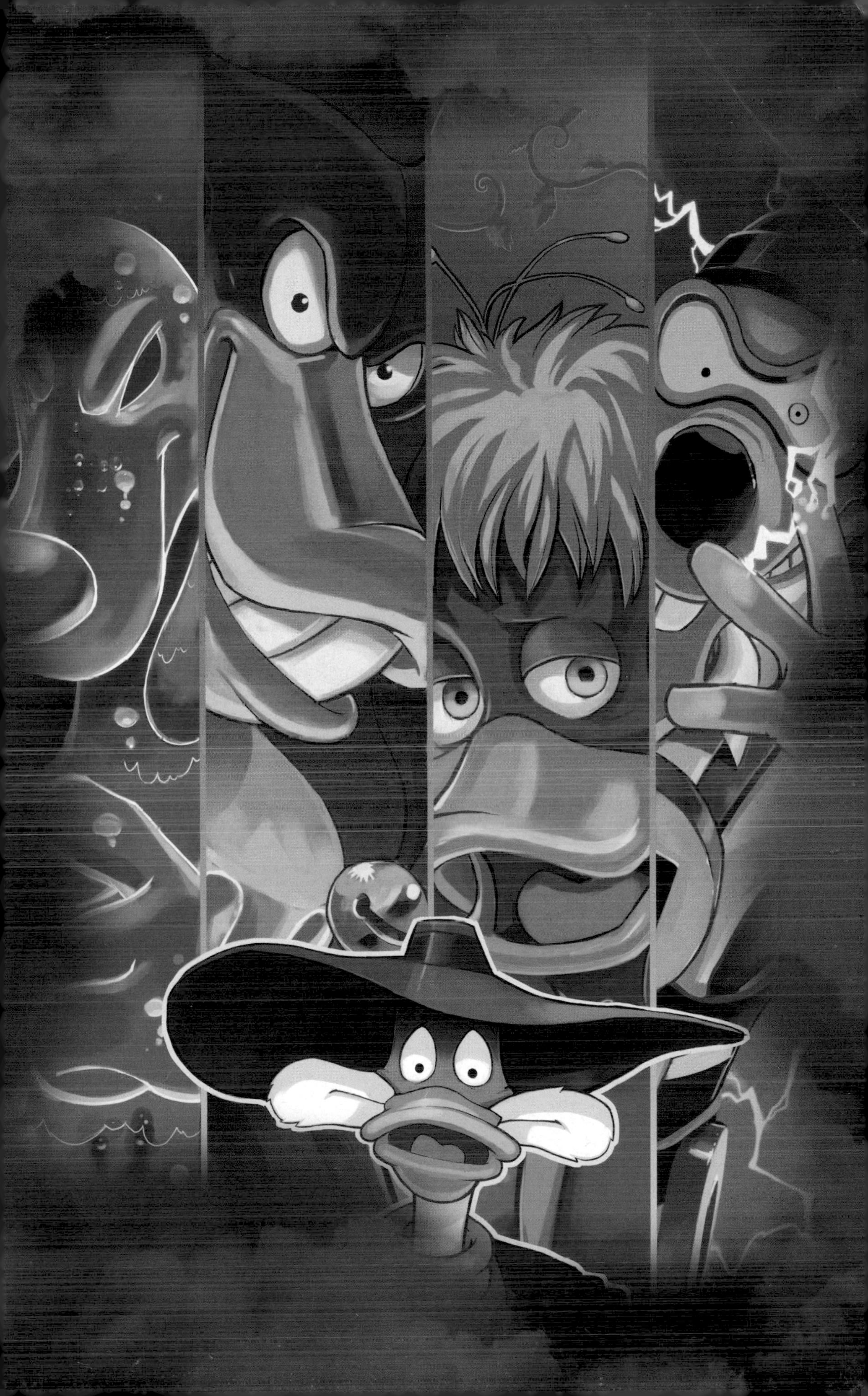

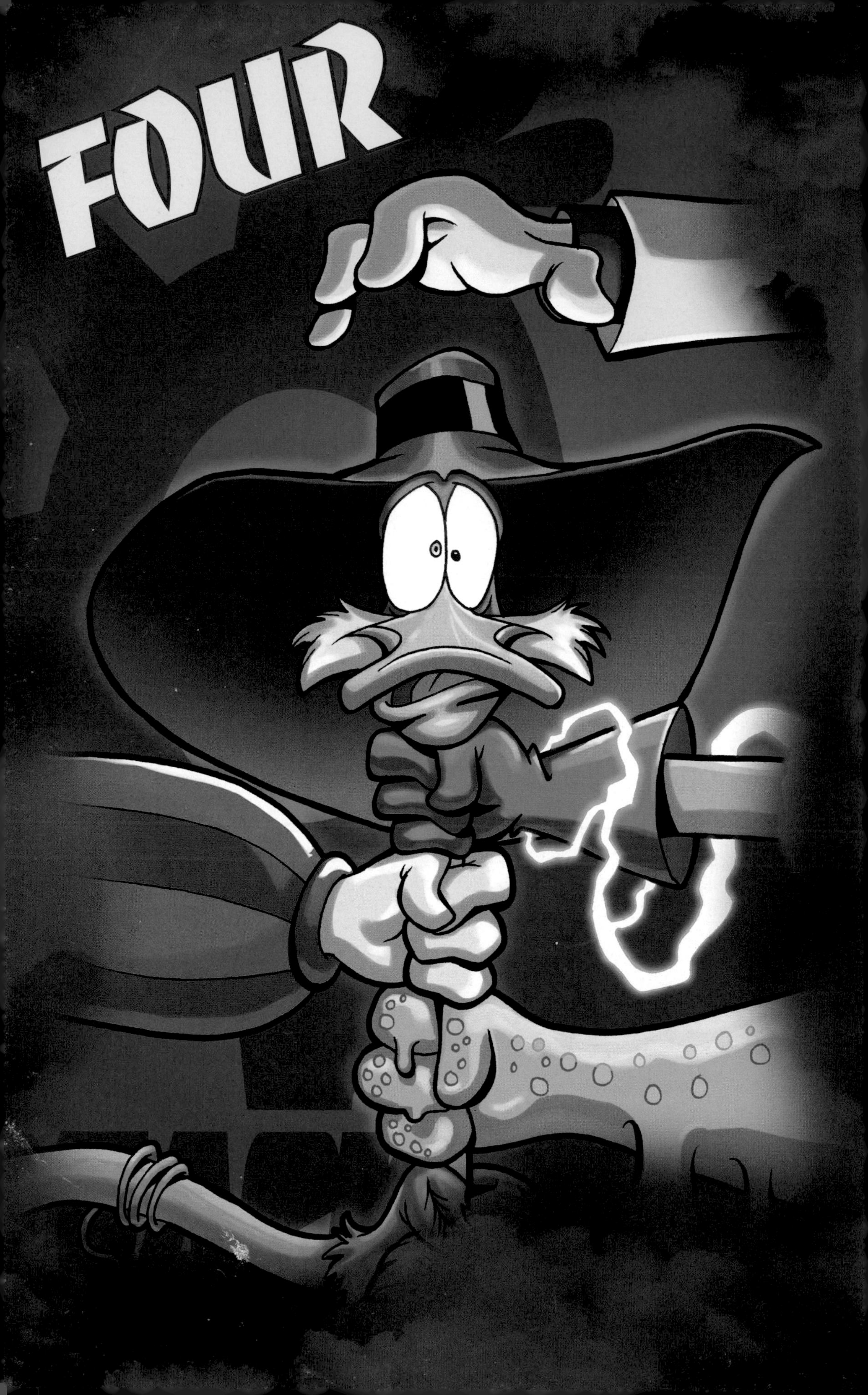
FOUR

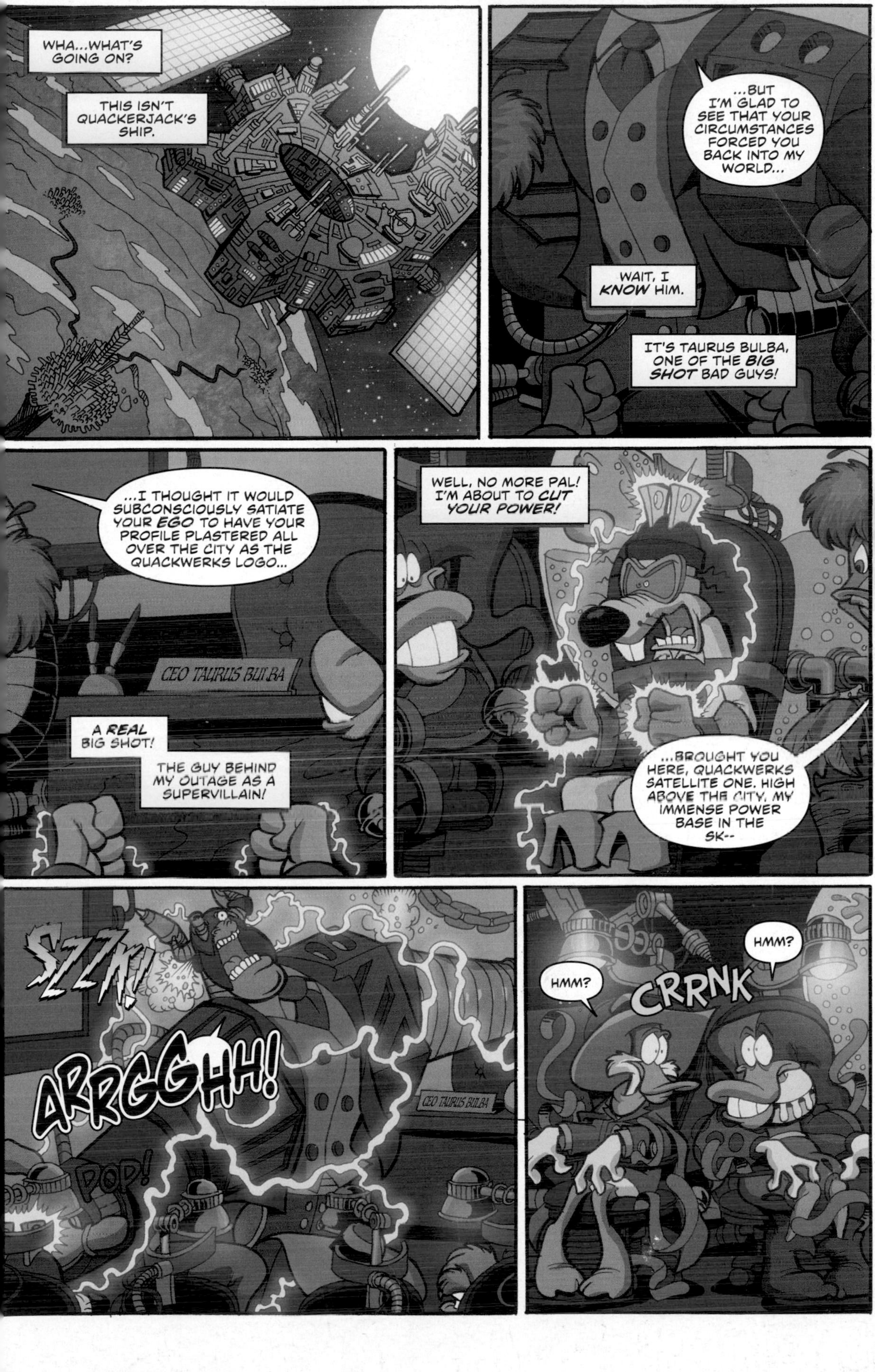
WHA...WHAT'S GOING ON?
THIS ISN'T QUACKERJACK'S SHIP.
...BUT I'M GLAD TO SEE THAT YOUR CIRCUMSTANCES FORCED YOU BACK INTO MY WORLD...
WAIT, I KNOW HIM.
IT'S TAURUS BULBA, ONE OF THE BIG SHOT BAD GUYS!
...I THOUGHT IT WOULD SUBCONSCIOUSLY SATIATE YOUR EGO TO HAVE YOUR PROFILE PLASTERED ALL OVER THE CITY AS THE QUACKWERKS LOGO...
CEO TAURUS BULBA
A REAL BIG SHOT!
THE GUY BEHIND MY OUTAGE AS A SUPERVILLAIN!
WELL, NO MORE PAL! I'M ABOUT TO CUT YOUR POWER!
...BROUGHT YOU HERE, QUACKWERKS SATELLITE ONE. HIGH ABOVE THE CITY. MY IMMENSE POWER BASE IN THE SK--
SZZK!
ARRGGHH!
CEO TAURUS BULBA
POP!
HMM?
HMM?
CRRNK

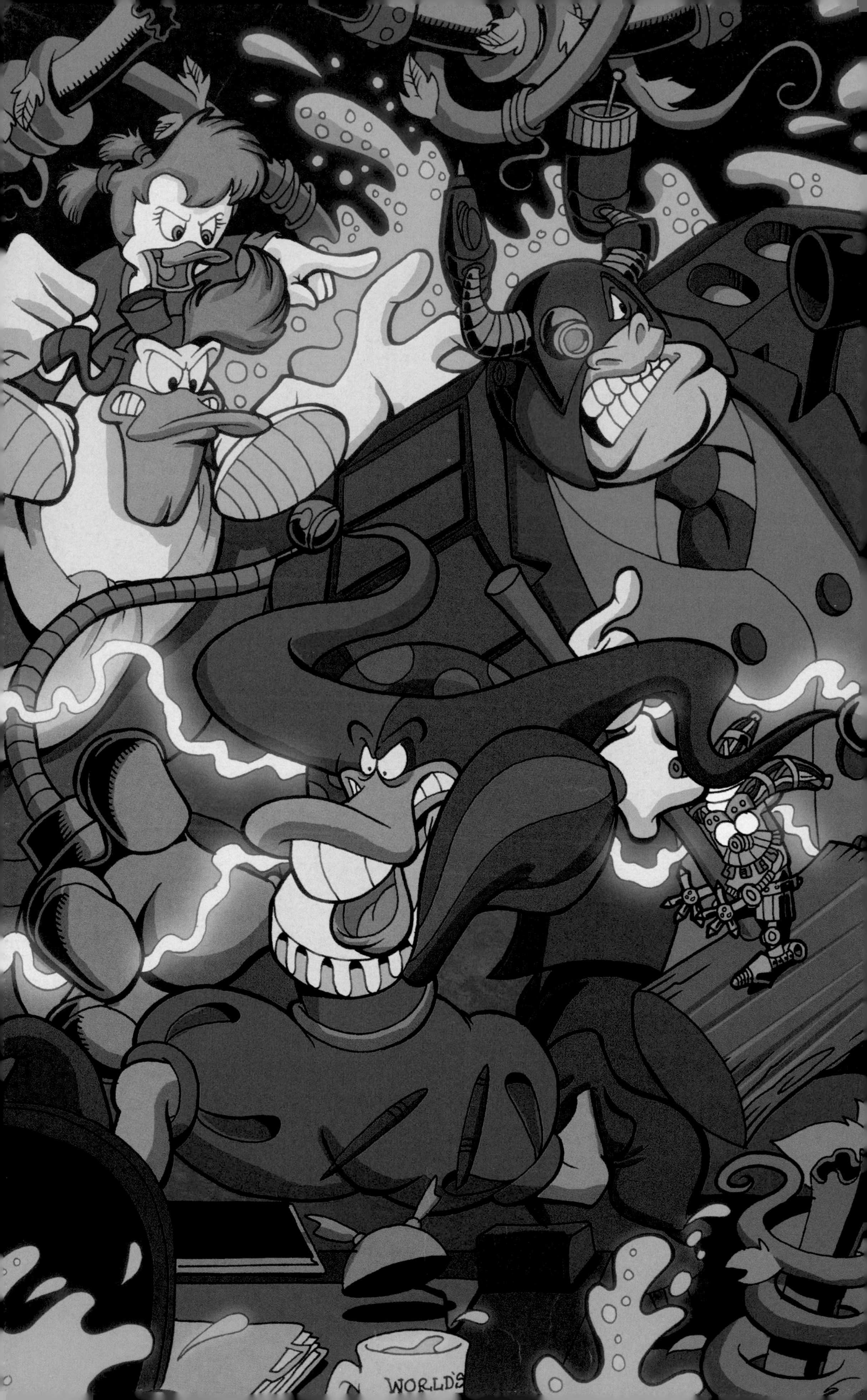
WORLD'S

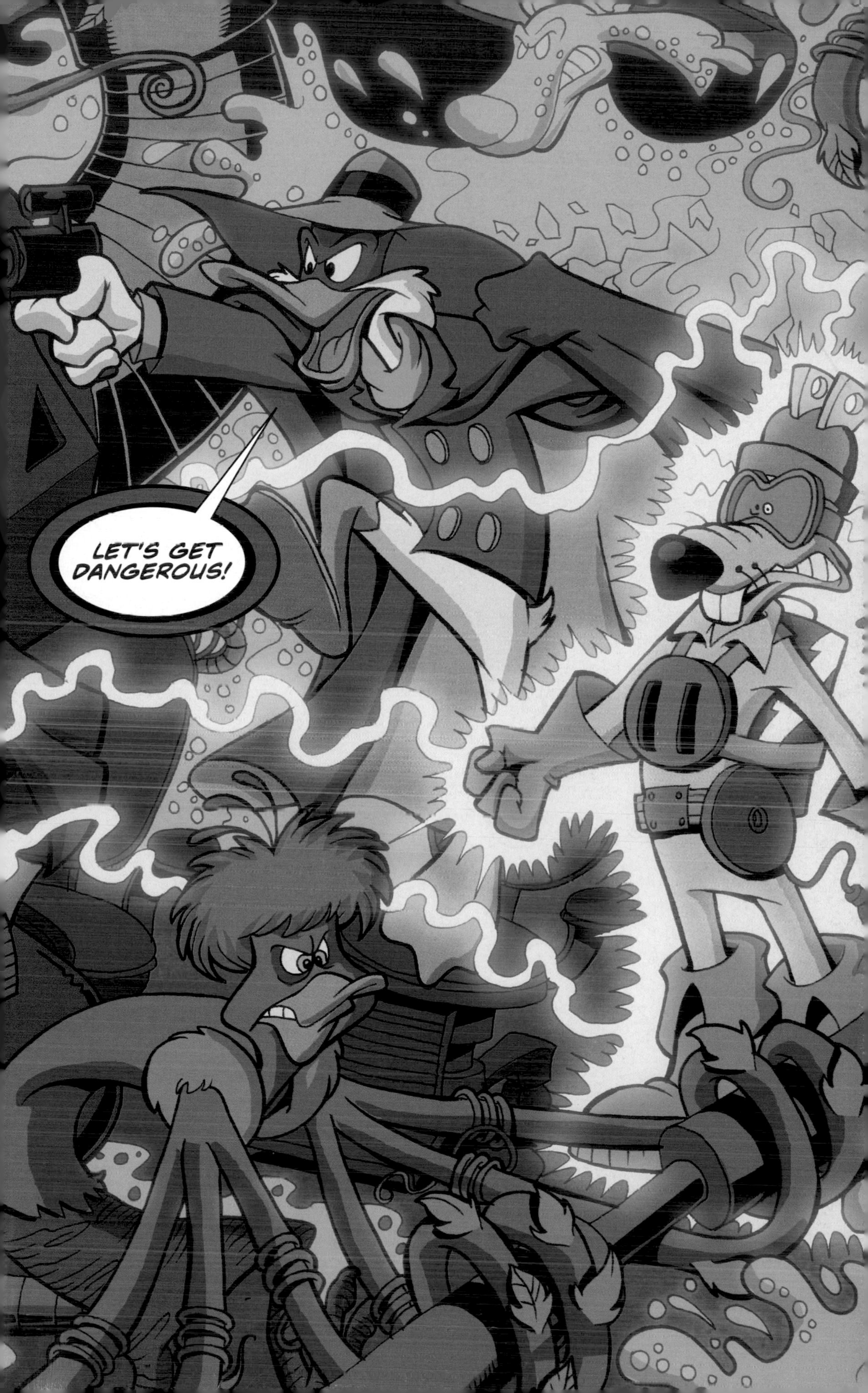
LET'S GET DANGEROUS!

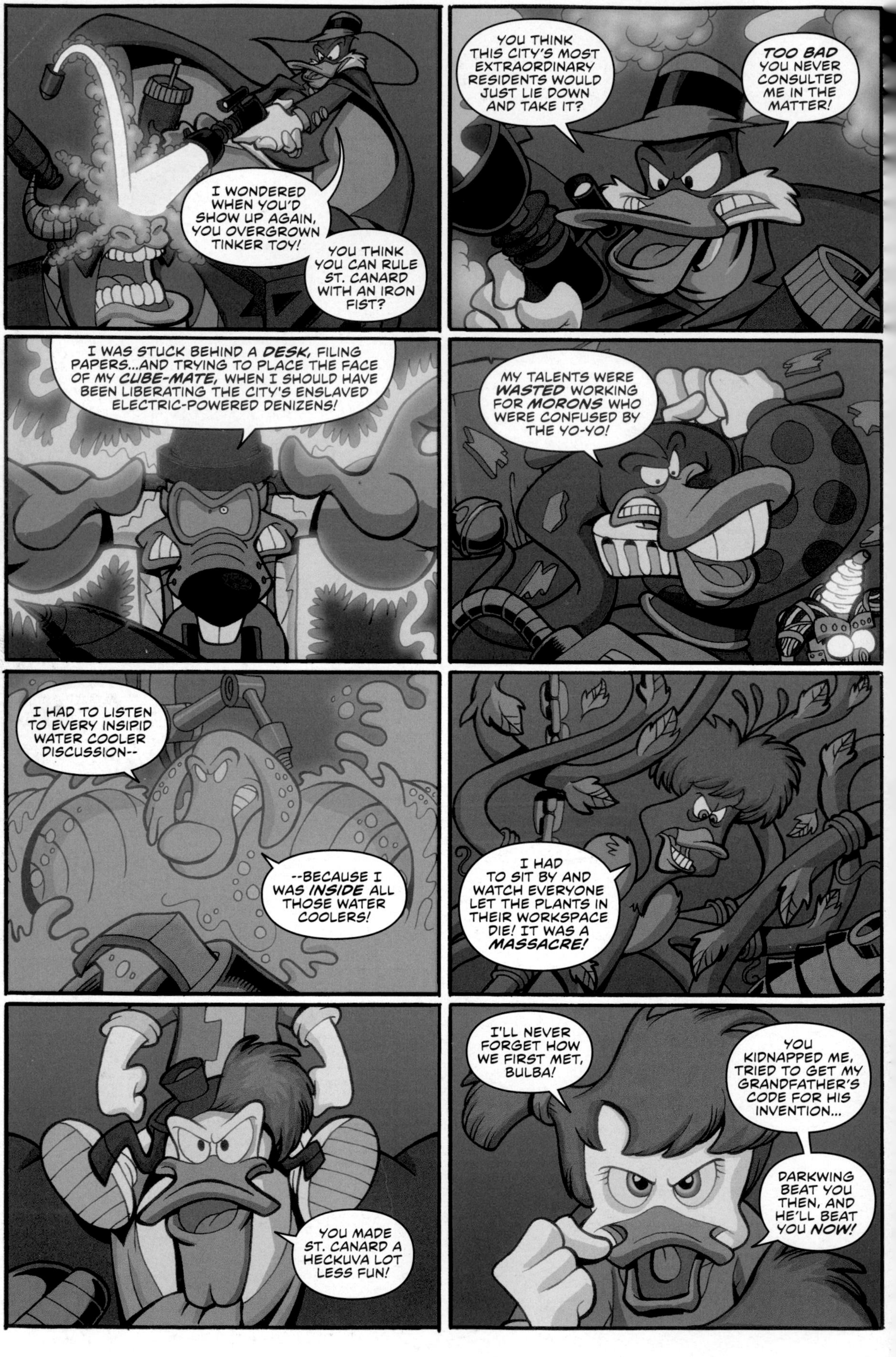
I WONDERED WHEN YOU'D SHOW UP AGAIN, YOU OVERGROWN TINKER TOY!
YOU THINK YOU CAN RULE ST. CANARD WITH AN IRON FIST?
YOU THINK THIS CITY'S MOST EXTRAORDINARY RESIDENTS WOULD JUST LIE DOWN AND TAKE IT?
TOO BAD YOU NEVER CONSULTED ME IN THE MATTER!
I WAS STUCK BEHIND A DESK, FILING PAPERS...AND TRYING TO PLACE THE FACE OF MY CUBE-MATE, WHEN I SHOULD HAVE BEEN LIBERATING THE CITY'S ENSLAVED ELECTRIC-POWERED DENIZENS!
MY TALENTS WERE WASTED WORKING FOR MORONS WHO WERE CONFUSED BY THE YO-YO!
I HAD TO LISTEN TO EVERY INSIPID WATER COOLER DISCUSSION--
--BECAUSE I WAS INSIDE ALL THOSE WATER COOLERS!
I HAD TO SIT BY AND WATCH EVERYONE LET THE PLANTS IN THEIR WORKSPACE DIE! IT WAS A MASSACRE!
YOU MADE ST. CANARD A HECKUVA LOT LESS FUN!
I'LL NEVER FORGET HOW WE FIRST MET, BULBA!
YOU KIDNAPPED ME, TRIED TO GET MY GRANDFATHER'S CODE FOR HIS INVENTION...
DARKWING BEAT YOU THEN, AND HE'LL BEAT YOU NOW!

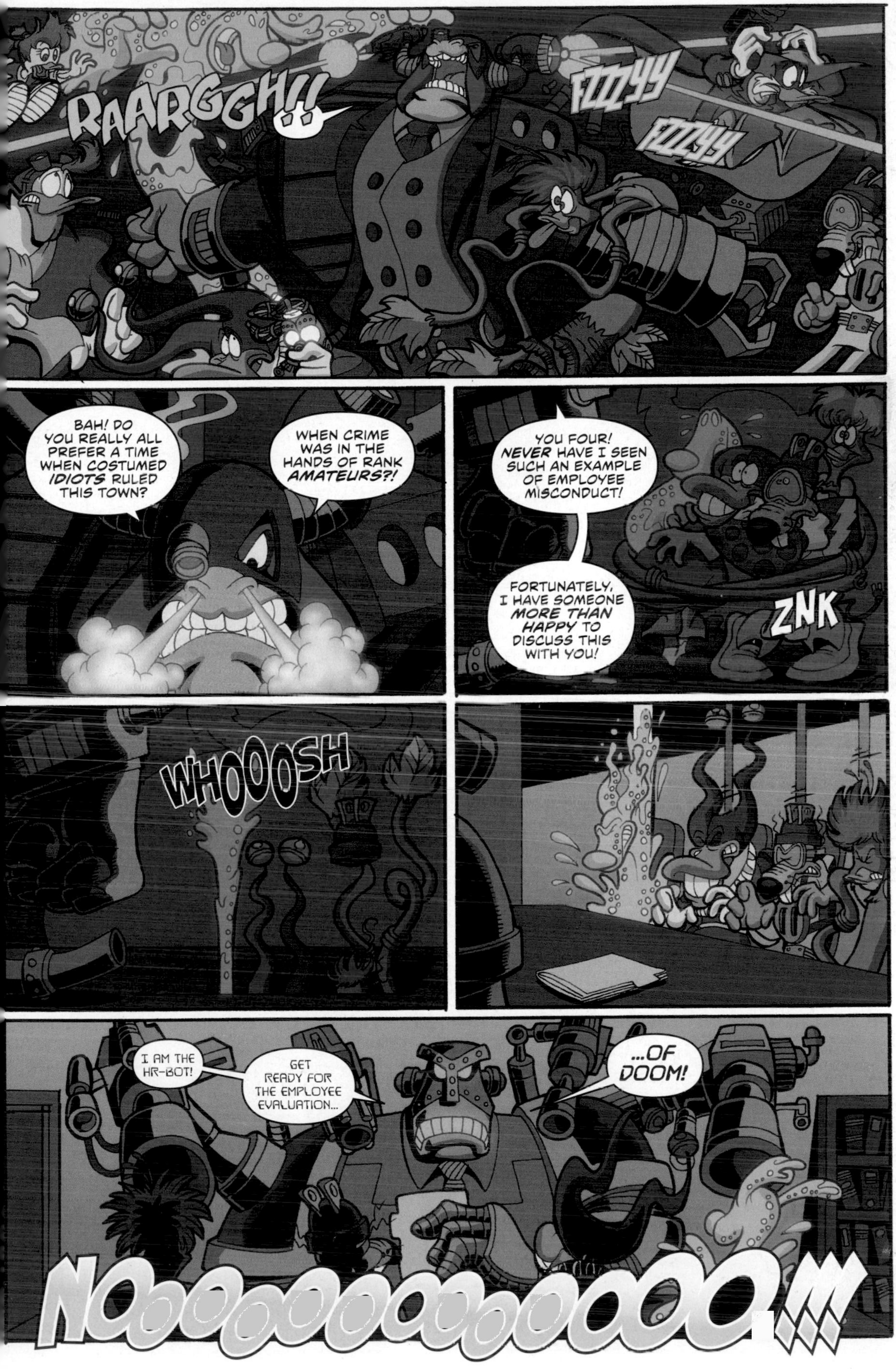
RAARGGH!!
FZZZYY
FZZZYY
BAH! DO YOU REALLY ALL PREFER A TIME WHEN COSTUMED IDIOTS RULED THIS TOWN?
WHEN CRIME WAS IN THE HANDS OF RANK AMATEURS?!
YOU FOUR! NEVER HAVE I SEEN SUCH AN EXAMPLE OF EMPLOYEE MISCONDUCT!
FORTUNATELY, I HAVE SOMEONE MORE THAN HAPPY TO DISCUSS THIS WITH YOU!
ZNK
WHOOOSH
I AM THE HR-BOT!
GET READY FOR THE EMPLOYEE EVALUATION...
...OF DOOM!
NOOOOOOOOOOOOO!!!

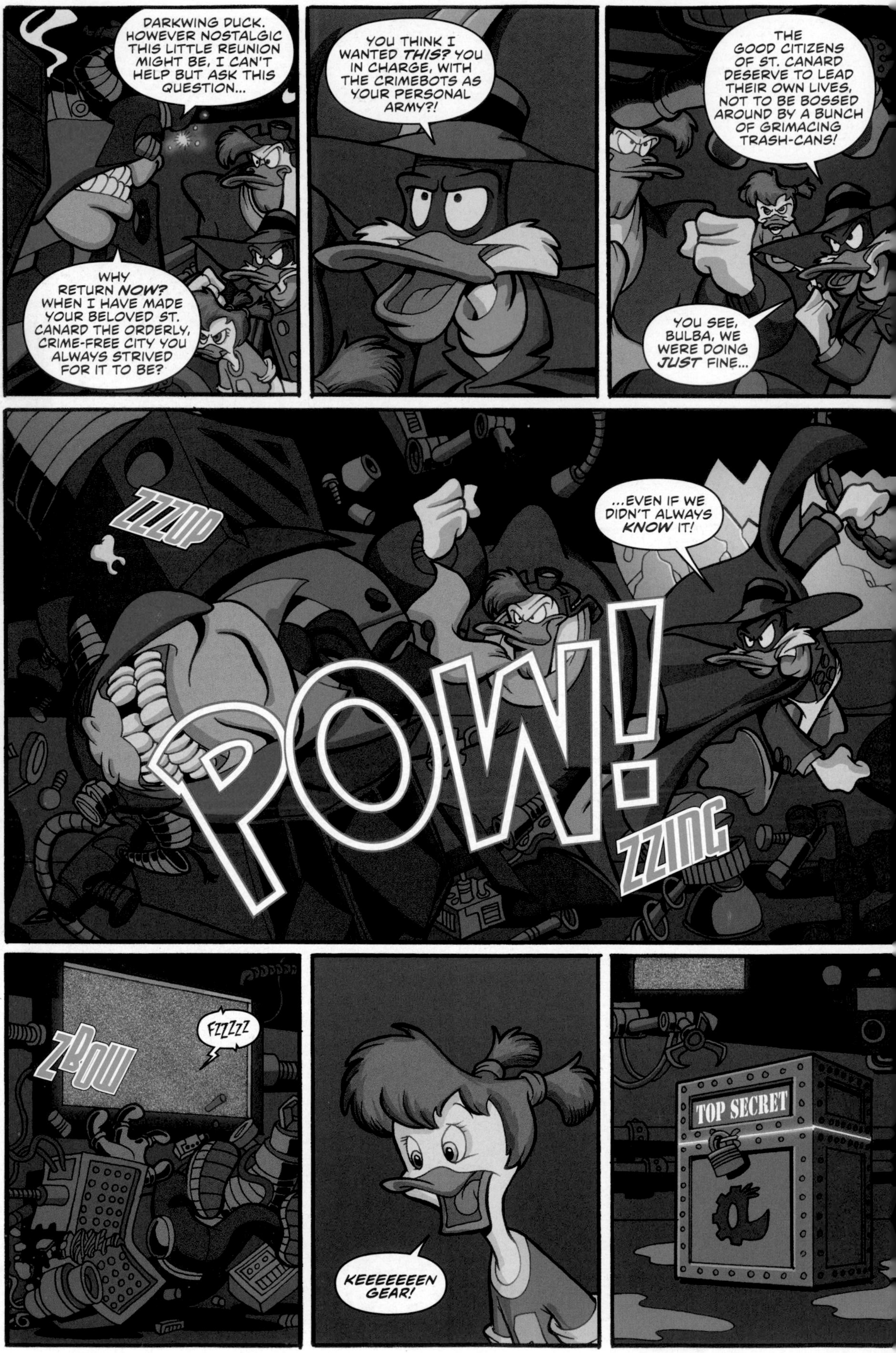
DARKWING DUCK. HOWEVER NOSTALGIC THIS LITTLE REUNION MIGHT BE, I CAN'T HELP BUT ASK THIS QUESTION...
WHY RETURN NOW? WHEN I HAVE MADE YOUR BELOVED ST. CANARD THE ORDERLY, CRIME-FREE CITY YOU ALWAYS STRIVED FOR IT TO BE?
YOU THINK I WANTED THIS? YOU IN CHARGE, WITH THE CRIMEBOTS AS YOUR PERSONAL ARMY?!
THE GOOD CITIZENS OF ST. CANARD DESERVE TO LEAD THEIR OWN LIVES, NOT TO BE BOSSED AROUND BY A BUNCH OF GRIMACING TRASH-CANS!
YOU SEE, BULBA, WE WERE DOING JUST FINE...
ZZZOP
...EVEN IF WE DIDN'T ALWAYS KNOW IT!
POW!
ZZING
ZBOW
FZZZZZ
KEEEEEEEN GEAR!
TOP SECRET

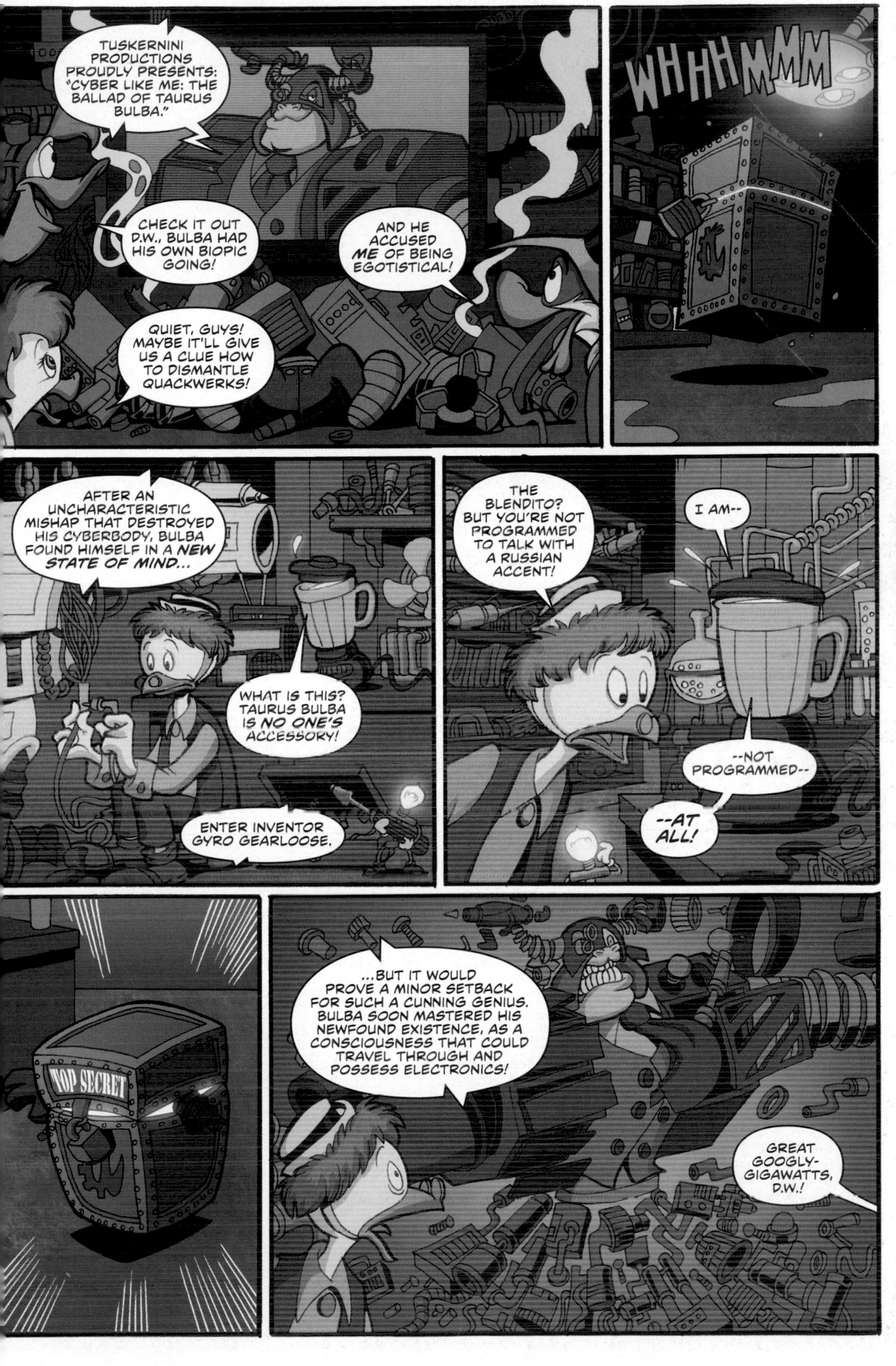
TUSKERNINI PRODUCTIONS PROUDLY PRESENTS: "CYBER LIKE ME: THE BALLAD OF TAURUS BULBA."
CHECK IT OUT D.W., BULBA HAD HIS OWN BIOPIC GOING!
AND HE ACCUSED ME OF BEING EGOTISTICAL!
QUIET, GUYS! MAYBE IT'LL GIVE US A CLUE HOW TO DISMANTLE QUACKWERKS!
WHHHMMMM
AFTER AN UNCHARACTERISTIC MISHAP THAT DESTROYED HIS CYBERBODY, BULBA FOUND HIMSELF IN A NEW STATE OF MIND...
WHAT IS THIS? TAURUS BULBA IS NO ONE'S ACCESSORY!
ENTER INVENTOR GYRO GEARLOOSE.
THE BLENDITO? BUT YOU'RE NOT PROGRAMMED TO TALK WITH A RUSSIAN ACCENT!
I AM--
--NOT PROGRAMMED--
--AT ALL!
TOP SECRET
...BUT IT WOULD PROVE A MINOR SETBACK FOR SUCH A CUNNING GENIUS. BULBA SOON MASTERED HIS NEWFOUND EXISTENCE, AS A CONSCIOUSNESS THAT COULD TRAVEL THROUGH AND POSSESS ELECTRONICS!
GREAT GOOGLY-GIGAWATTS, D.W.!

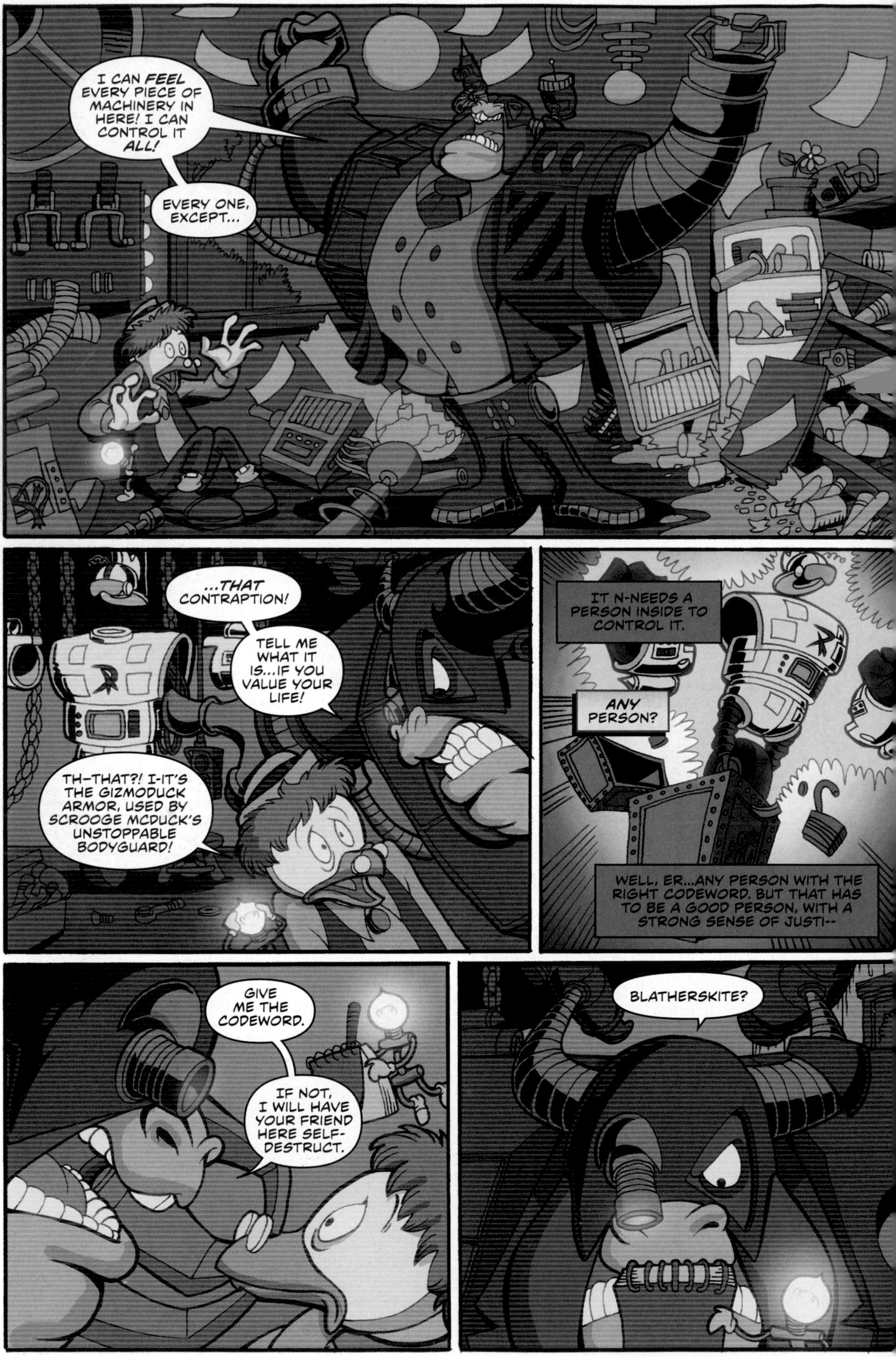

I CAN FEEL EVERY PIECE OF MACHINERY IN HERE! I CAN CONTROL IT ALL!
EVERY ONE, EXCEPT...
...THAT CONTRAPTION!
TELL ME WHAT IT IS...IF YOU VALUE YOUR LIFE!
TH–THAT?! I-IT'S THE GIZMODUCK ARMOR, USED BY SCROOGE McDUCK'S UNSTOPPABLE BODYGUARD!
IT N-NEEDS A PERSON INSIDE TO CONTROL IT.
ANY PERSON?
WELL, ER...ANY PERSON WITH THE RIGHT CODEWORD. BUT THAT HAS TO BE A GOOD PERSON, WITH A STRONG SENSE OF JUSTI--
GIVE ME THE CODEWORD.
IF NOT, I WILL HAVE YOUR FRIEND HERE SELF-DESTRUCT.
BLATHERSKITE?

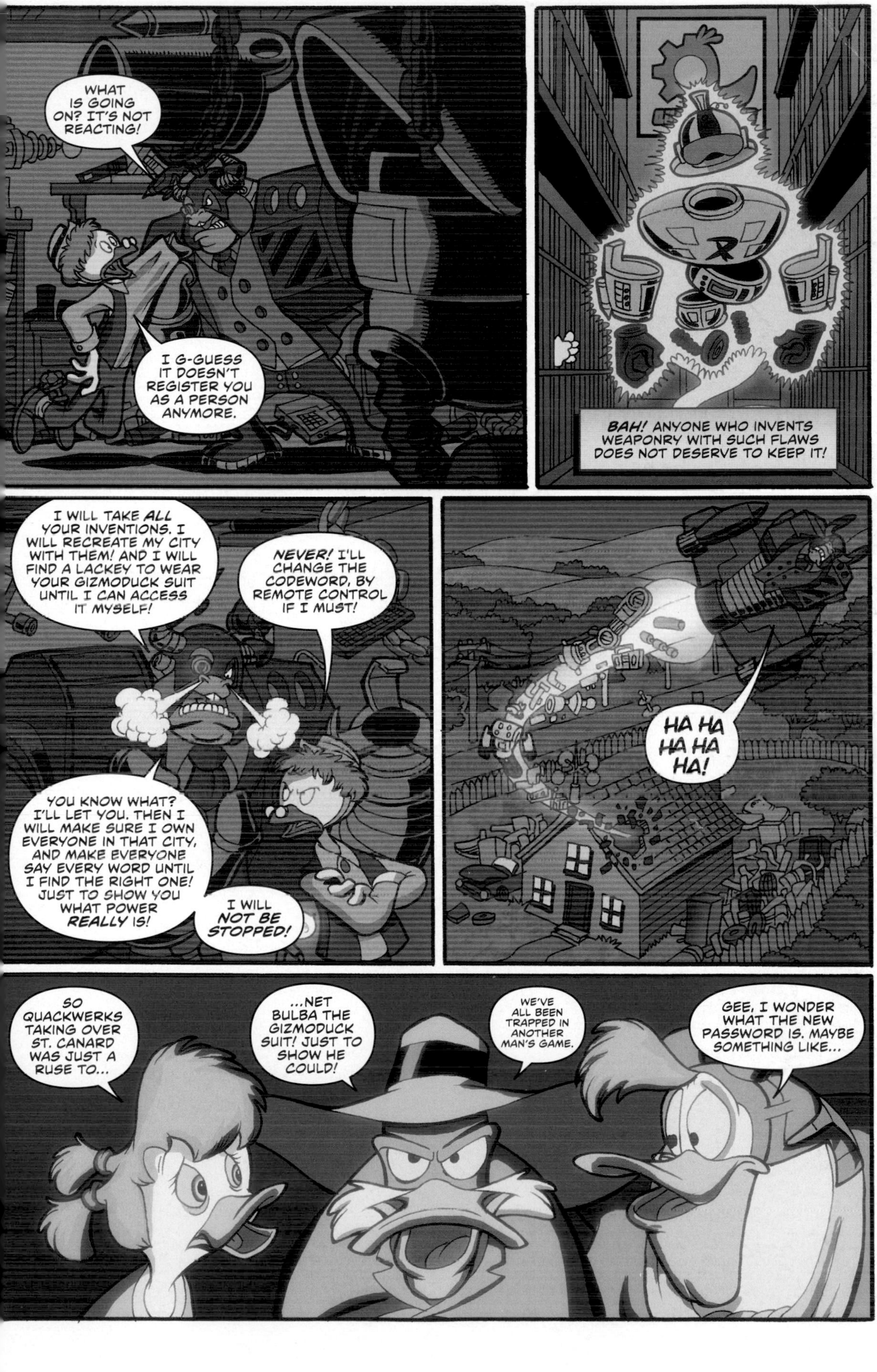
WHAT IS GOING ON? IT'S NOT REACTING!
I G-GUESS IT DOESN'T REGISTER YOU AS A PERSON ANYMORE.
BAH! ANYONE WHO INVENTS WEAPONRY WITH SUCH FLAWS DOES NOT DESERVE TO KEEP IT!
I WILL TAKE ALL YOUR INVENTIONS. I WILL RECREATE MY CITY WITH THEM! AND I WILL FIND A LACKEY TO WEAR YOUR GIZMODUCK SUIT UNTIL I CAN ACCESS IT MYSELF!
NEVER! I'LL CHANGE THE CODEWORD, BY REMOTE CONTROL IF I MUST!
YOU KNOW WHAT? I'LL LET YOU. THEN I WILL MAKE SURE I OWN EVERYONE IN THAT CITY, AND MAKE EVERYONE SAY EVERY WORD UNTIL I FIND THE RIGHT ONE! JUST TO SHOW YOU WHAT POWER REALLY IS!
I WILL NOT BE STOPPED!
HA HA HA HA HA!
SO QUACKWERKS TAKING OVER ST. CANARD WAS JUST A RUSE TO...
...NET BULBA THE GIZMODUCK SUIT! JUST TO SHOW HE COULD!
WE'VE ALL BEEN TRAPPED IN ANOTHER MAN'S GAME.
GEE, I WONDER WHAT THE NEW PASSWORD IS. MAYBE SOMETHING LIKE...

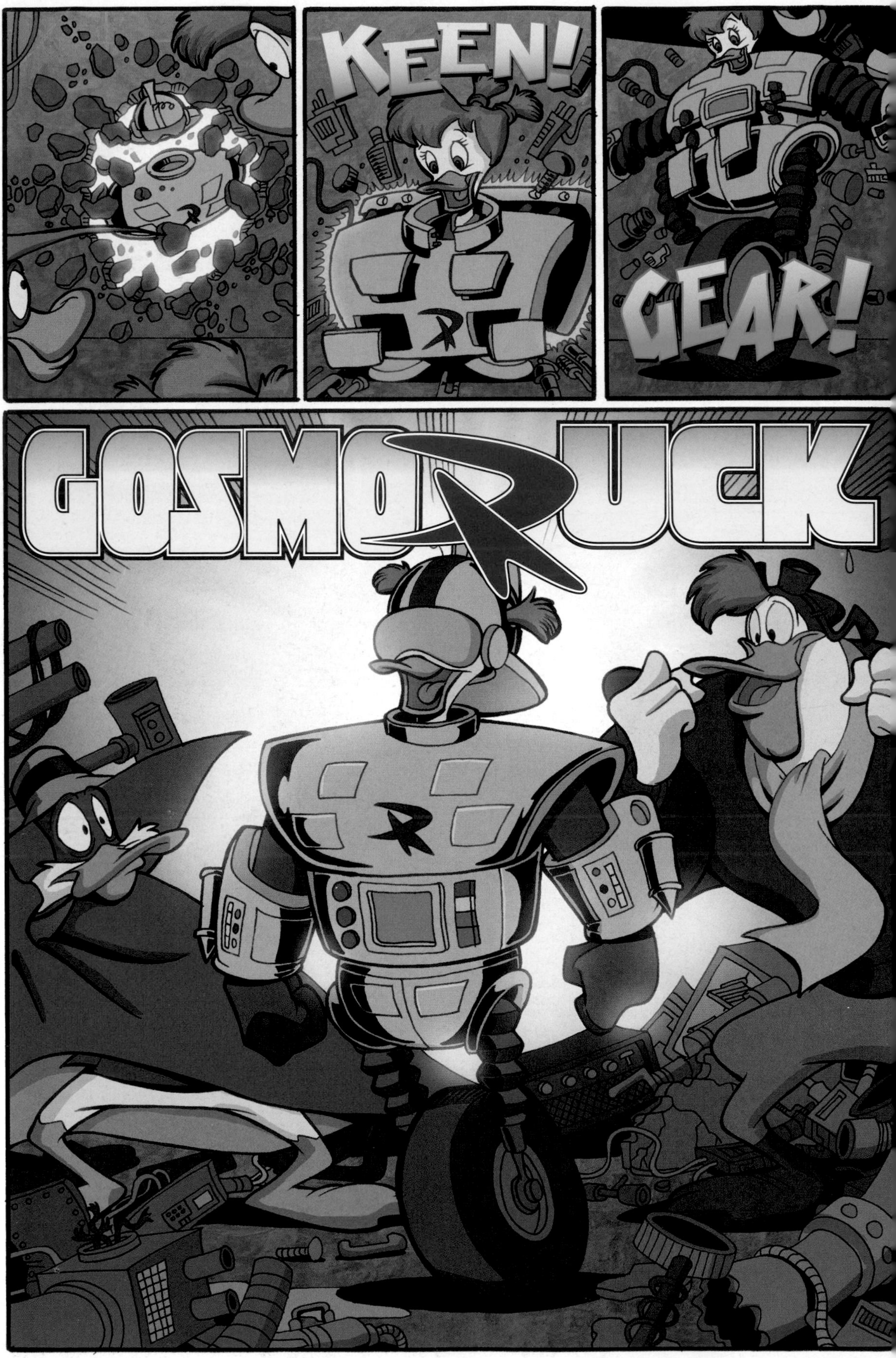
KEEN!
GEAR!
GOSMO DUCK

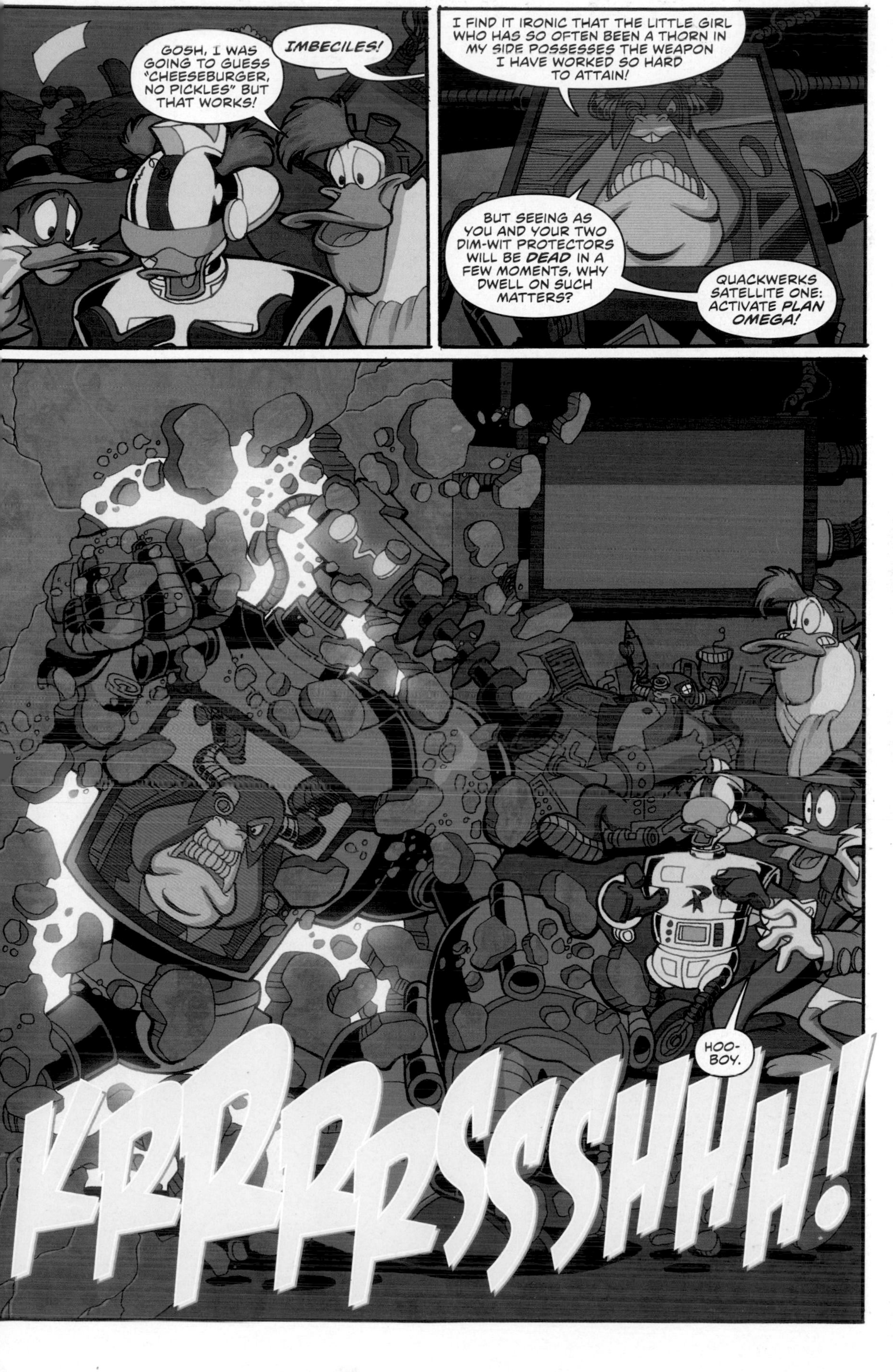
IMBECILES!
GOSH, I WAS GOING TO GUESS "CHEESEBURGER, NO PICKLES" BUT THAT WORKS!
I FIND IT IRONIC THAT THE LITTLE GIRL WHO HAS SO OFTEN BEEN A THORN IN MY SIDE POSSESSES THE WEAPON I HAVE WORKED SO HARD TO ATTAIN!
BUT SEEING AS YOU AND YOUR TWO DIM-WIT PROTECTORS WILL BE DEAD IN A FEW MOMENTS, WHY DWELL ON SUCH MATTERS?
QUACKWERKS SATELLITE ONE: ACTIVATE PLAN OMEGA!
HOO-BOY.
KRRRRSSSHHH!

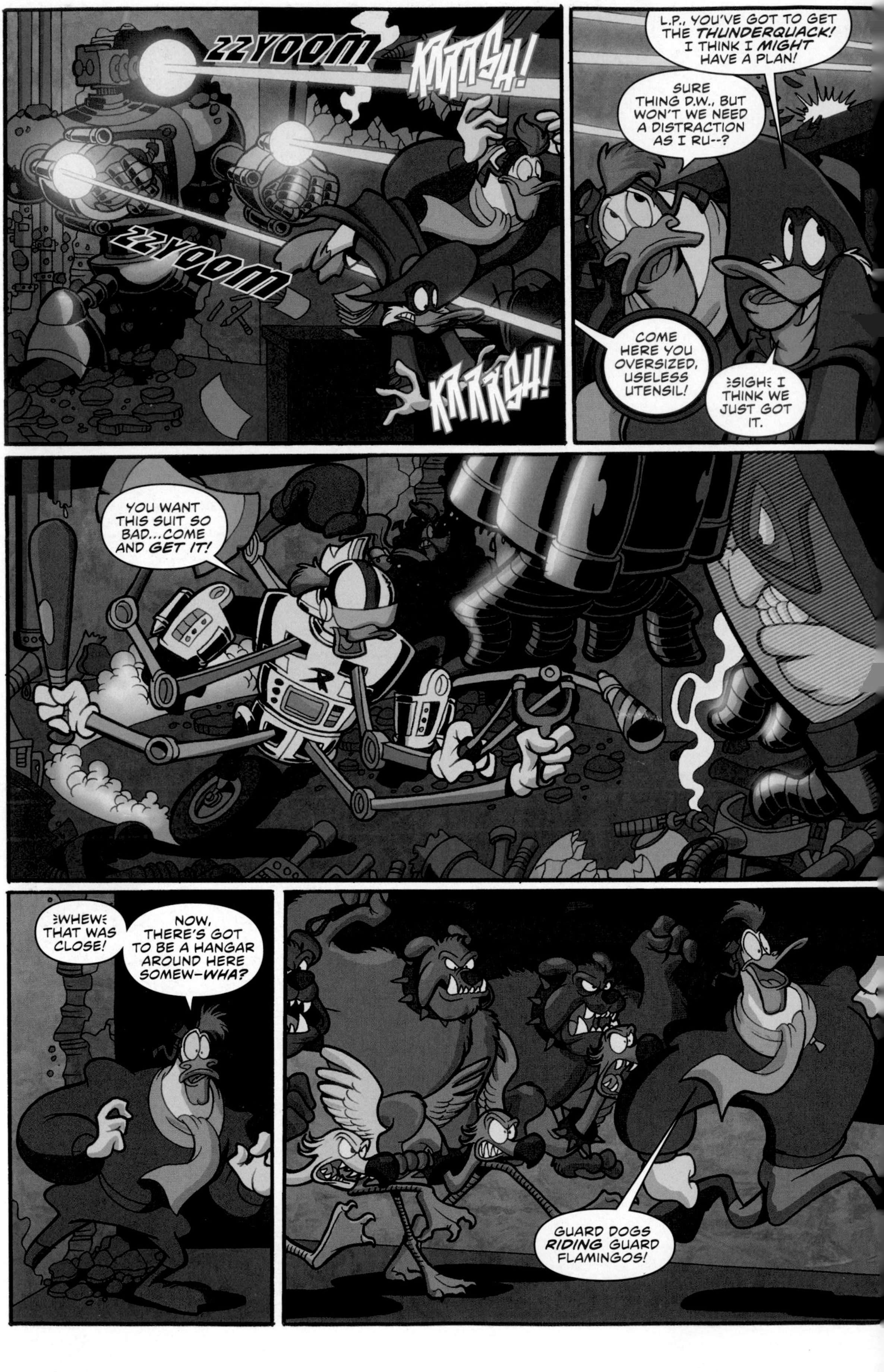
ZZYOOM
KRRRSH!
ZZYOOM
KRRRSH!
L.P., YOU'VE GOT TO GET THE THUNDERQUACK! I THINK I MIGHT HAVE A PLAN!
SURE THING D.W., BUT WON'T WE NEED A DISTRACTION AS I RU--?
COME HERE YOU OVERSIZED, USELESS UTENSIL!
SIGH I THINK WE JUST GOT IT.
YOU WANT THIS SUIT SO BAD...COME AND GET IT!
WHEW THAT WAS CLOSE!
NOW, THERE'S GOT TO BE A HANGAR AROUND HERE SOMEW-WHA?
GUARD DOGS RIDING GUARD FLAMINGOS!

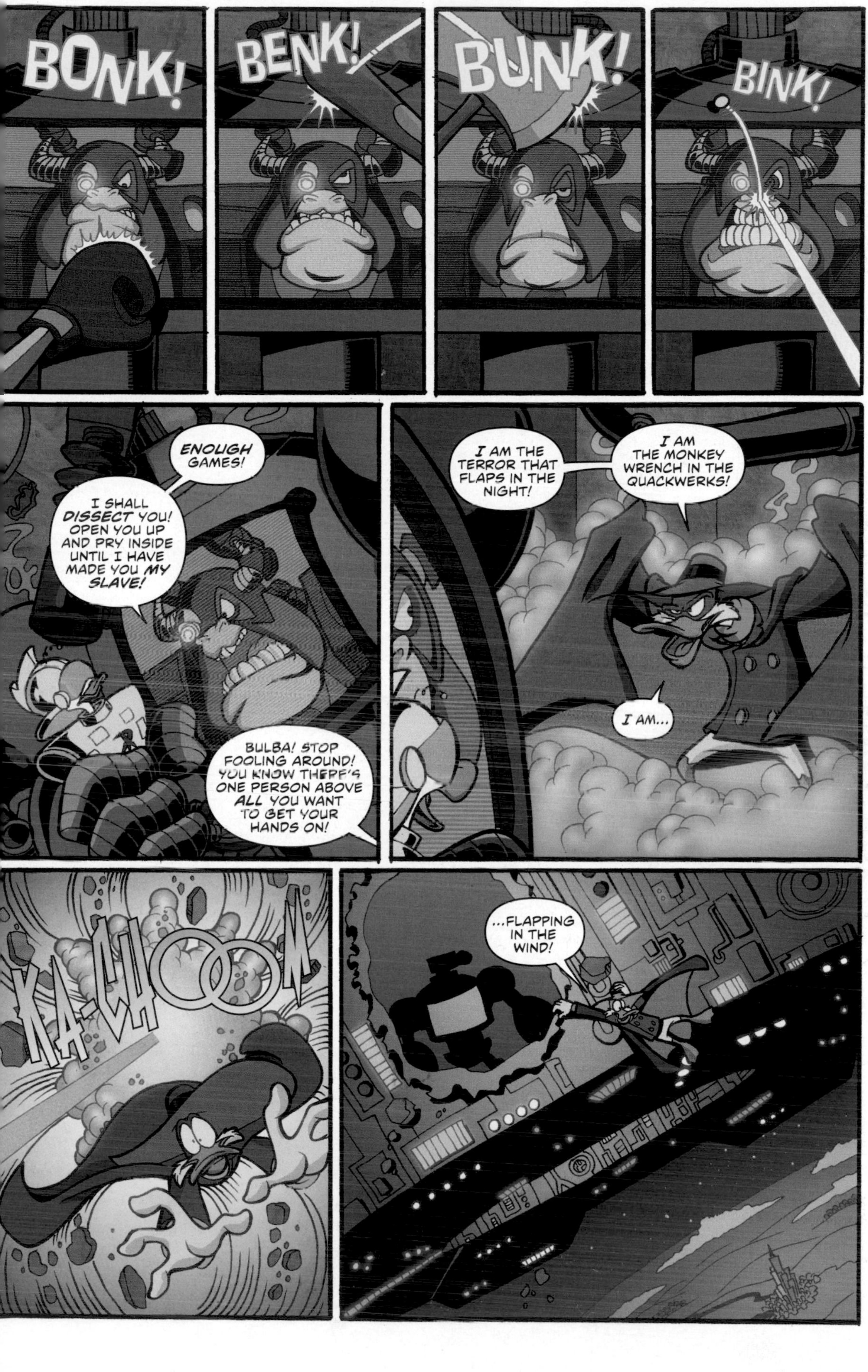
BONK!
BENK!
BUNK!
BINK!
ENOUGH GAMES!
I SHALL DISSECT YOU! OPEN YOU UP AND PRY INSIDE UNTIL I HAVE MADE YOU MY SLAVE!
BULBA! STOP FOOLING AROUND! YOU KNOW THERE'S ONE PERSON ABOVE ALL YOU WANT TO GET YOUR HANDS ON!
I AM THE TERROR THAT FLAPS IN THE NIGHT!
I AM THE MONKEY WRENCH IN THE QUACKWERKS!
I AM...
KA-CHOOOM
...FLAPPING IN THE WIND!

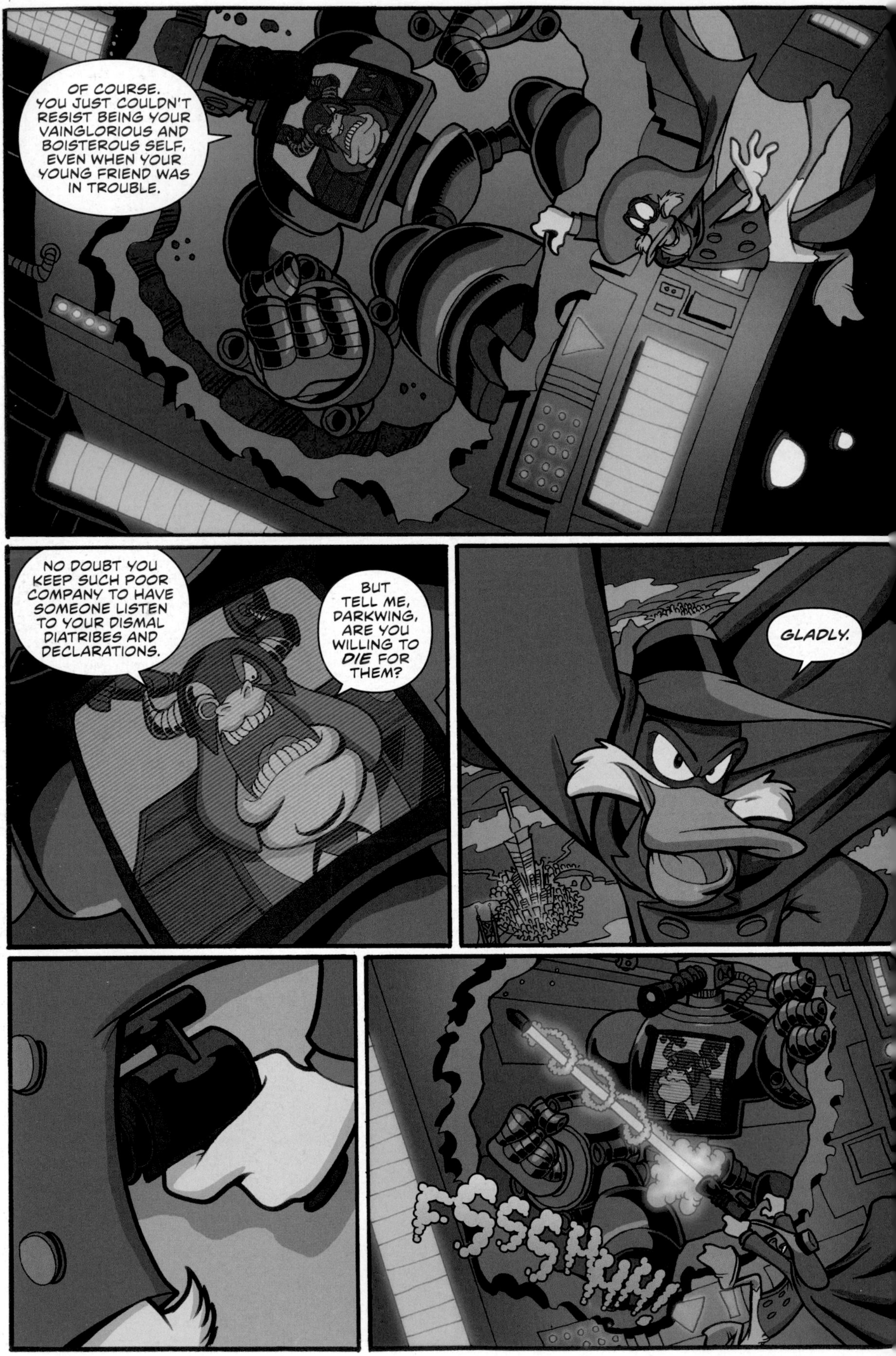
OF COURSE. YOU JUST COULDN'T RESIST BEING YOUR VAINGLORIOUS AND BOISTEROUS SELF, EVEN WHEN YOUR YOUNG FRIEND WAS IN TROUBLE.
NO DOUBT YOU KEEP SUCH POOR COMPANY TO HAVE SOMEONE LISTEN TO YOUR DISMAL DIATRIBES AND DECLARATIONS.
BUT TELL ME, DARKWING, ARE YOU WILLING TO DIE FOR THEM?
GLADLY.
FSSSHHH!

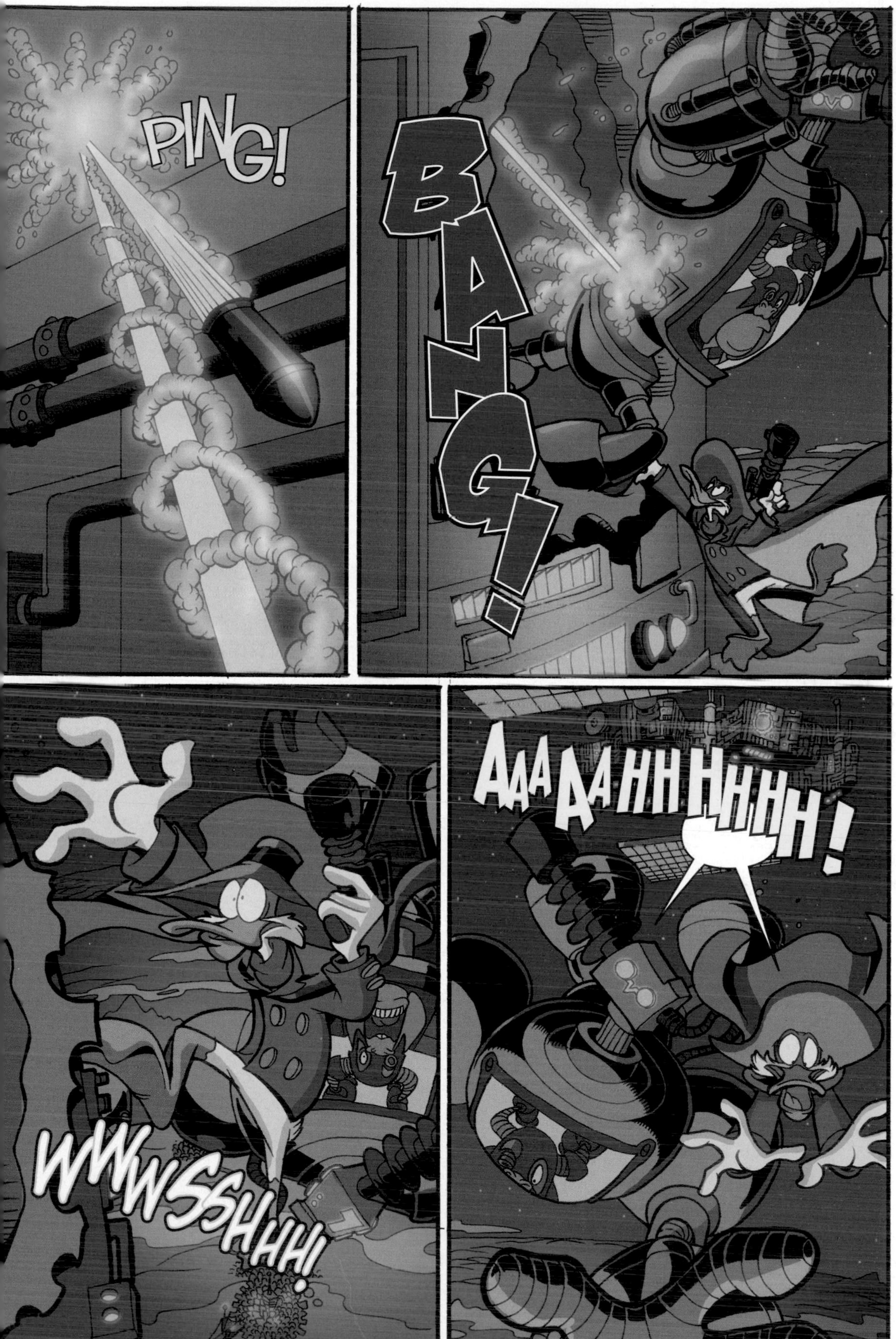
PING!
BANG!
WWWSSHHH!
AAAAAHHHHHHH!

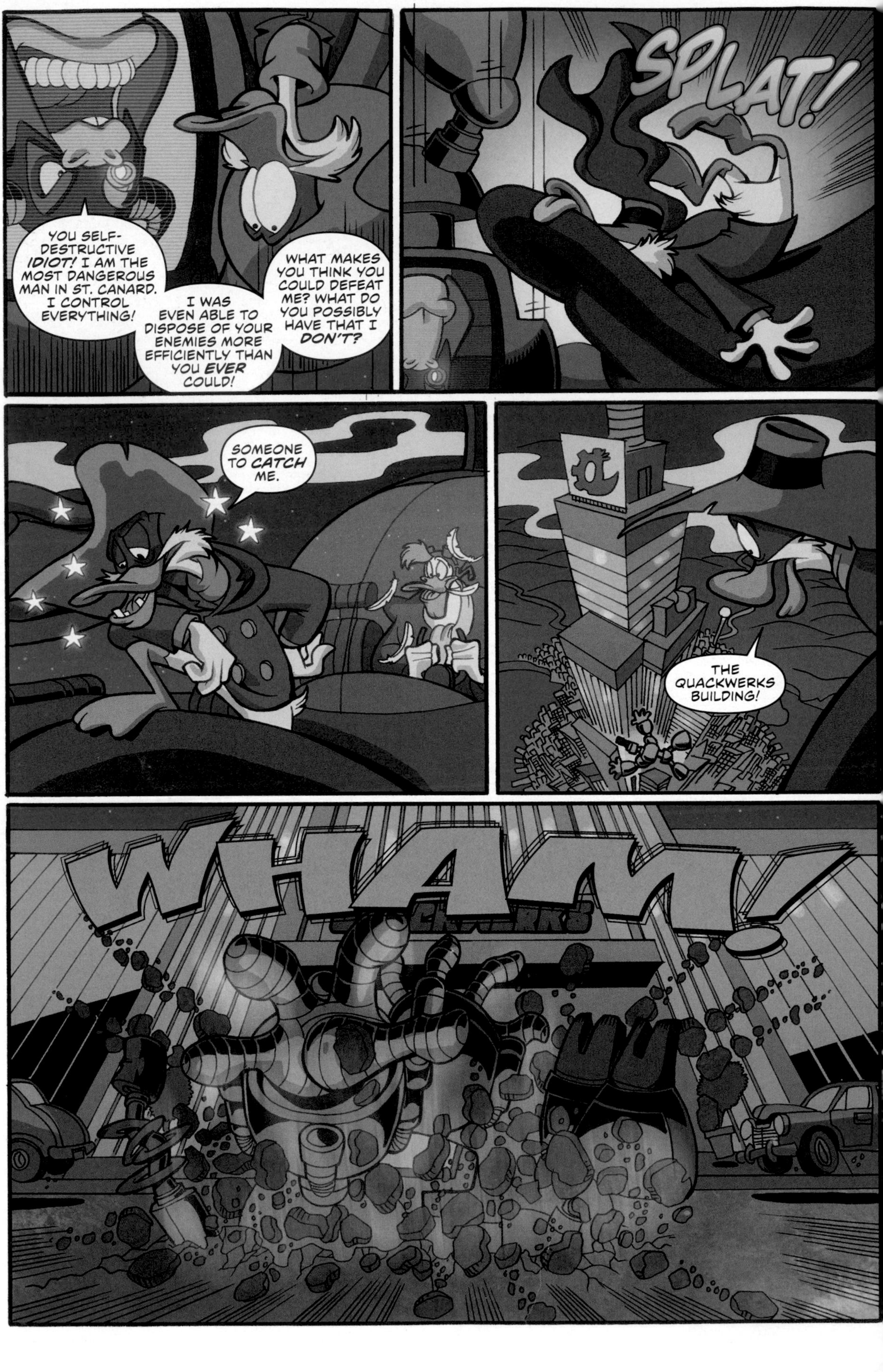

YOU SELF-DESTRUCTIVE IDIOT! I AM THE MOST DANGEROUS MAN IN ST. CANARD. I CONTROL EVERYTHING!
I WAS EVEN ABLE TO DISPOSE OF YOUR ENEMIES MORE EFFICIENTLY THAN YOU EVER COULD!
WHAT MAKES YOU THINK YOU COULD DEFEAT ME? WHAT DO YOU POSSIBLY HAVE THAT I DON'T?
SPLAT!
SOMEONE TO CATCH ME.
THE QUACKWERKS BUILDING!
WHAM!

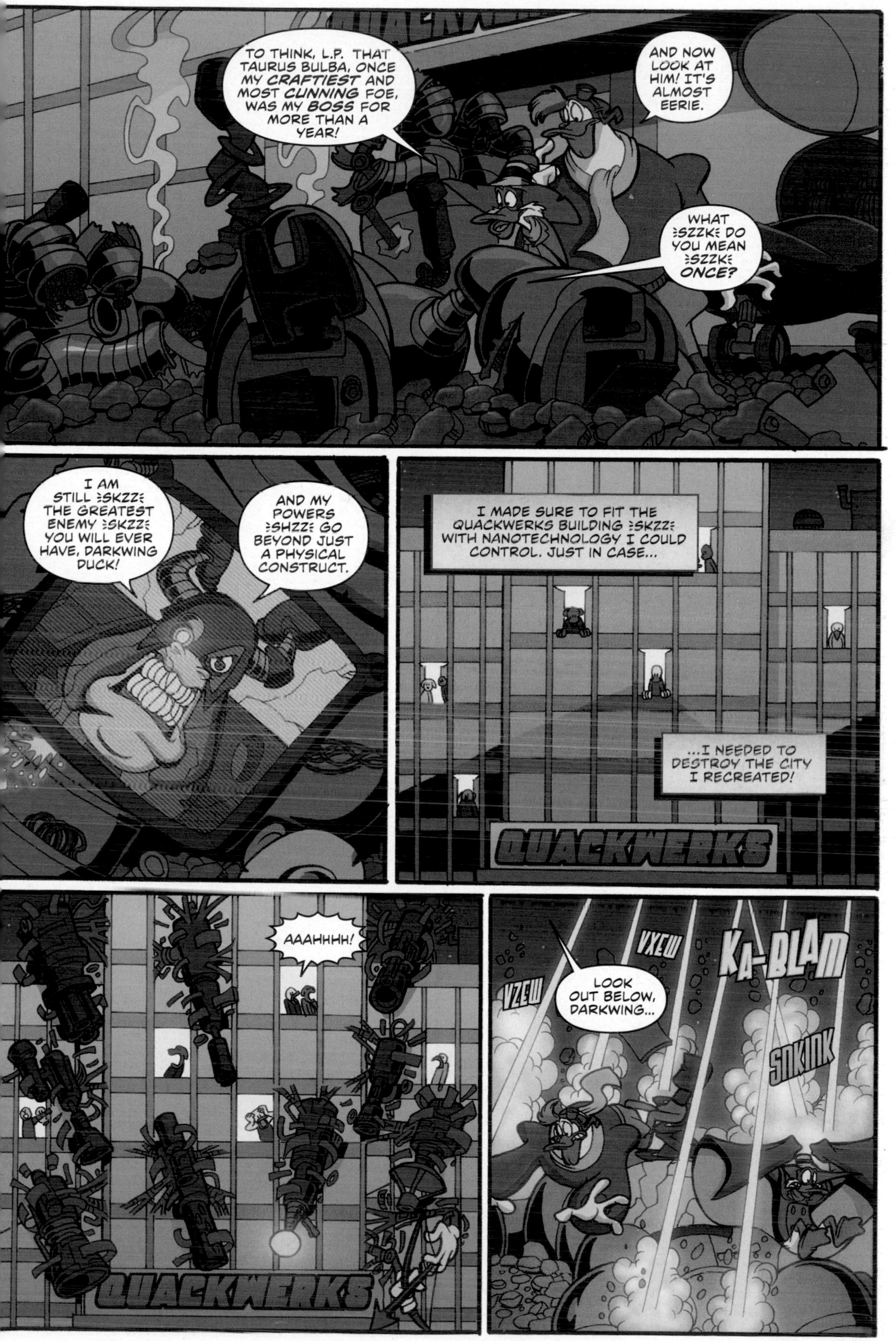
TO THINK, L.P. THAT TAURUS BULBA, ONCE MY CRAFTIEST AND MOST CUNNING FOE, WAS MY BOSS FOR MORE THAN A YEAR!
AND NOW LOOK AT HIM! IT'S ALMOST EERIE.
WHAT SZZK DO YOU MEAN SZZK ONCE?
I AM STILL SKZZ THE GREATEST ENEMY SKZZ YOU WILL EVER HAVE, DARKWING DUCK!
AND MY POWERS SHZZ GO BEYOND JUST A PHYSICAL CONSTRUCT.
I MADE SURE TO FIT THE QUACKWERKS BUILDING SKZZ WITH NANOTECHNOLOGY I COULD CONTROL. JUST IN CASE...
...I NEEDED TO DESTROY THE CITY I RECREATED!
QUACKWERKS
AAAHHHH!
QUACKWERKS
VZEW
VXEW
KA-BLAM
LOOK OUT BELOW, DARKWING...
SNKINK

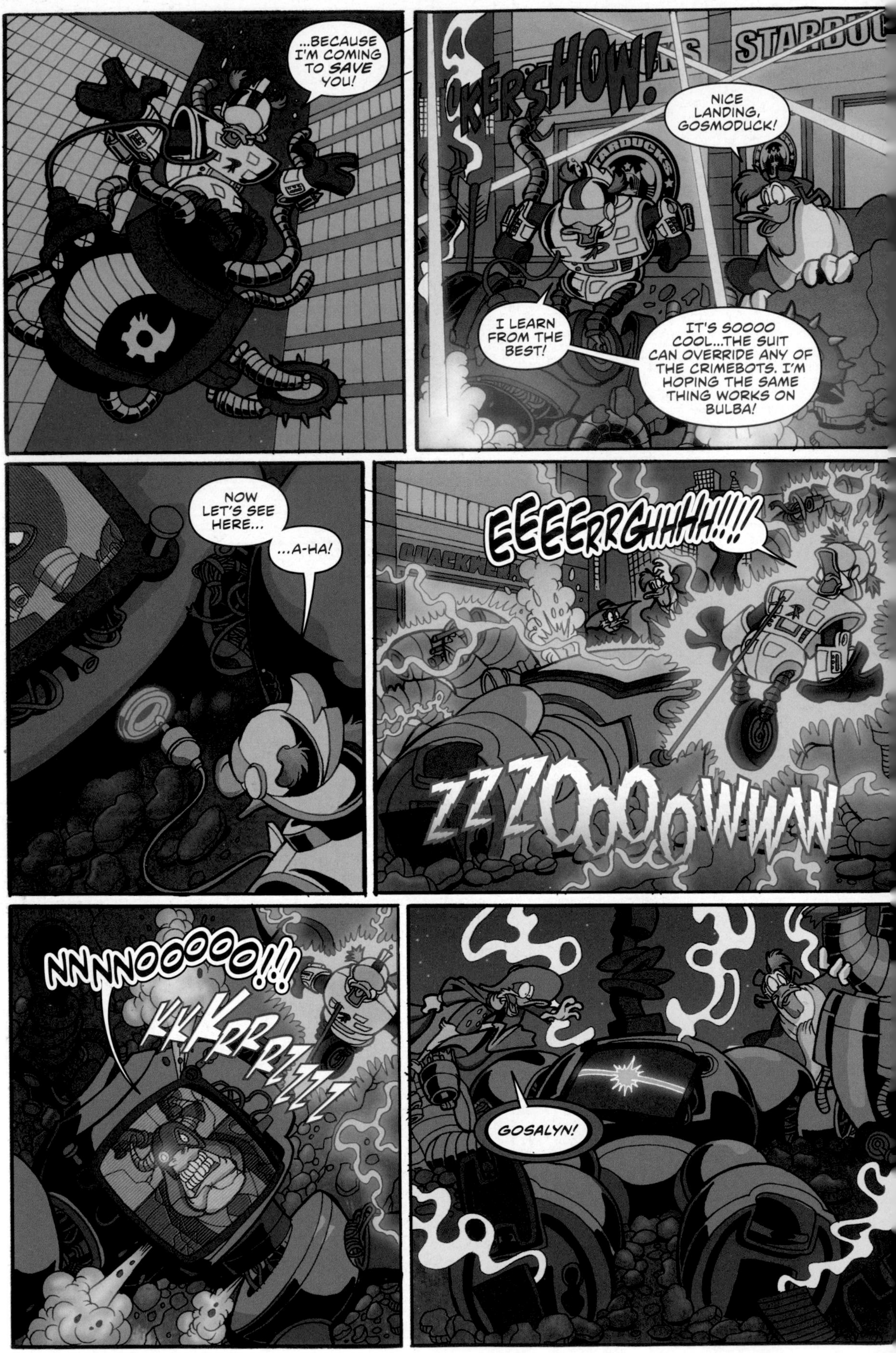
...BECAUSE I'M COMING TO SAVE YOU!
KERSHOW!
STARBUCKS
NICE LANDING, GOSMODUCK!
I LEARN FROM THE BEST!
IT'S SOOOO COOL...THE SUIT CAN OVERRIDE ANY OF THE CRIMEBOTS. I'M HOPING THE SAME THING WORKS ON BULBA!
NOW LET'S SEE HERE...
...A-HA!
EEEERRGHHHH!!!!
ZZZOOOOWWAN
NNNNOOOOOO!!!
KKKRRRZZZZ
GOSALYN!

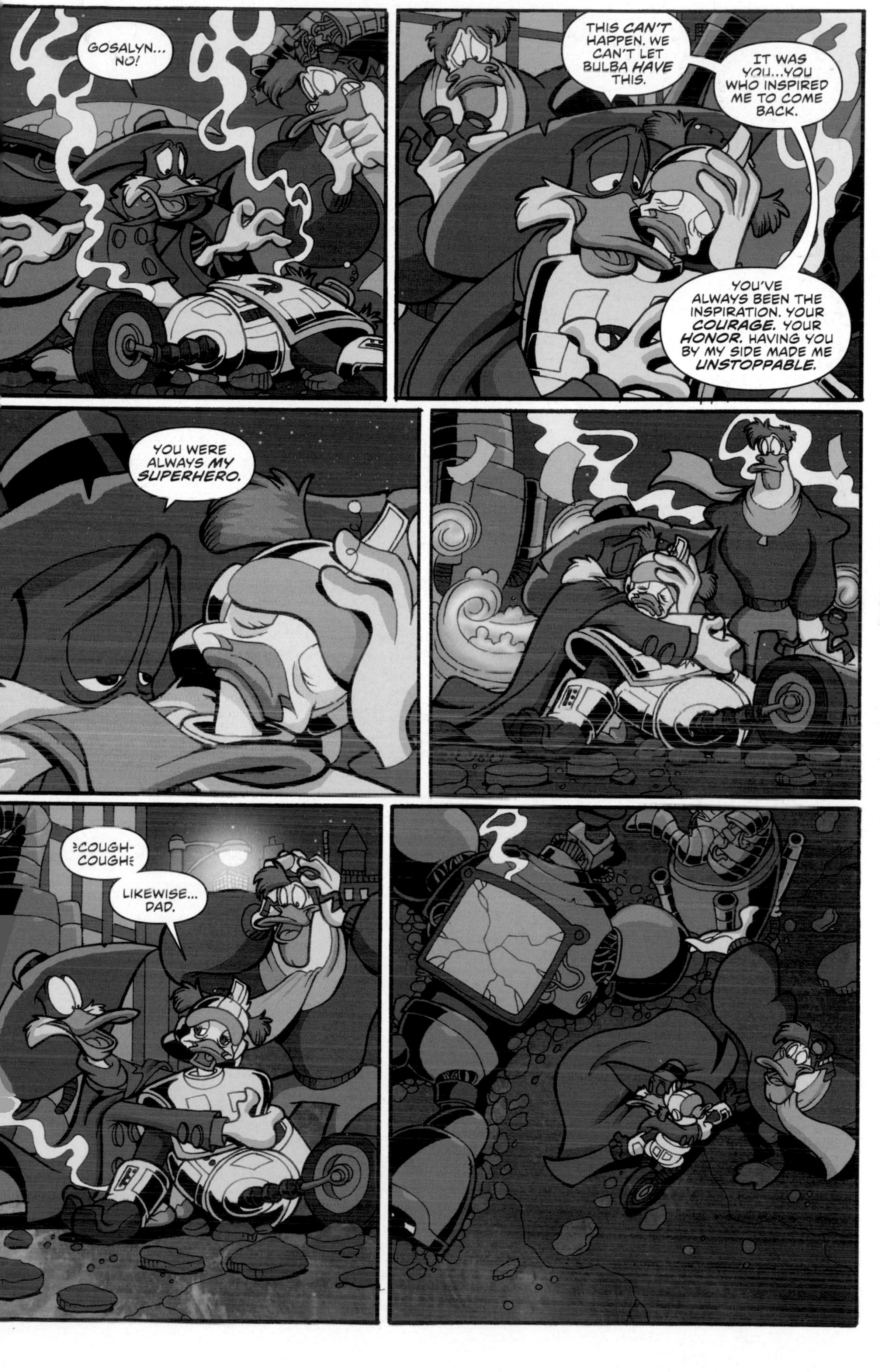

GOSALYN... NO!
THIS CAN'T HAPPEN. WE CAN'T LET BULBA HAVE THIS.
IT WAS YOU...YOU WHO INSPIRED ME TO COME BACK.
YOU'VE ALWAYS BEEN THE INSPIRATION. YOUR COURAGE. YOUR HONOR. HAVING YOU BY MY SIDE MADE ME UNSTOPPABLE.
YOU WERE ALWAYS MY SUPERHERO.
COUGH-COUGH
LIKEWISE... DAD.

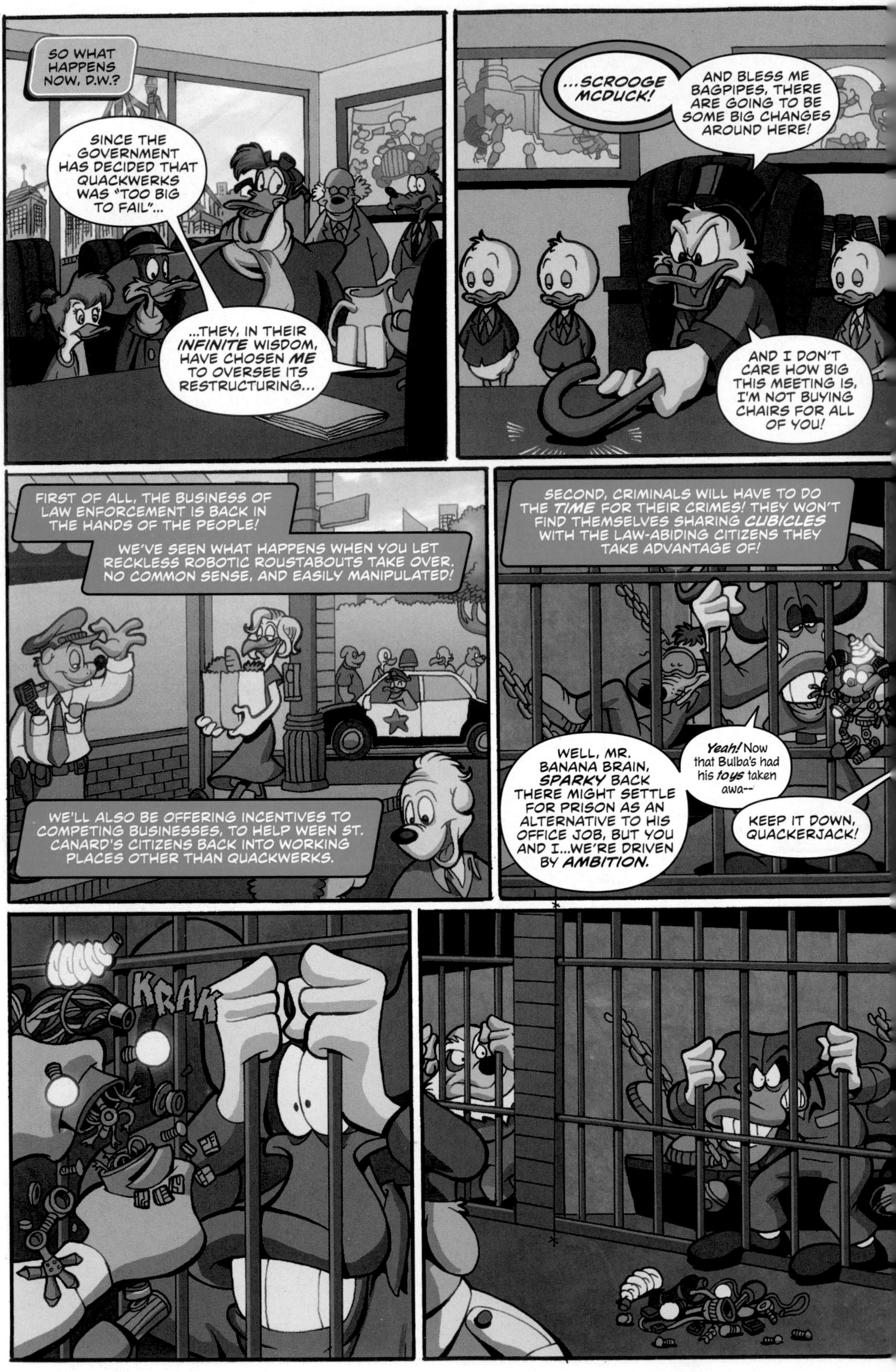
SO WHAT HAPPENS NOW, D.W.?
SINCE THE GOVERNMENT HAS DECIDED THAT QUACKWERKS WAS "TOO BIG TO FAIL"...
...THEY, IN THEIR INFINITE WISDOM, HAVE CHOSEN ME TO OVERSEE ITS RESTRUCTURING...
...SCROOGE MCDUCK!
AND BLESS ME BAGPIPES, THERE ARE GOING TO BE SOME BIG CHANGES AROUND HERE!
AND I DON'T CARE HOW BIG THIS MEETING IS, I'M NOT BUYING CHAIRS FOR ALL OF YOU!
FIRST OF ALL, THE BUSINESS OF LAW ENFORCEMENT IS BACK IN THE HANDS OF THE PEOPLE!
WE'VE SEEN WHAT HAPPENS WHEN YOU LET RECKLESS ROBOTIC ROUSTABOUTS TAKE OVER. NO COMMON SENSE, AND EASILY MANIPULATED!
WE'LL ALSO BE OFFERING INCENTIVES TO COMPETING BUSINESSES, TO HELP WEEN ST. CANARD'S CITIZENS BACK INTO WORKING PLACES OTHER THAN QUACKWERKS.
SECOND, CRIMINALS WILL HAVE TO DO THE TIME FOR THEIR CRIMES! THEY WON'T FIND THEMSELVES SHARING CUBICLES WITH THE LAW-ABIDING CITIZENS THEY TAKE ADVANTAGE OF!
WELL, MR. BANANA BRAIN, SPARKY BACK THERE MIGHT SETTLE FOR PRISON AS AN ALTERNATIVE TO HIS OFFICE JOB, BUT YOU AND I...WE'RE DRIVEN BY AMBITION.
Yeah! Now that Bulba's had his toys taken awa--
KEEP IT DOWN, QUACKERJACK!
KRAK

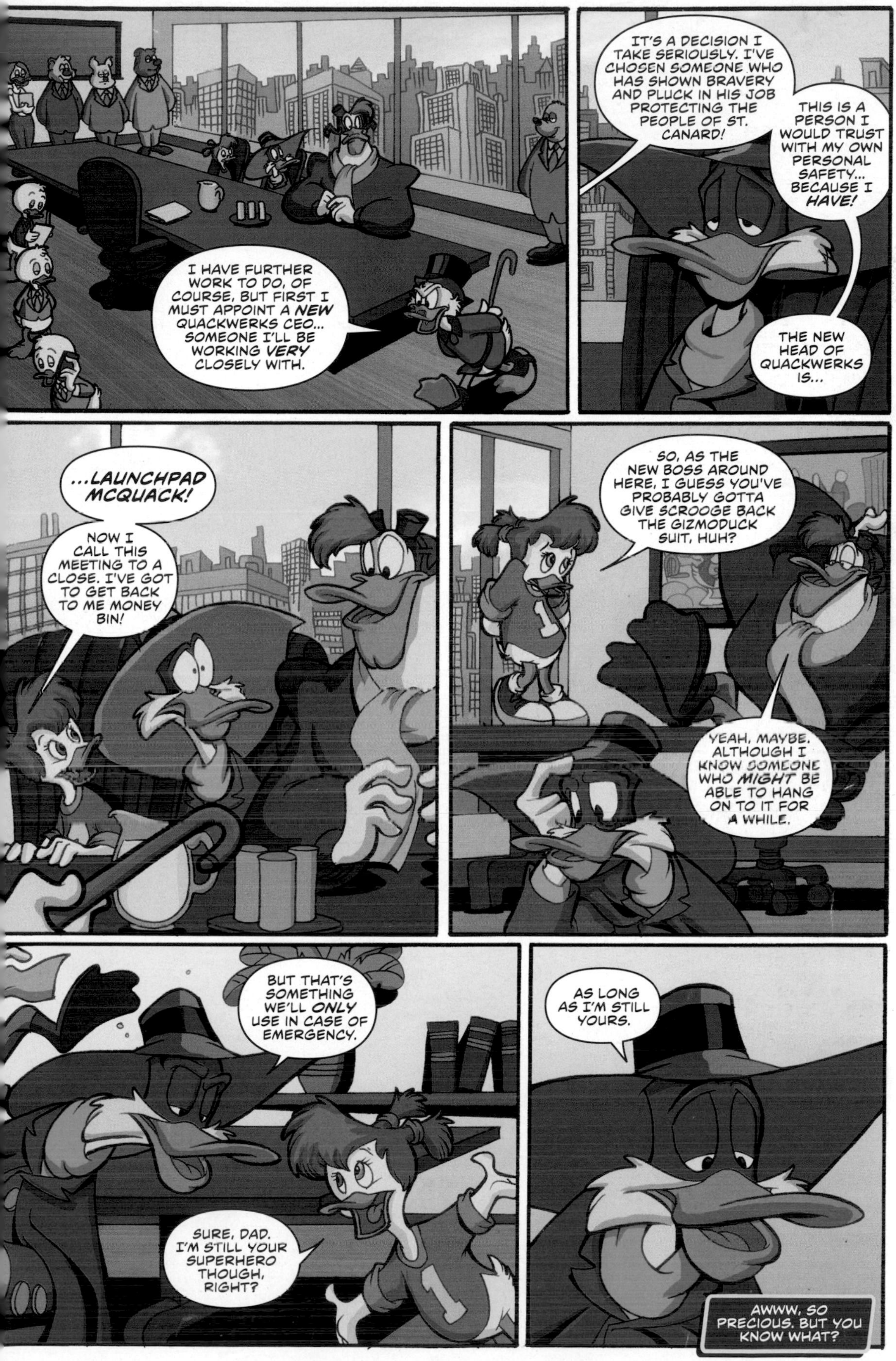
I HAVE FURTHER WORK TO DO, OF COURSE, BUT FIRST I MUST APPOINT A NEW QUACKWERKS CEO... SOMEONE I'LL BE WORKING VERY CLOSELY WITH.
IT'S A DECISION I TAKE SERIOUSLY. I'VE CHOSEN SOMEONE WHO HAS SHOWN BRAVERY AND PLUCK IN HIS JOB PROTECTING THE PEOPLE OF ST. CANARD!
THIS IS A PERSON I WOULD TRUST WITH MY OWN PERSONAL SAFETY... BECAUSE I HAVE!
THE NEW HEAD OF QUACKWERKS IS...
...LAUNCHPAD MCQUACK!
NOW I CALL THIS MEETING TO A CLOSE. I'VE GOT TO GET BACK TO ME MONEY BIN!
SO, AS THE NEW BOSS AROUND HERE, I GUESS YOU'VE PROBABLY GOTTA GIVE SCROOGE BACK THE GIZMODUCK SUIT, HUH?
YEAH, MAYBE. ALTHOUGH I KNOW SOMEONE WHO MIGHT BE ABLE TO HANG ON TO IT FOR A WHILE.
BUT THAT'S SOMETHING WE'LL ONLY USE IN CASE OF EMERGENCY.
SURE, DAD. I'M STILL YOUR SUPERHERO THOUGH, RIGHT?
AS LONG AS I'M STILL YOURS.
AWWW, SO PRECIOUS. BUT YOU KNOW WHAT?

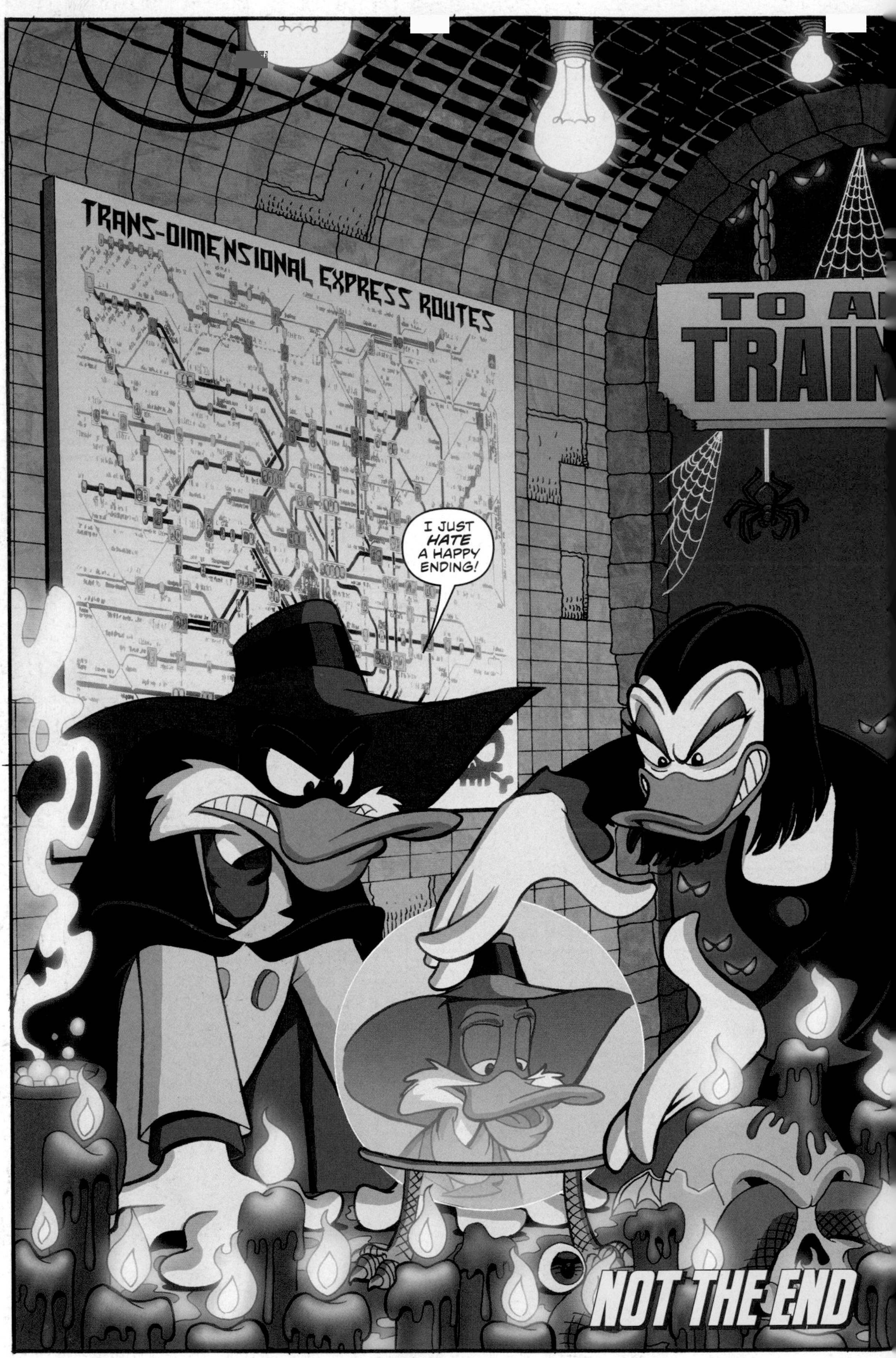
TRANS-DIMENSIONAL EXPRESS ROUTES
TO A
TRAIN
I JUST HATE A HAPPY ENDING!
NOT THE END

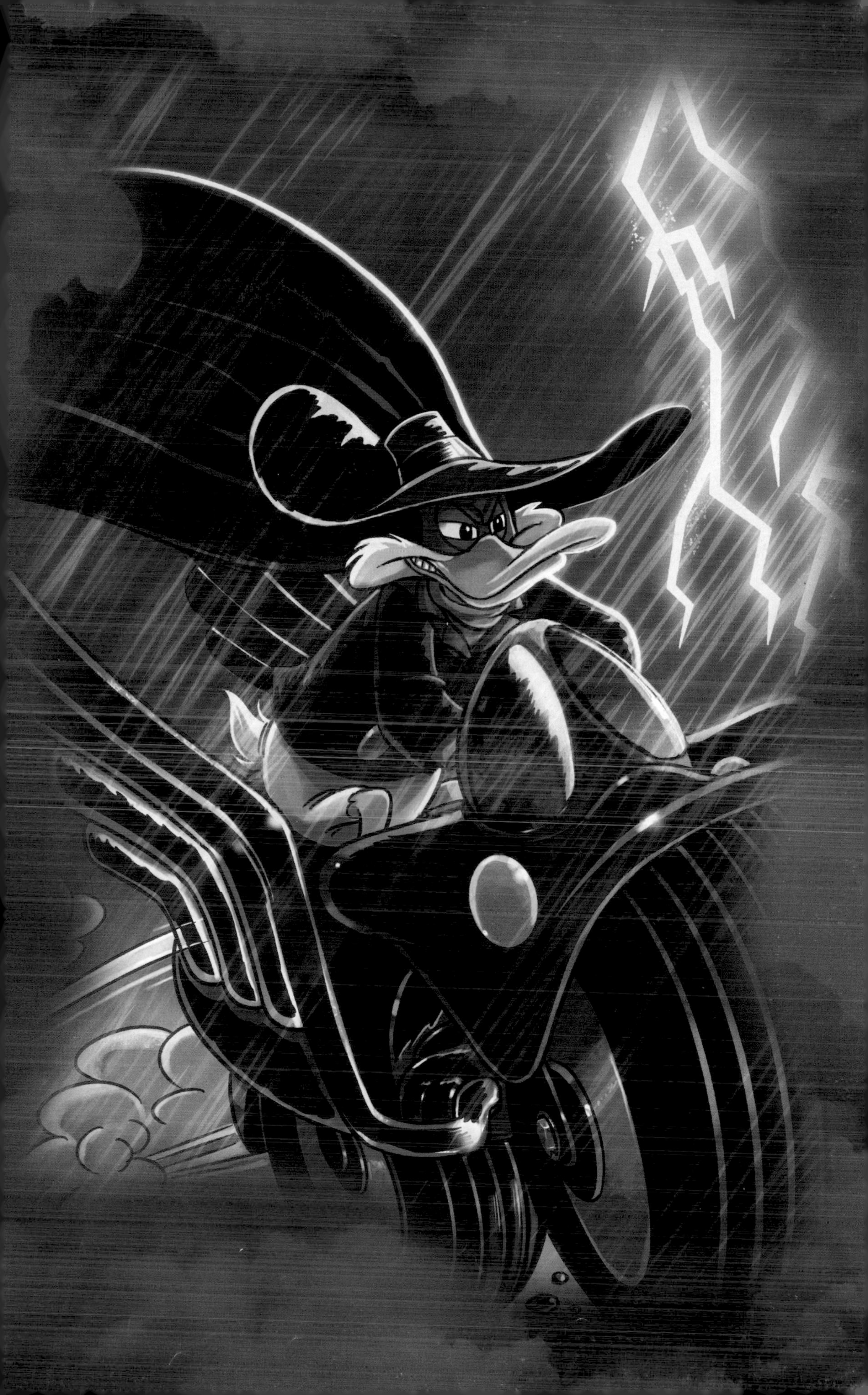

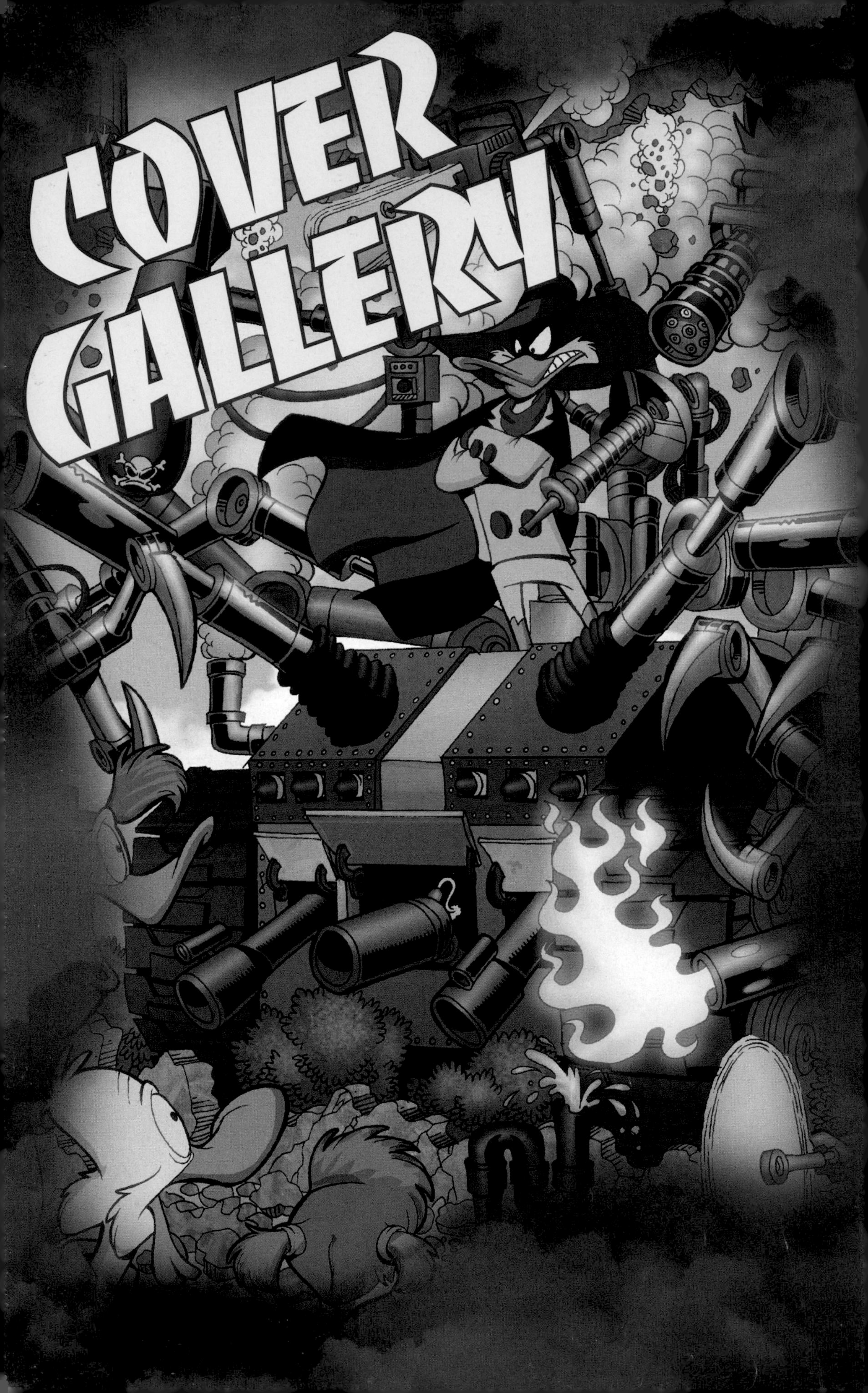
COVER GALLERY

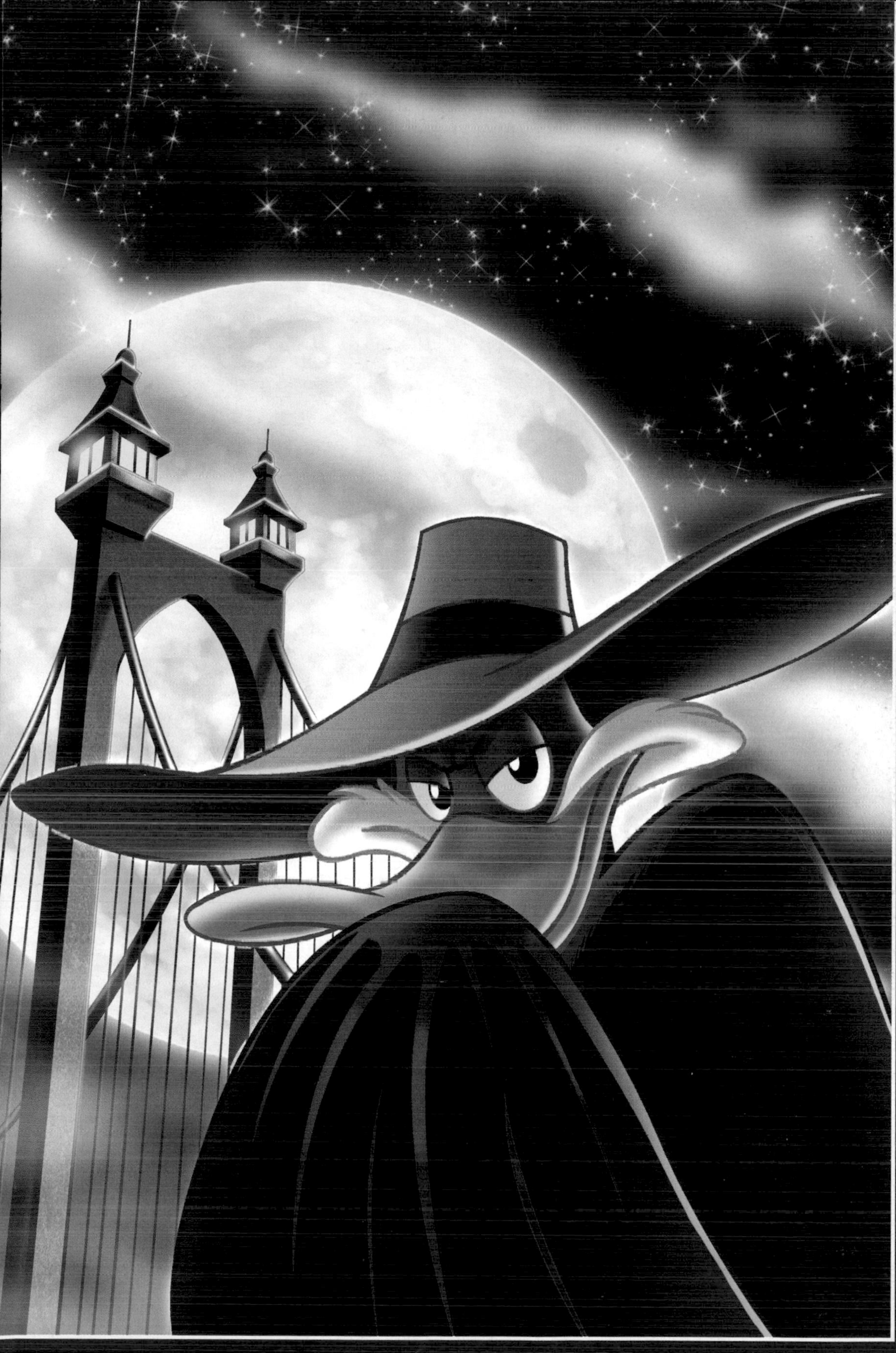

COVER 1A
MAGIC EYE STUDIOS

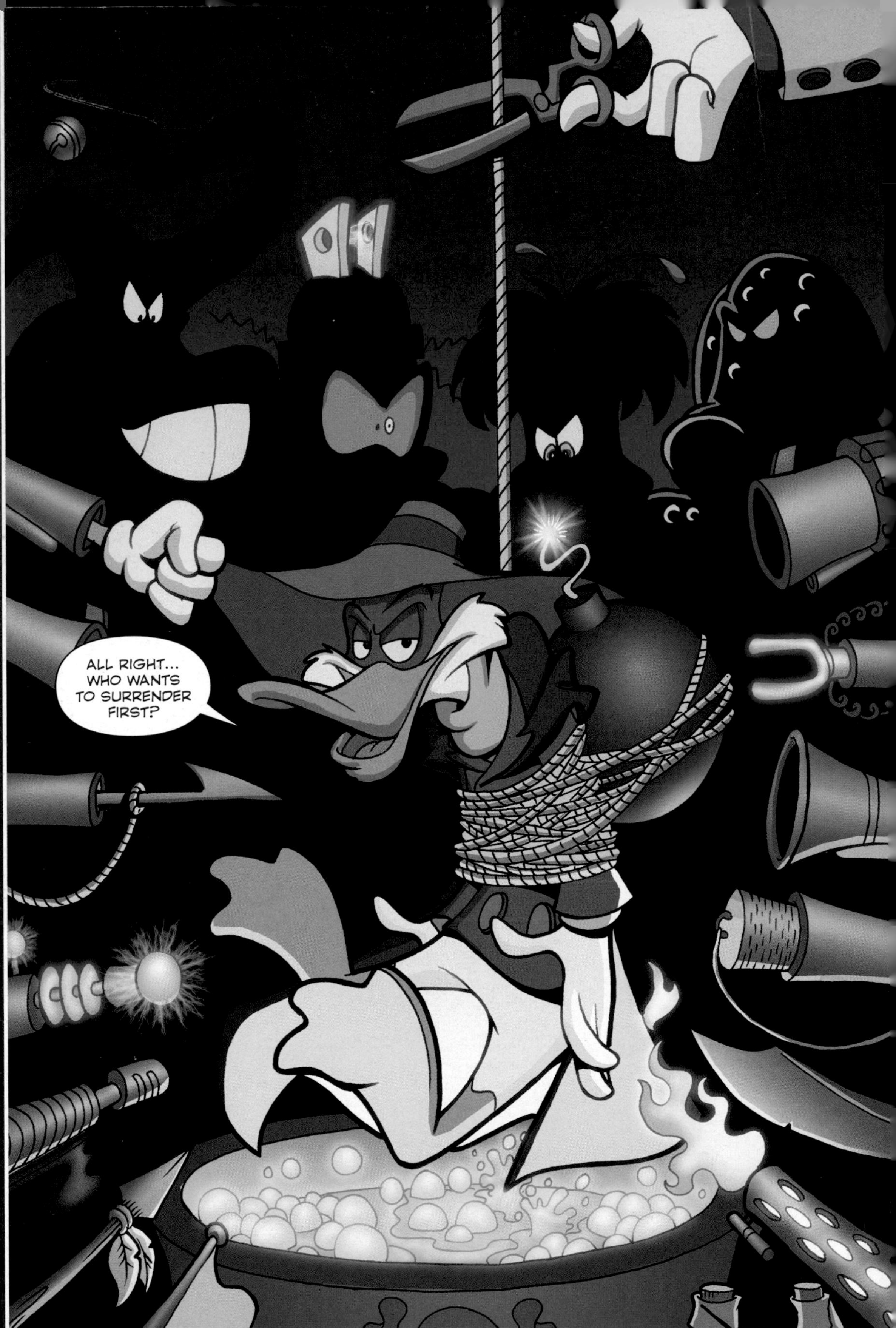
ALL RIGHT... WHO WANTS TO SURRENDER FIRST?

COVER 1B
JAMES SILVANI
COLORS: ANDREW DALHOUSE

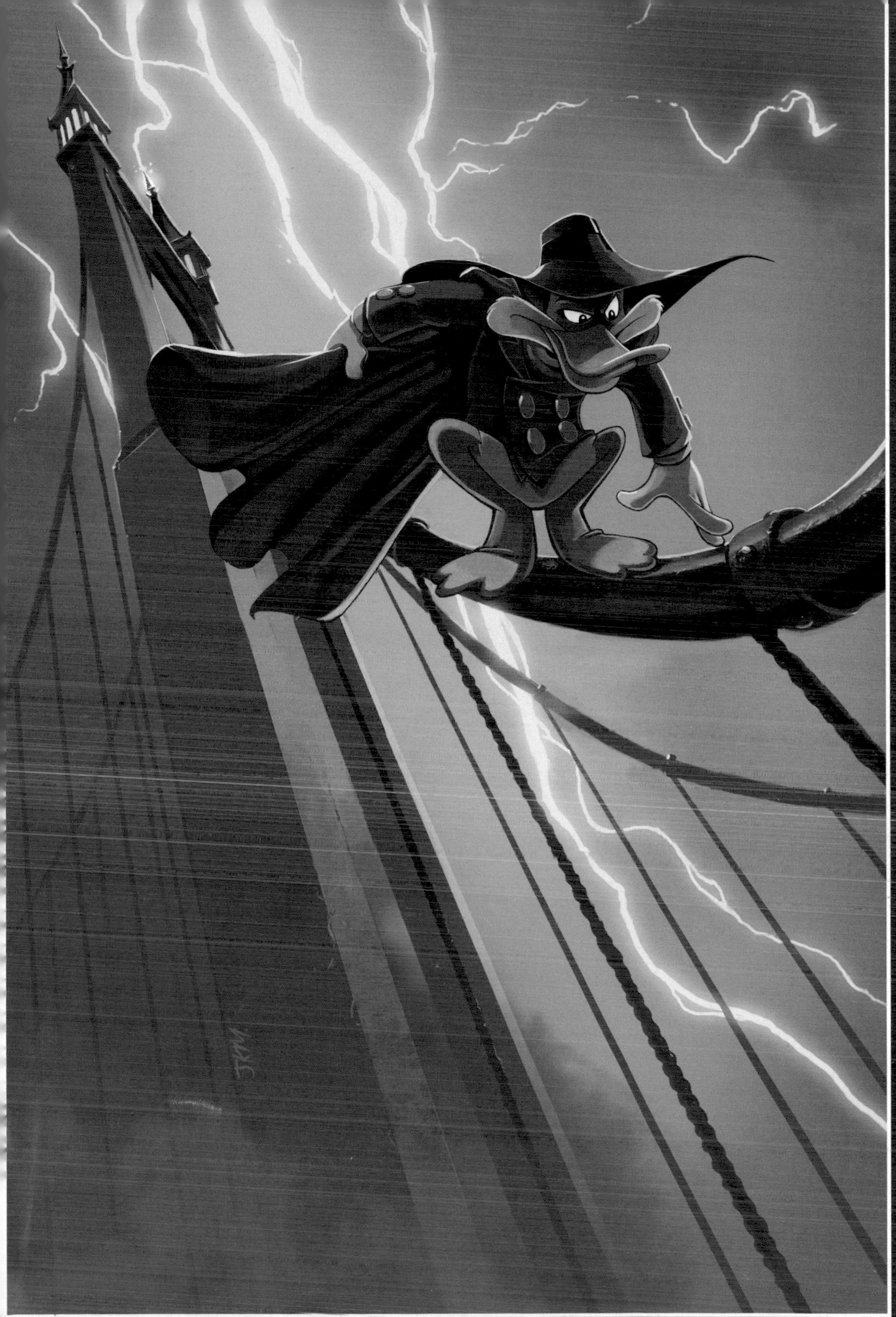

COVER 1C
JAMES SILVANI & JAKE MYLER
COLORS: JAKE MYLER

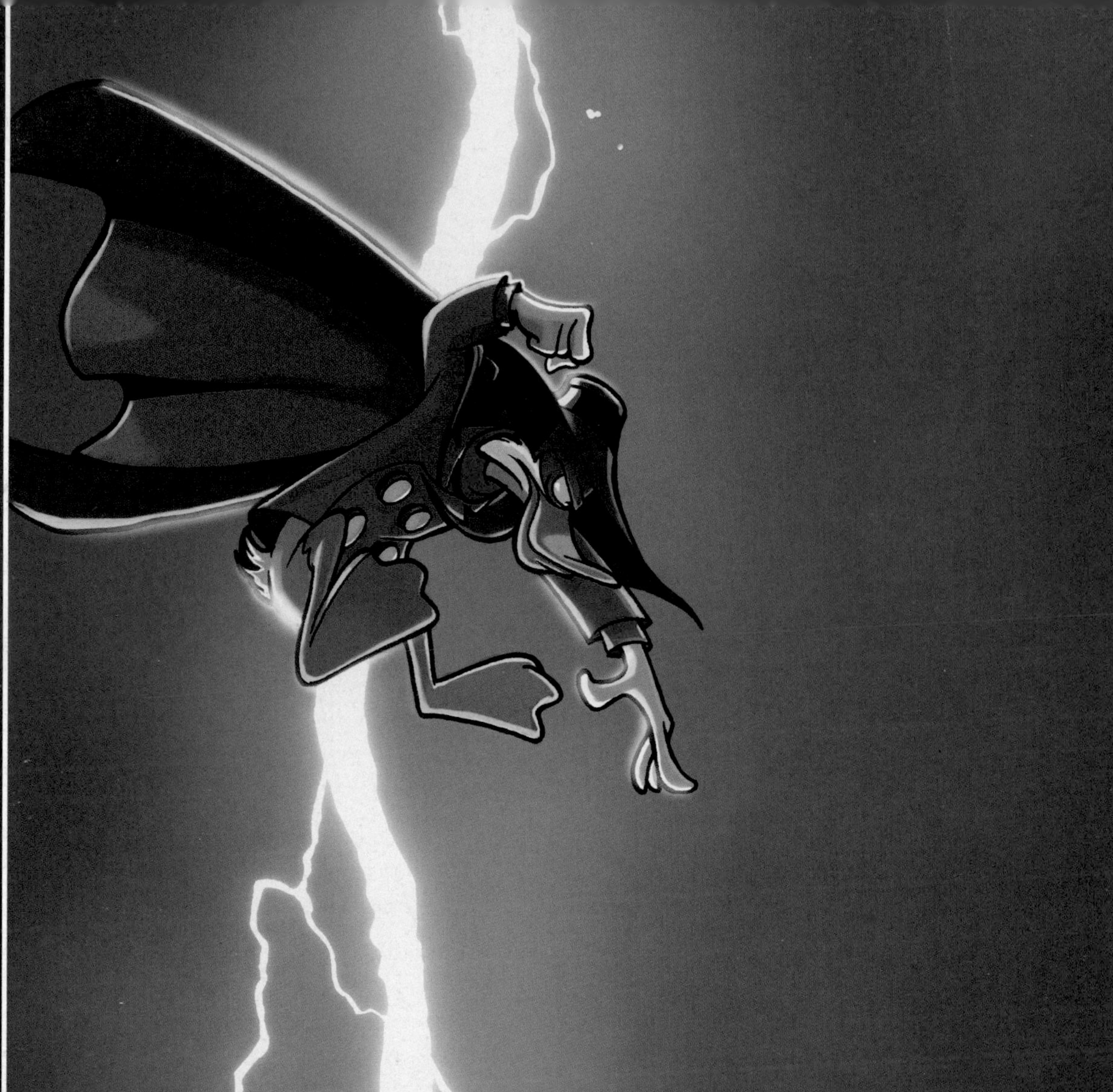

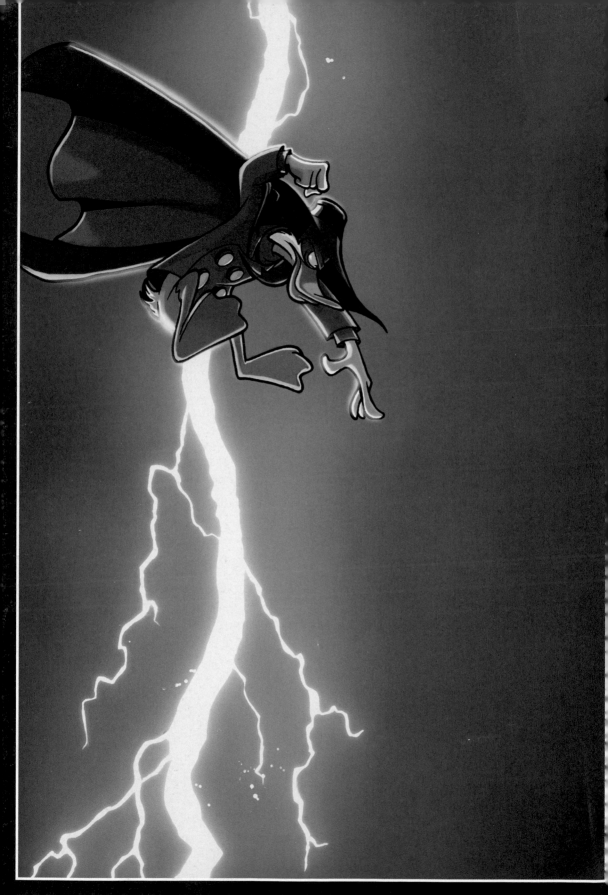

ISSUE # 1 SAN DIEGO COMIC-CON EXCLUSIVE
JAMES SILVANI
COLORS: JAKE MYLER

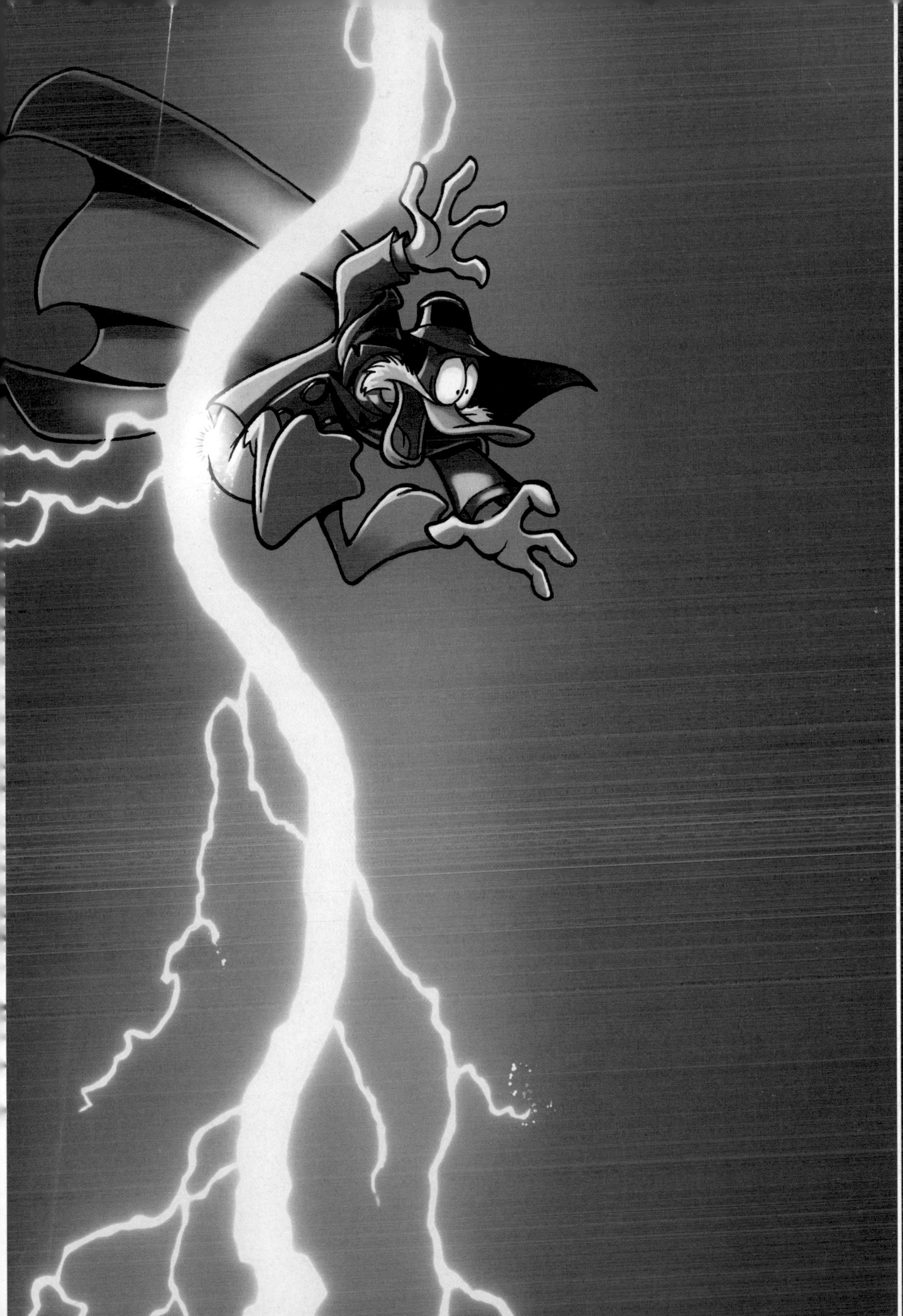

ISSUE # 1 SECOND PRINT
JAMES SILVANI
COLORS: JAKE MYLER

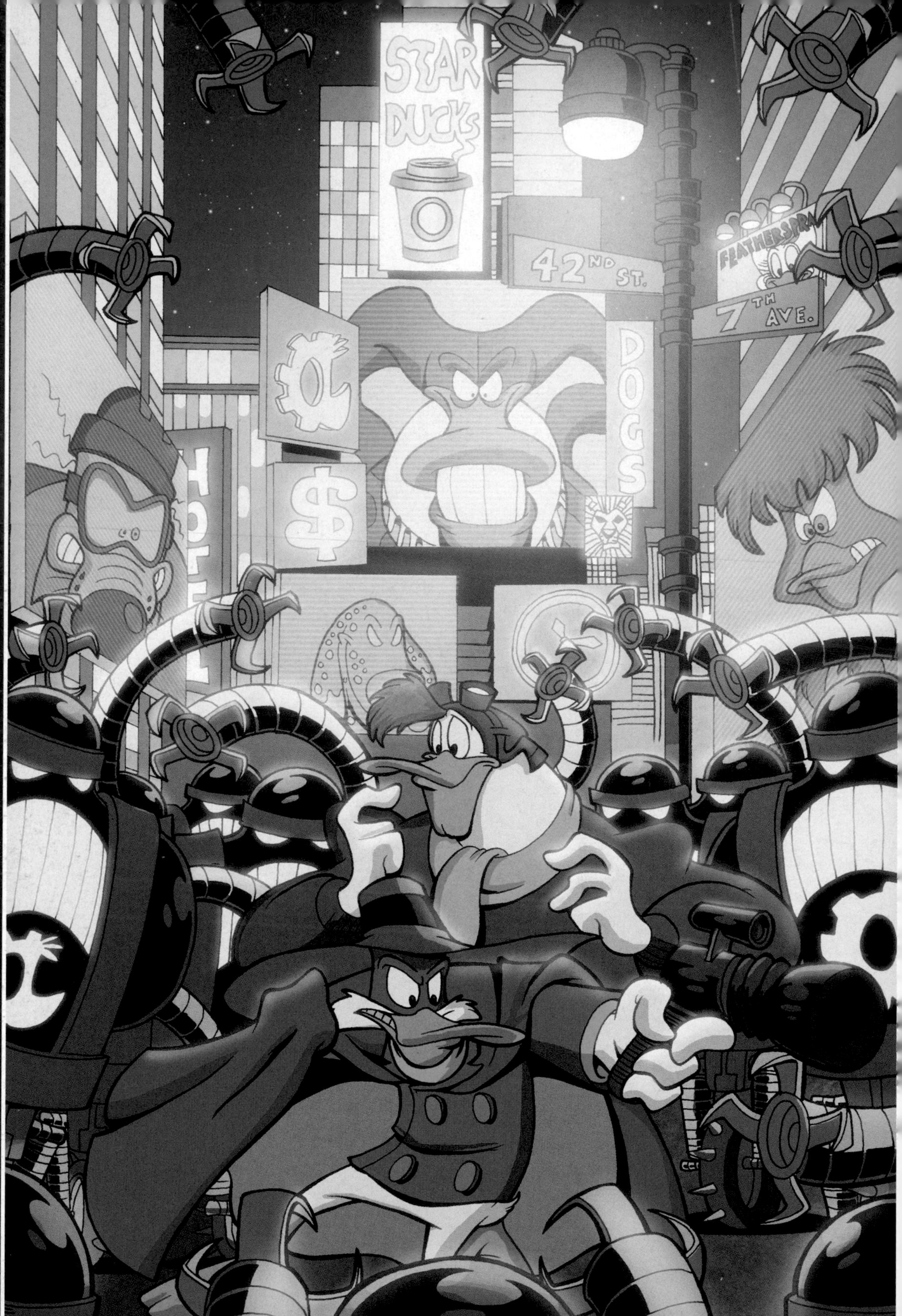
STAR DUCKS
42ND ST.
FEATHERSPRA
7TH AVE.
DOGS
$

ISSUE # 1 NEW YORK COMIC CON EXCLUSIVE
JAMES SILVANI
COLORS: ANDREW DALHOUSE

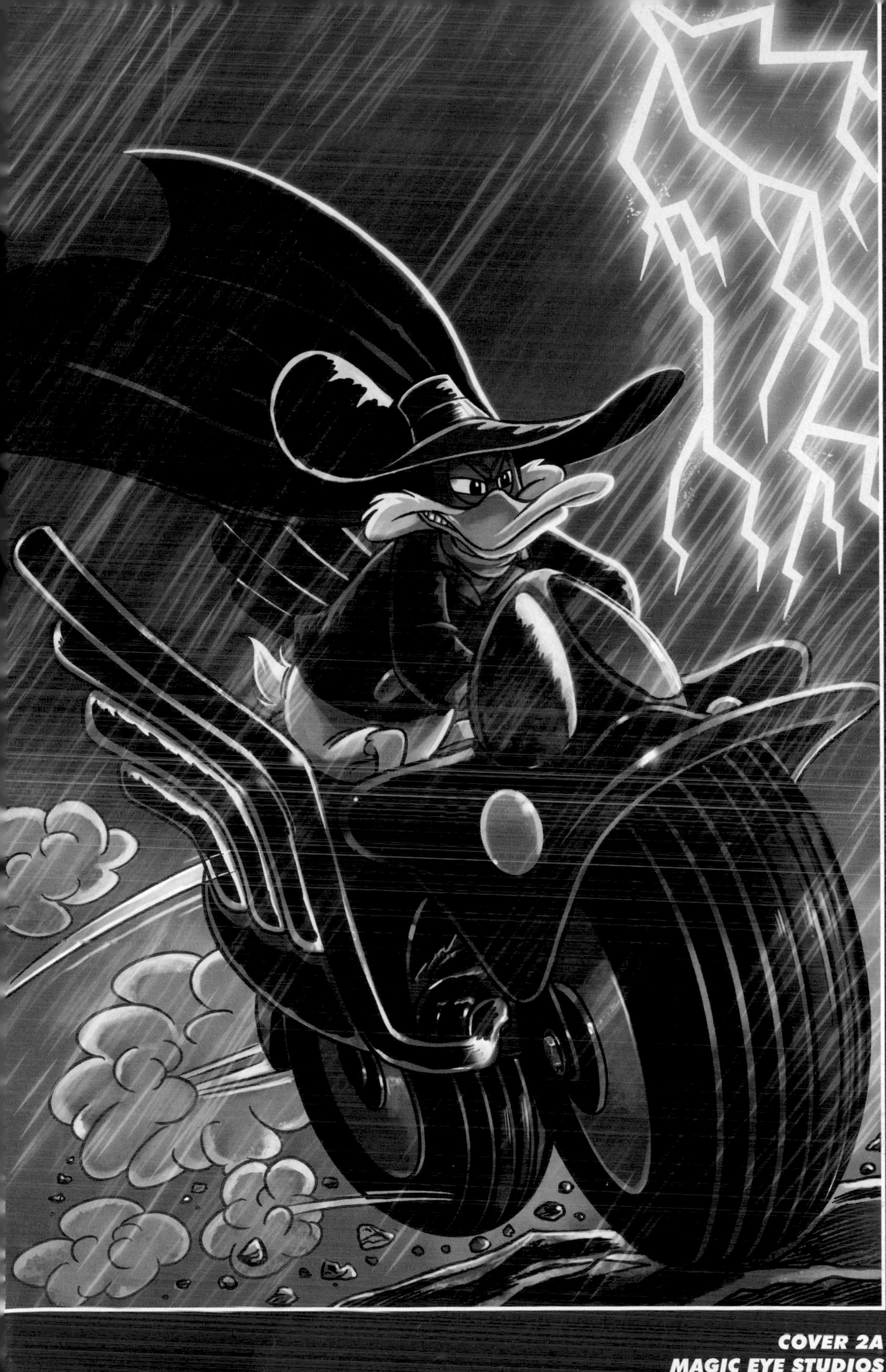

COVER 2A
MAGIC EYE STUDIOS
COLORS: JAKE MYLER

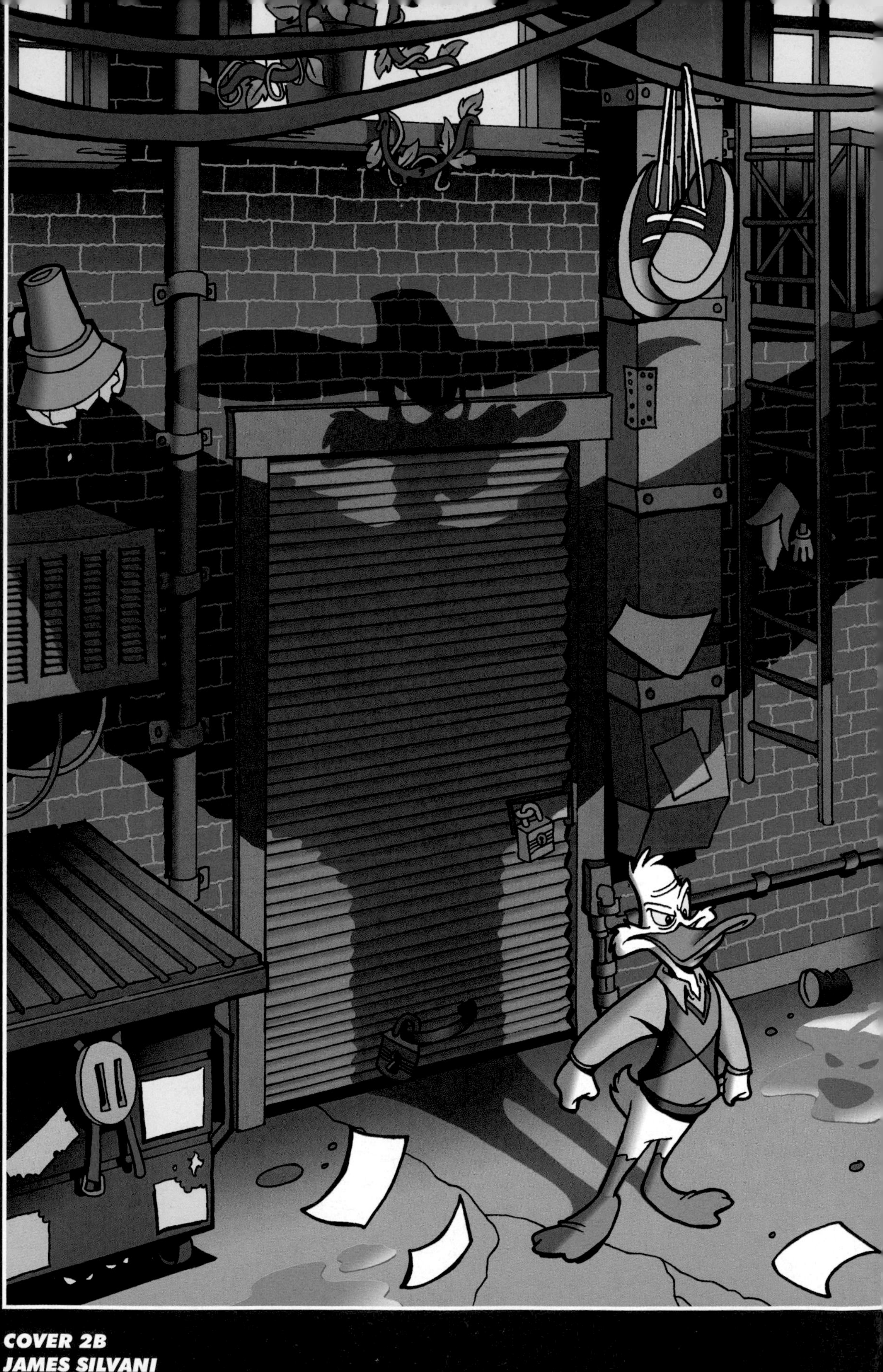

COVER 2B
JAMES SILVANI

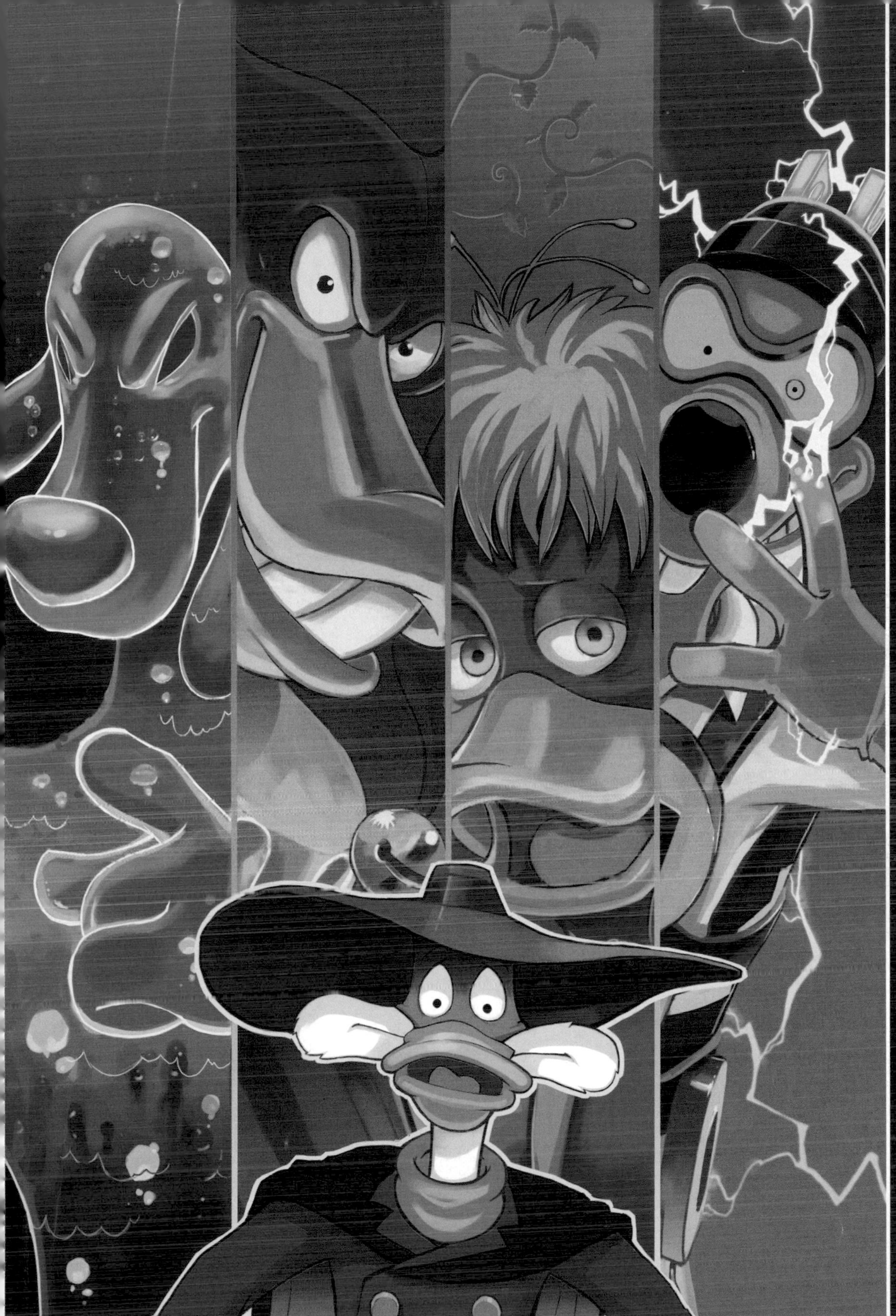

COVER 2C
JAKE MYLER

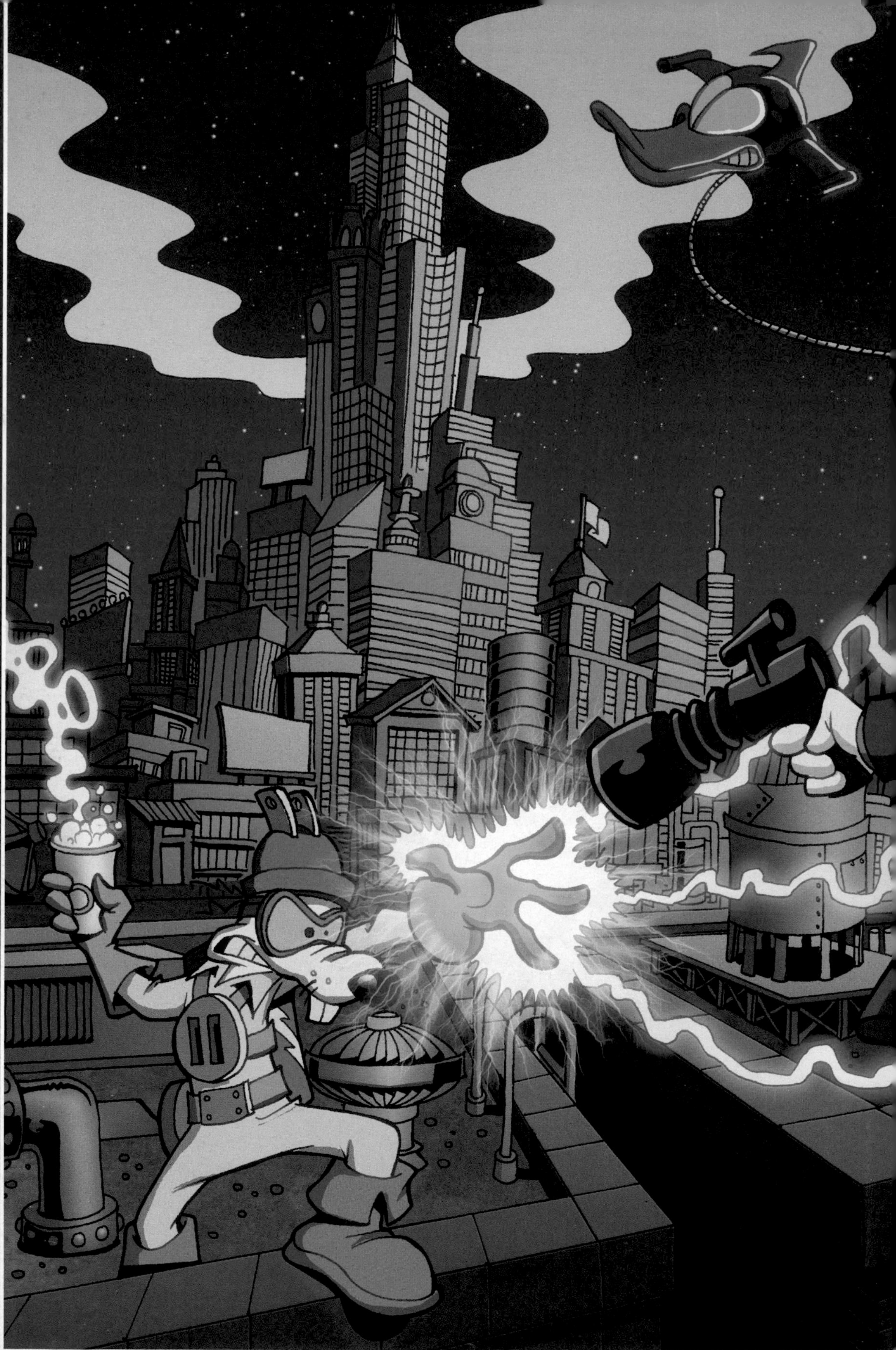

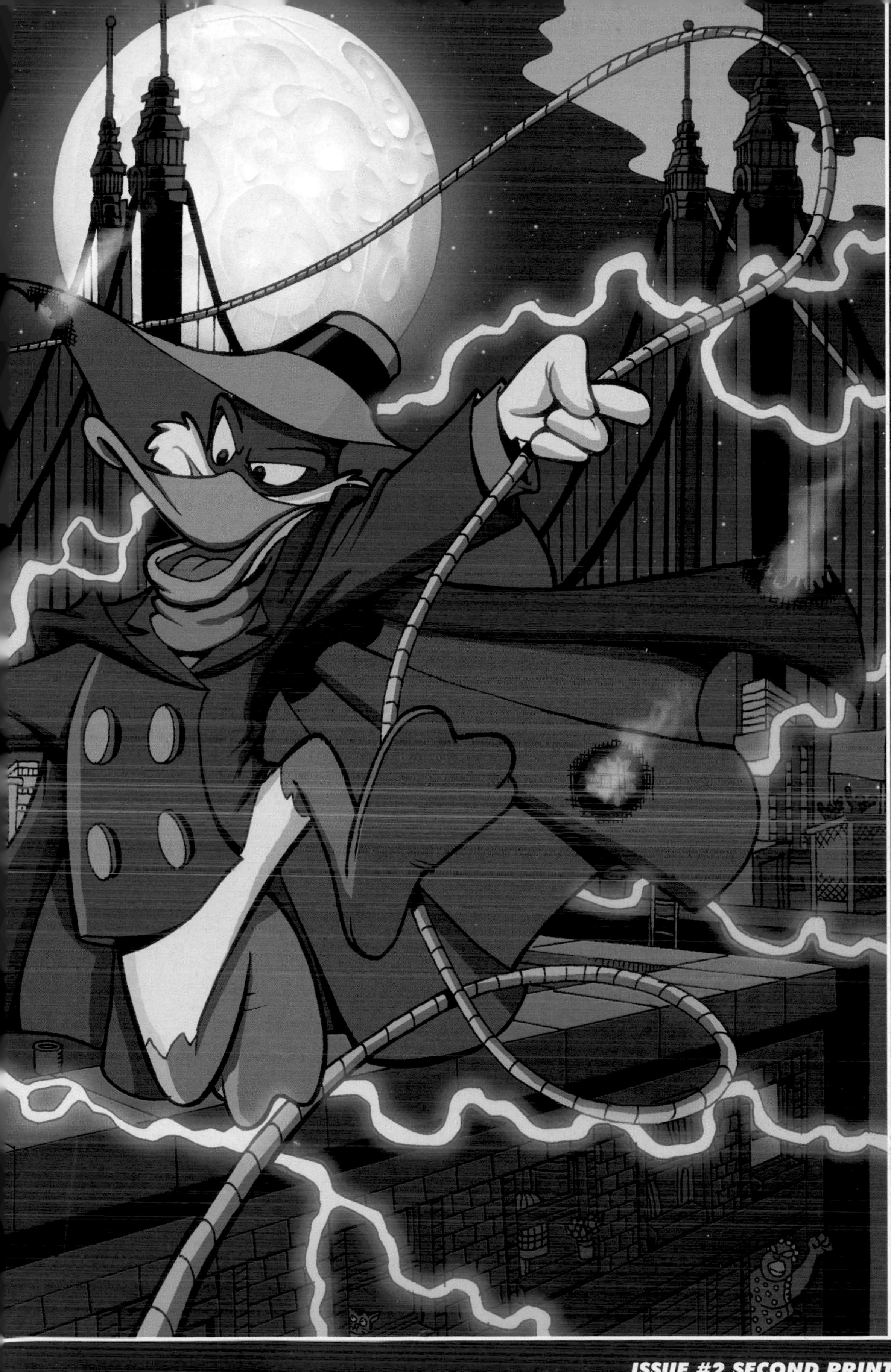

ISSUE #2 SECOND PRINT
JAMES SILVANI
COLORS: ANDREW DALHOUSE

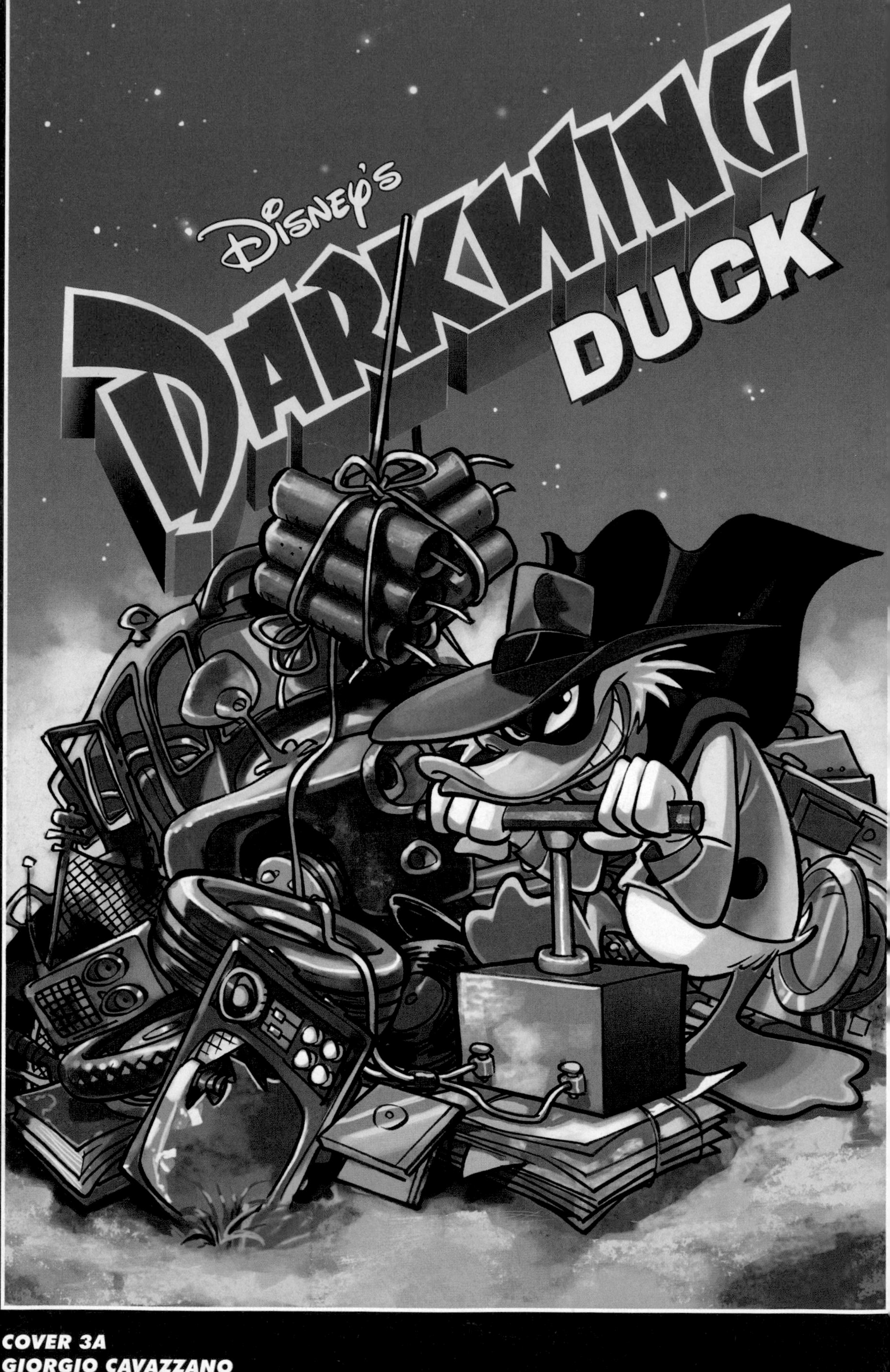
DISNEY'S
DARKWING
DUCK

COVER 3A
GIORGIO CAVAZZANO
COLORS: JAKE MYLER

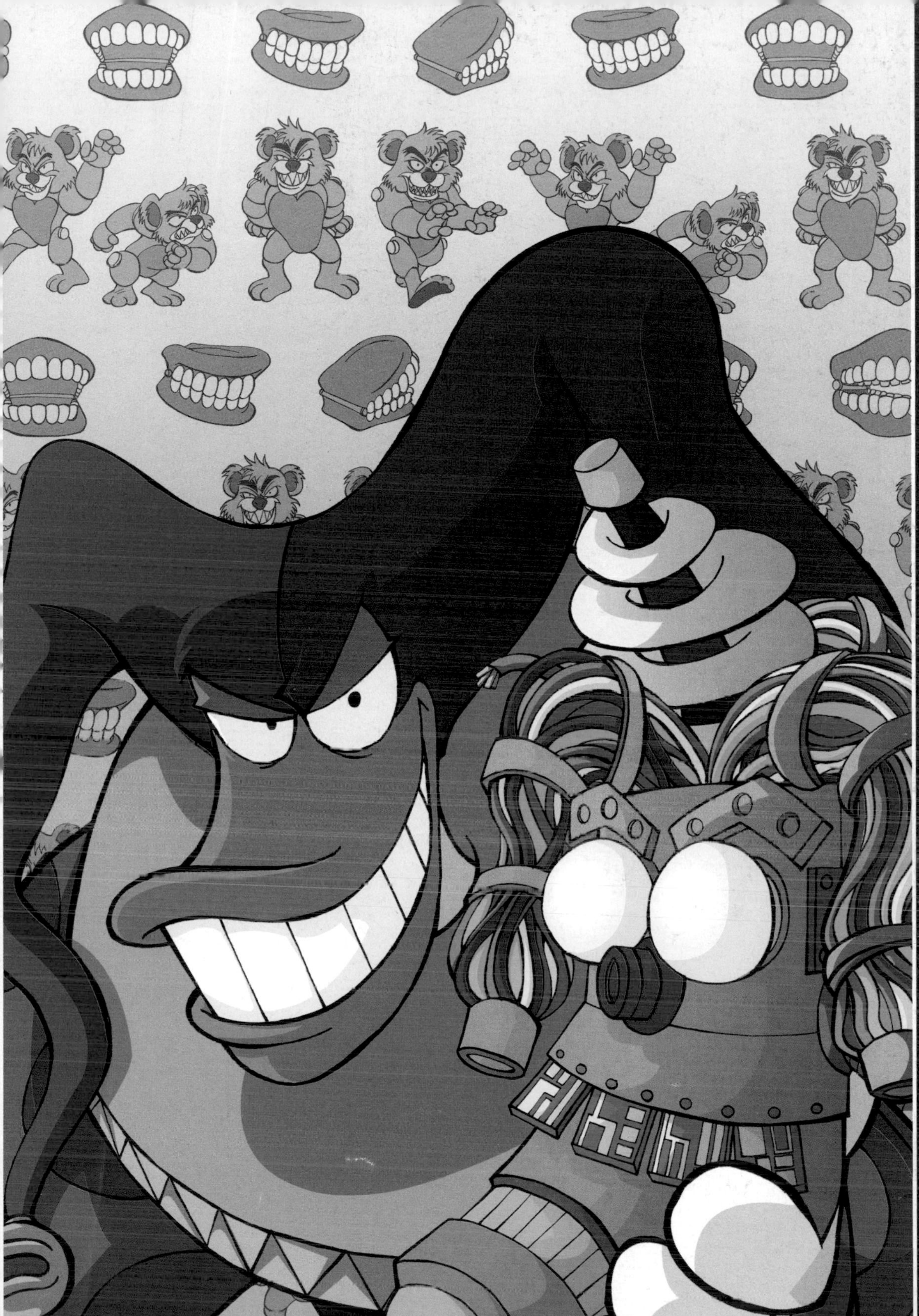

COVER 3B
JOSE MACASOCOL, JR.

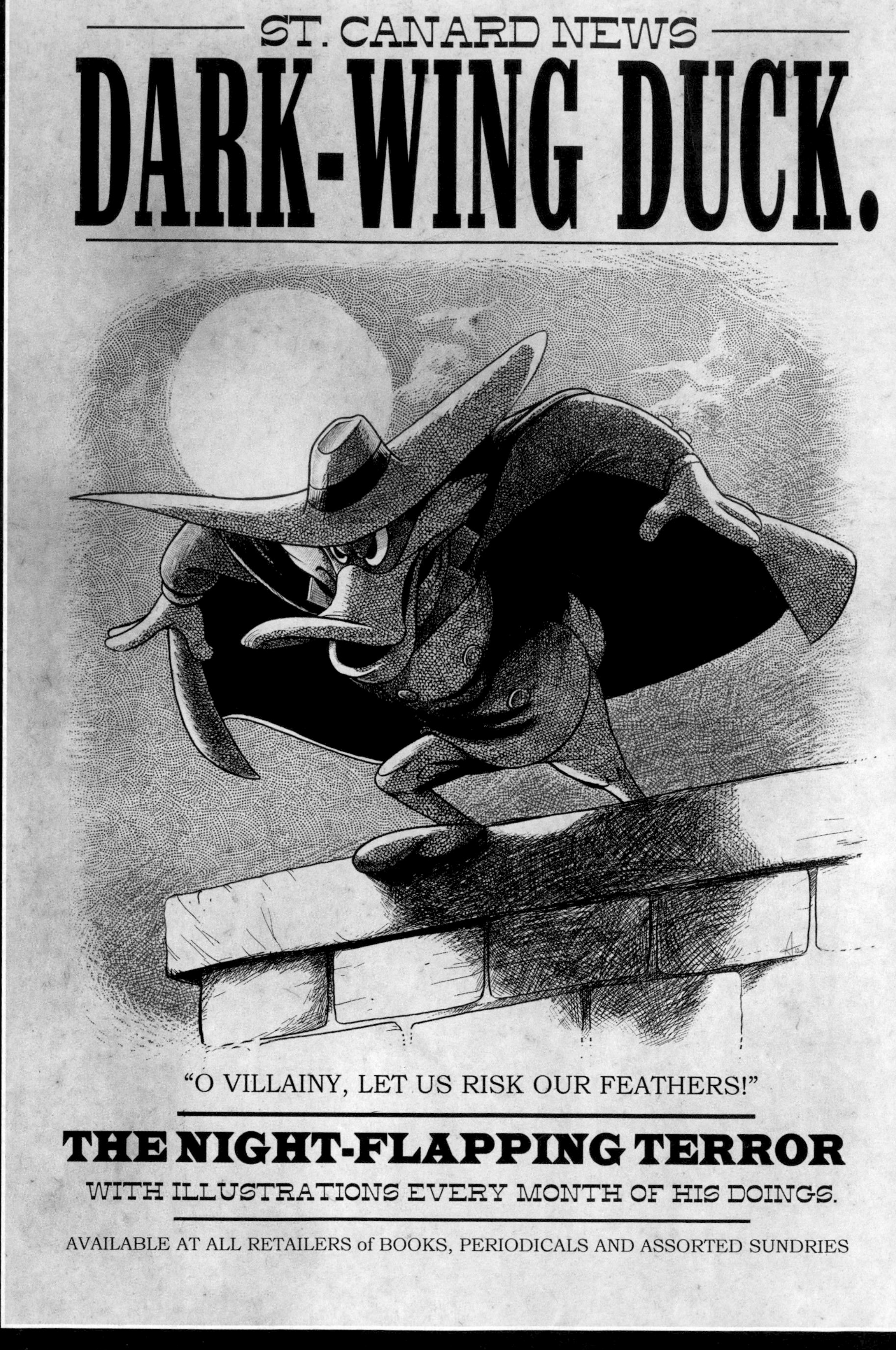

COVER 3C
AMY MEBBERSON

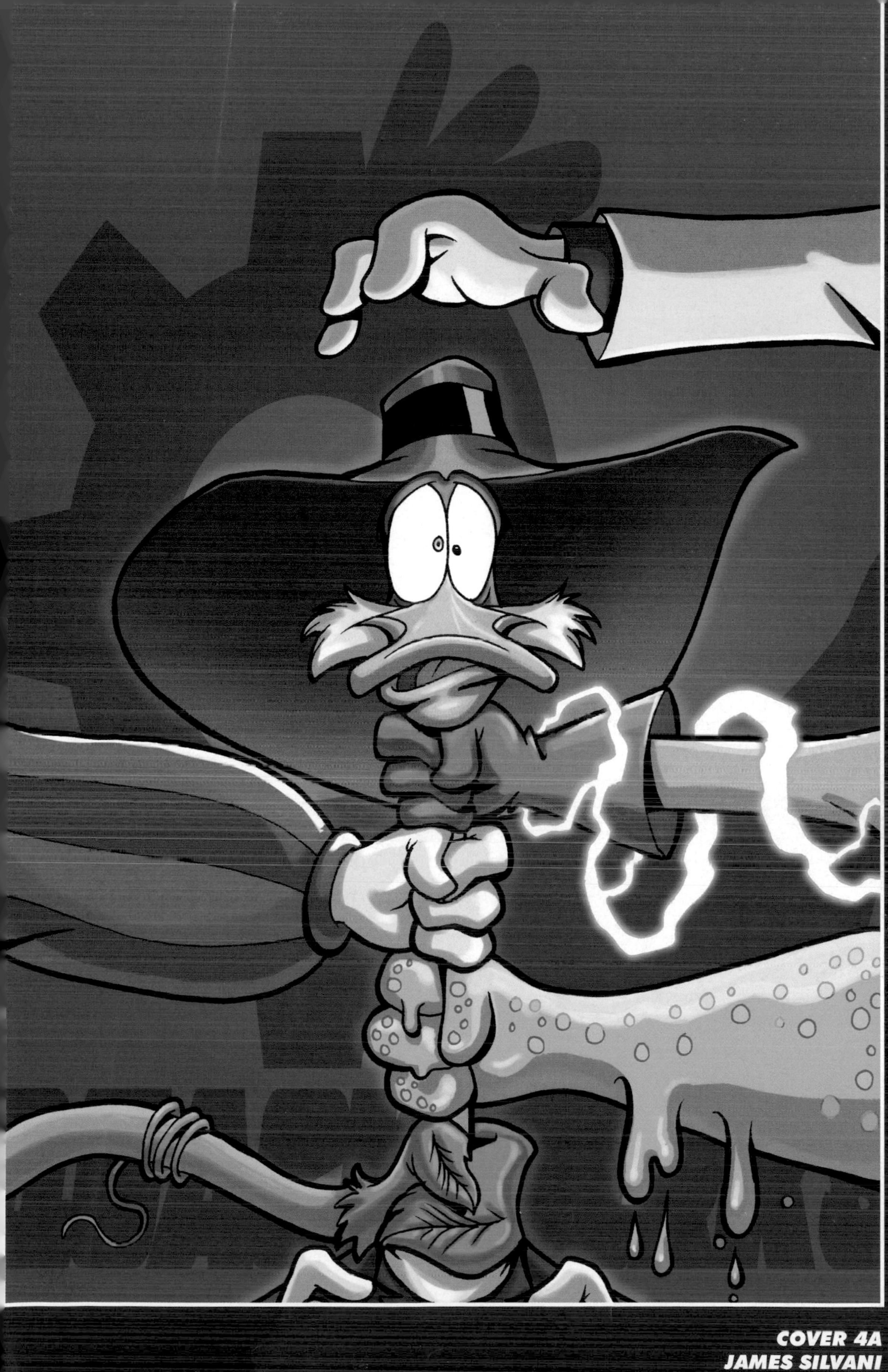

COVER 4A
JAMES SILVANI
COLORS: ANDREW DALHOUSE

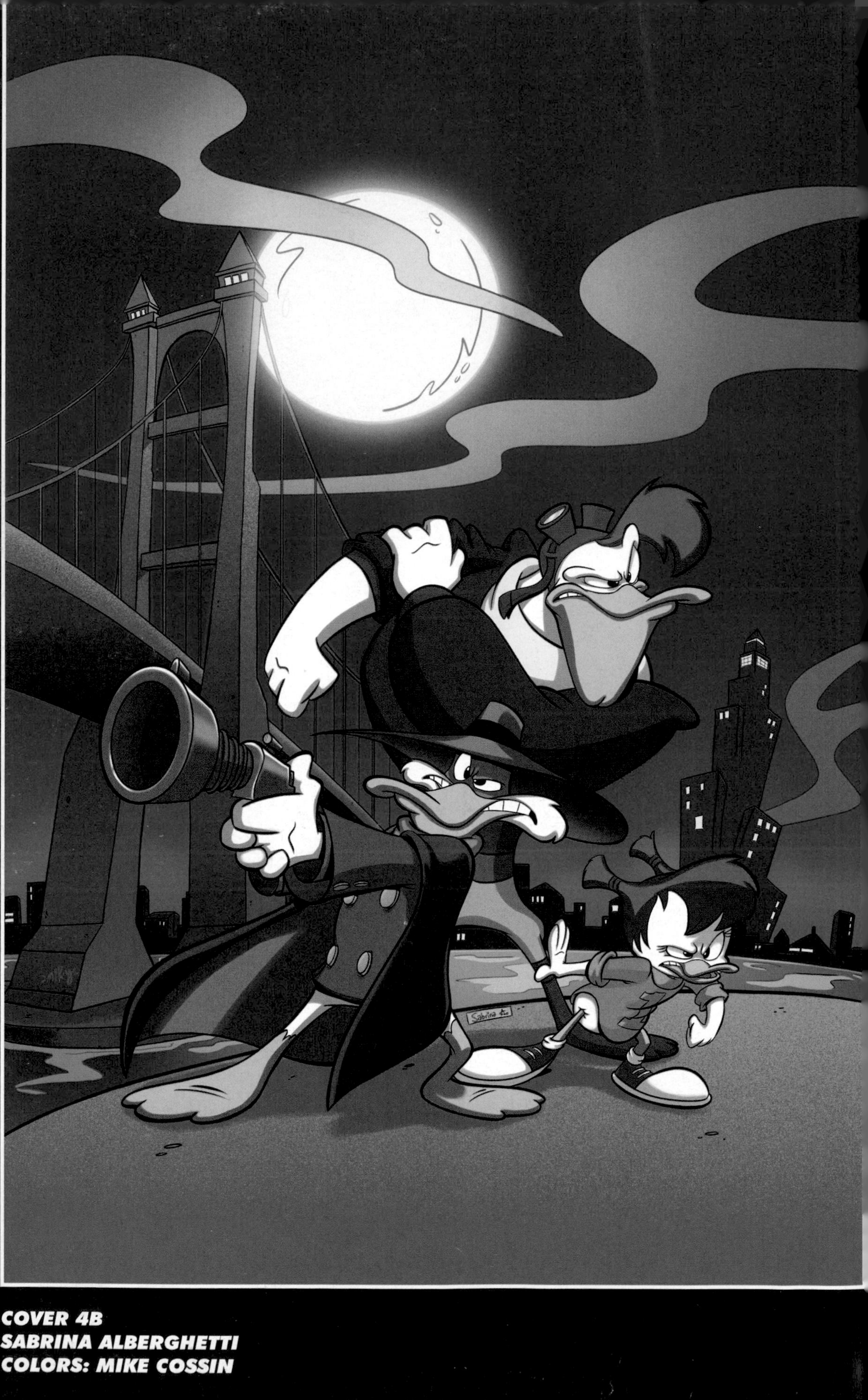

COVER 4B
SABRINA ALBERGHETTI
COLORS: MIKE COSSIN

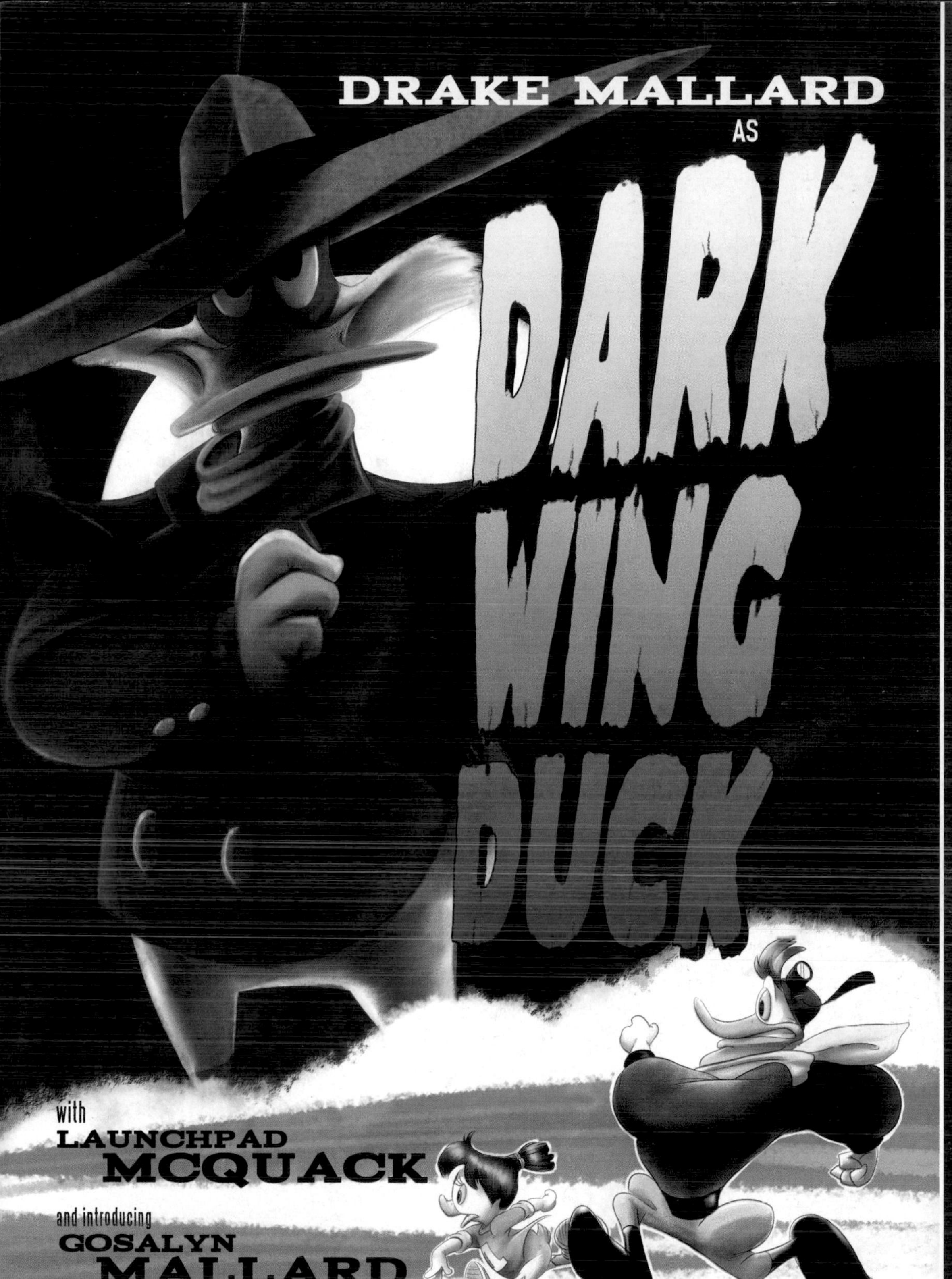
DRAKE MALLARD
AS
DARK WING DUCK
with
LAUNCHPAD MCQUACK
and introducing
GOSALYN MALLARD
Produced by CHRISTOPHER BURNS
Screenplay by IAN BRILL
Directed by JAMES SILVANI

COVER 4C
AMY MEBBERSON

JAMES SILVANI ORIGINAL SKETCHES

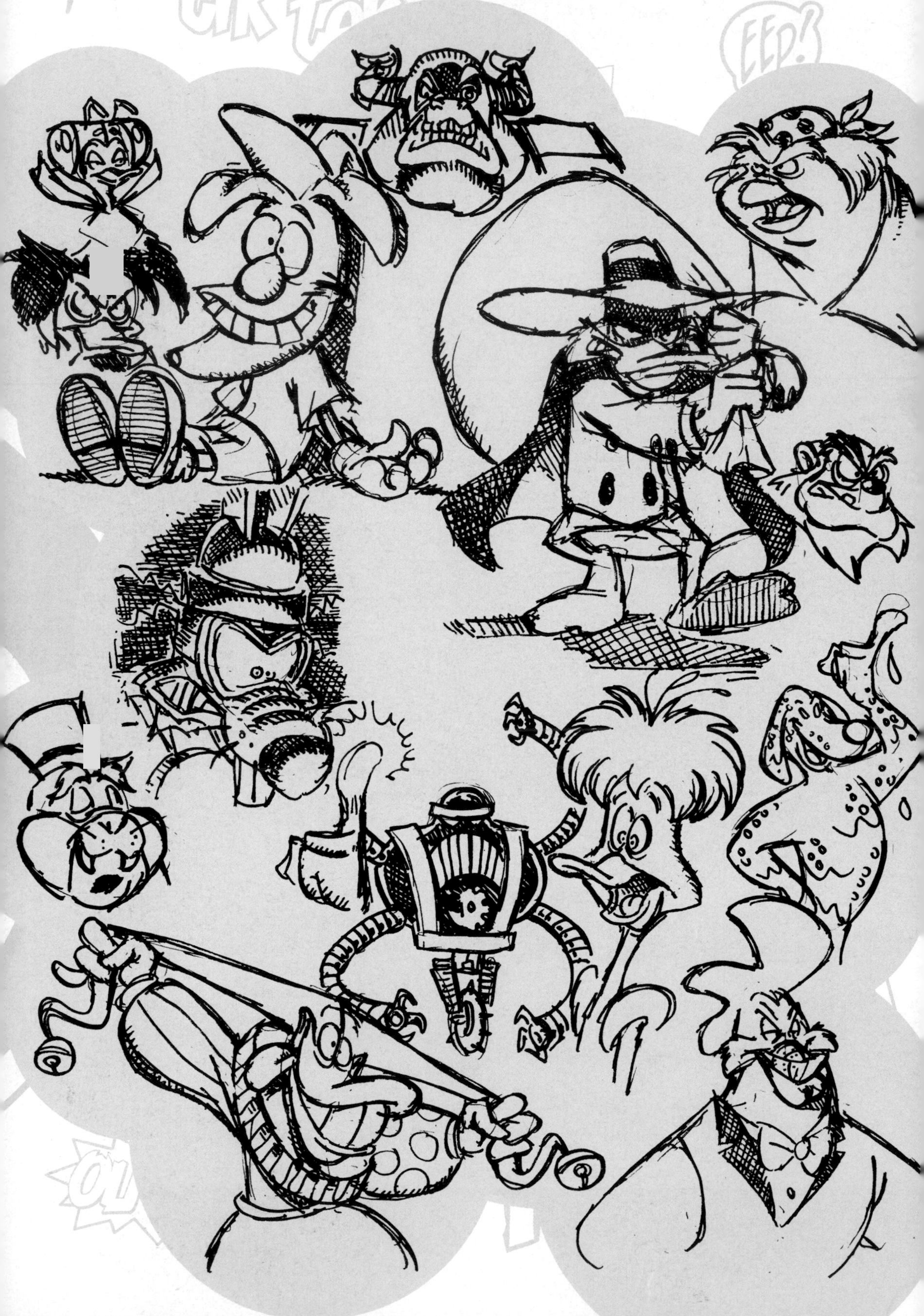
EEP!

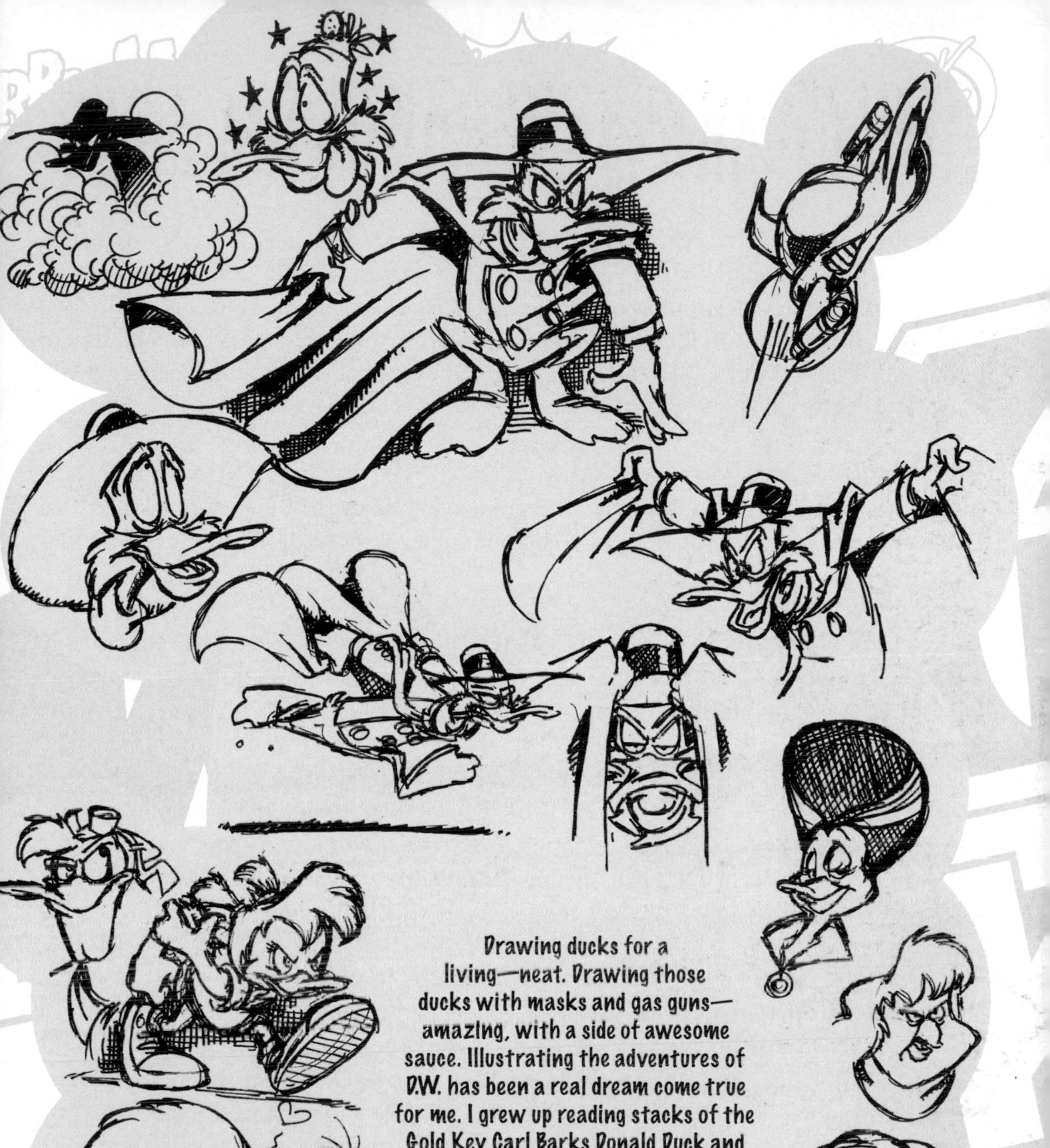

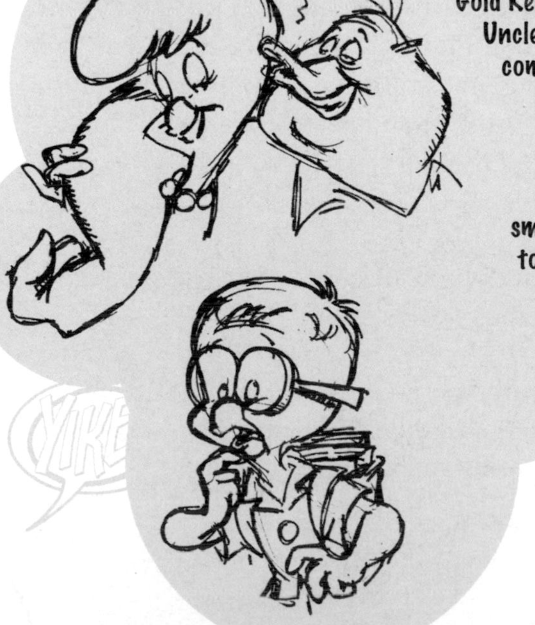

Drawing ducks for a living—neat. Drawing those ducks with masks and gas guns—amazing, with a side of awesome sauce. Illustrating the adventures of D.W. has been a real dream come true for me. I grew up reading stacks of the Gold Key Carl Barks Donald Duck and Uncle Scrooge collections . Those comics, with their perfect blend of humor and adventure, were exactly the kinds of stories I wanted to draw.

I'm proud to say that, in some small way, I was able to contribute to the legacy of the Disney Ducks comics.

-James Silvani

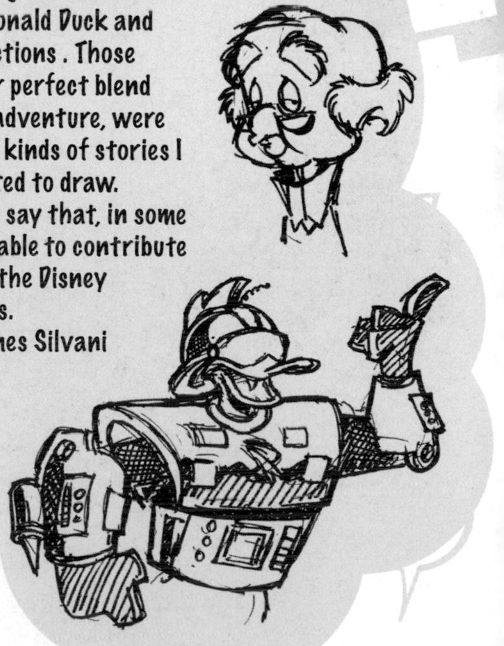

THE ORIGIN(S) OF DARKWING DUCK

In the shadows of his hidden lair, Drake Mallard ponders his role in bringing justice to the city of St. Canard, "Criminals are a superstitious, cowardly lot, so my disguise must be able to strike terror into their hearts! I must be a creature of the night…" As if in answer, a duck flies in the open window. Mallard vaults to his feet, "It's an omen! I shall become a DUCK!" He pauses a moment and ponders further, "Wait. I AM a duck. How is this going to work?"

Just what is the "real" origin of Darkwing Duck? You won't get it from me and the duck's not talkin'. If you watched all the episodes of the TV show, you know that Darkwing had at least four origins. Had we another season, he might have had four more.

Any origin I created for D.W. would have been a pale reflection of something already out there in popular culture. He doesn't have superpowers so there wasn't much to explain. At least the multiple origins were an excuse to play with the tropes of comic book icons.

The writers and artists working on the series focused on finding the most entertaining stories for the Duck Knight, not adhering to a strict continuity. It was much like the early superheroes were handled. In fact, although he was created in the nineties, Darkwing Duck is largely a product of the Silver Age of Comics, the comics I read as a kid when they only cost a dime!

In the late fifties, comics were about big concepts, outrageous action and most of all, fun. Darkwing and I owe a huge load of thanks to the famous DC editor, Julius Schwartz, who filled the covers of his comics with a giant, turtle-mutated Jimmy Olsen, ginormous-headed Lois Lane, and any number of super-powered gorillas. Flip through the covers of Carmine Infantino's run on The Flash and you can almost see the duck struggling to break free of the staples. Fat Flash, Old Man Flash, Flash of two worlds? Although I didn't remember the stories, those images have stayed with me my entire life. I even instructed my story editors to "pitch me the comic book cover," meaning the visual, high concept, central idea of the story. An actual Darkwing Duck comic book seemed inevitable.

The origin I CAN tell you about is how the Darkwing Duck TV series was created. It all started with a studio executive who loved catchy titles.

There had been an episode of the fantastically popular DUCKTALES featuring Launchpad McQuack as a secret agent named "Double-O Duck." This executive thought that the concept could make for a hit series and assigned it to me.

I was not thrilled. James Bond had yet to be revitalized and it was years before Austin Powers would mine the inherent goofiness in the idea of a super secret agent. I felt an animated show would just be a parody with no heart or sense of family, ingredients we tried to include in all our shows.

I created a pitch that added Gizmoduck as a partner to Launchpad. It had the prerequisite beats of femme fatales, crazy gadgets and world-coveting villains. I presented it to the powers that be, who summed it up as being just a parody with no heart or sense of family.

For a brief second I felt that warm glow that happens when you are absolutely certain that you and your supremely powerful boss are on the exact same wavelength. That glow was extinguished in the next second when my boss said, "Do it over." You see, he loved that title.

So I did what I should've done in the first place, take the creation of the show seriously and not just do the expected. I threw out the Bond template and reconsidered the nature of a secret organization.

What came to mind was Doc Savage, a pulp hero with an eccentric band of assistants. That led to thoughts of The Shadow and suddenly I was engaged and enthusiastic about the idea. Artists Bob Kline and Mike Peraza, were assigned to the project and soon the world of Double-O Duck took shape. He was a duck of mystery whose motto was "Look good while doing good," a slogan that spoke to his tremendous ego.

My childhood Batman had a Batmobile, a Batplane and Bathelicopters that all sported a huge bat head on front, so of course Double-O Duck was given duck-themed modes of transportation. A mere car seemed boring, so I doodled a duck-beaked motorcycle that mirrored the earth-rattling street machine of Judge Dredd. Character-wise, we added a sidekick to avoid expositional monologues. Since he had been hanging around the series concept from the start, Launchpad was pressed into service.

But the show concept didn't click until we asked ourselves, "What if Batman had to raise a little girl?" Gosalyn was the perfect addition. An incorrigible ball of energy who refused to stay at home, she would complicate his life in all sorts of ways. More importantly she would play havoc with his ultra smooth and sophisticated self-image.

My superiors thought it was great, and Buena Vista Distribution, who would be selling the series around the world, were happy. They even gave enameled cloisonné pins featuring a masked, white tuxedoed, Double-O Duck to all the station owners. All the elements were in place.

Except we couldn't use the phrase, "Double-O."

Turns out Ian Fleming made that whole thing up. The phrase is owned by his estate and those who make the Bond movies. They weren't thrilled with the idea of a foible-filled fowl making light of it. Small setback.

In truth, I was never thrilled with the name because I worried potential viewers would make the same mistake I had and assume it to be a tired spy parody instead of the pulp infused, superheroic, action comedy we were planning. Problem was I couldn't come up with a name.

Disney TV Animation actually held a contest for its employees with a $500 dollar prize for naming the duck. The entries included Deadeye Duck, Danger Duck, the Fantom Fowl, every alliterative combination you can imagine. Interestingly, the winner was Alan Burnett who came up with "Darkwing." I added "Duck" and our star was on his way. Alan took the money and soon after left for Warner Brothers where he worked with Bruce Timm to create the award winning, BATMAN: THE ANIMATED SERIES.

Now development began in earnest. Double-O Duck looked like Donald Duck in a mask, hat and cape. Darkwing Duck needed his own look. Toby Shelton redesigned the entire cast, giving Darkwing Duck his distinctive cheeks and outrageously large hat. Other trademarks came as we started writing.

I could recite the Shadow's, "Who knows what evil lurks in the hearts of men?" speech long before I had ever heard an episode of his radio show. I wanted D.W. to have something similar and came up with "I am the terror that flaps in the night. I am Darkwiiiing Duck!" I told the writers that it must be included in every episode along with his call to action, "Let's… get… dangerous!"

But one of our early episodes required Launchpad to stand in for Darkwing and he could never get it right. The closest he got was, "I am the road salt that rusts the underside of your car!" I thought it was hilarious and said we needed to make that part of Darkwing's schtick.

Although I take credit for the creation of Darkwing Duck, you can see that some of the best loved details came from executive whims, development tangents, comic book covers, pulp culture and an incredibly talented staff of writers and artists. I was just smart enough to recognize the gold when it appeared in their pans.

The guys at BOOM! Studios have grasped the core of the Darkwing Duck TV series and adapted it to modern comic book storytelling. They were a little hesitant to approach me. After all they were taking over the legacy of my character (and by "my" I mean 100% Disney owned and operated). They were even giving him <gasp!> continuity.

I told them that Carl Barks worked on the old Donald Duck cartoons. If he had worried too much about adhering to the world of the animated shorts we would never

never have Scrooge McDuck, the Beagle Boys, Gladstone Gander, Magica DeSpell and the wonderful universe he created. Darkwing Duck and his family was theirs to play with and I'd help in any way I could.

This book contains the complete story that reintroduced Darkwing Duck to his fans. It received rave reviews from the fans of the show and even new readers who had never seen the original series. D.W., Launchpad and Gosalyn have landed in good hands and now their story is in yours.

Enjoy!
Tad Stones
September 2010

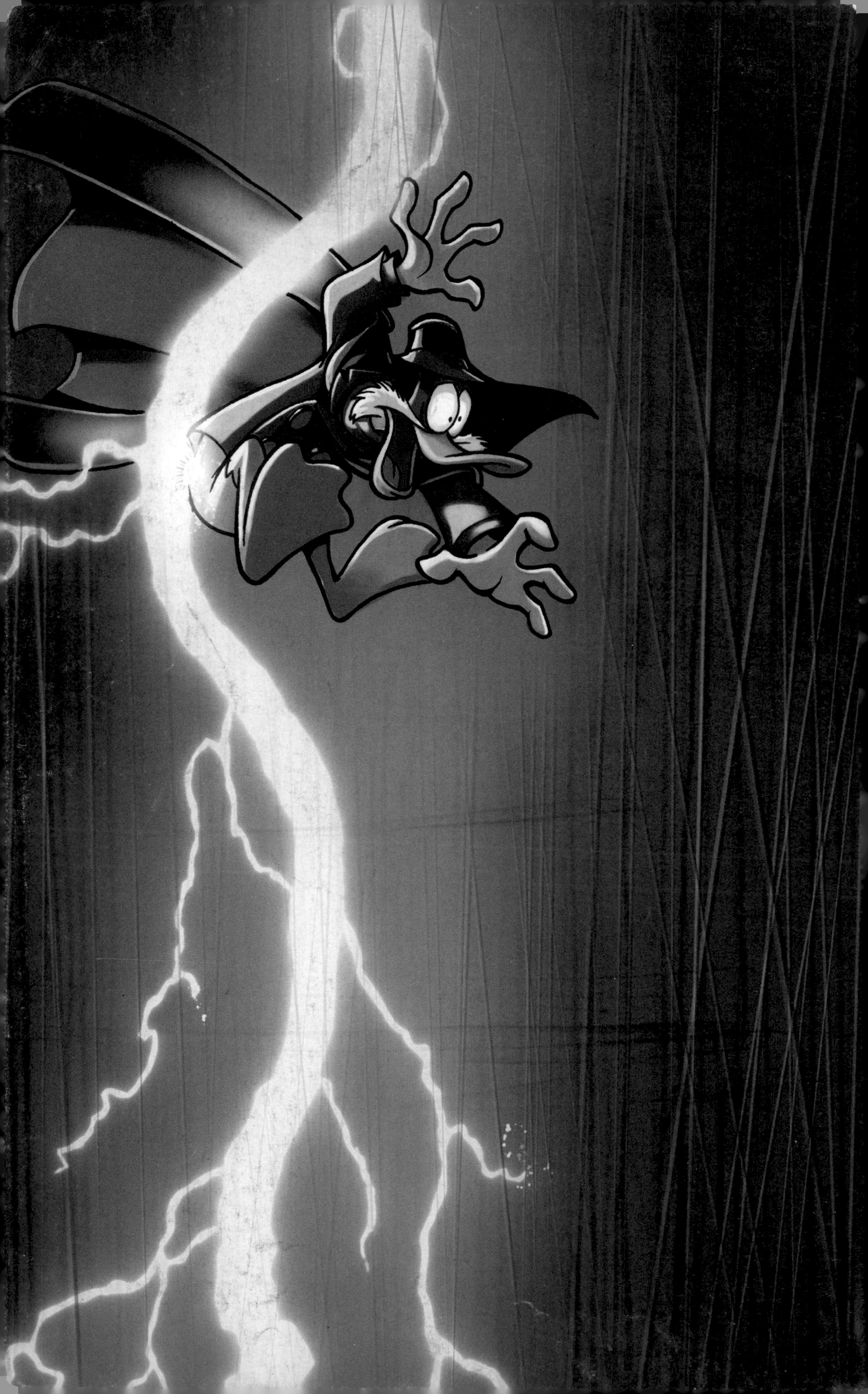

Disney's DARKWING DUCK

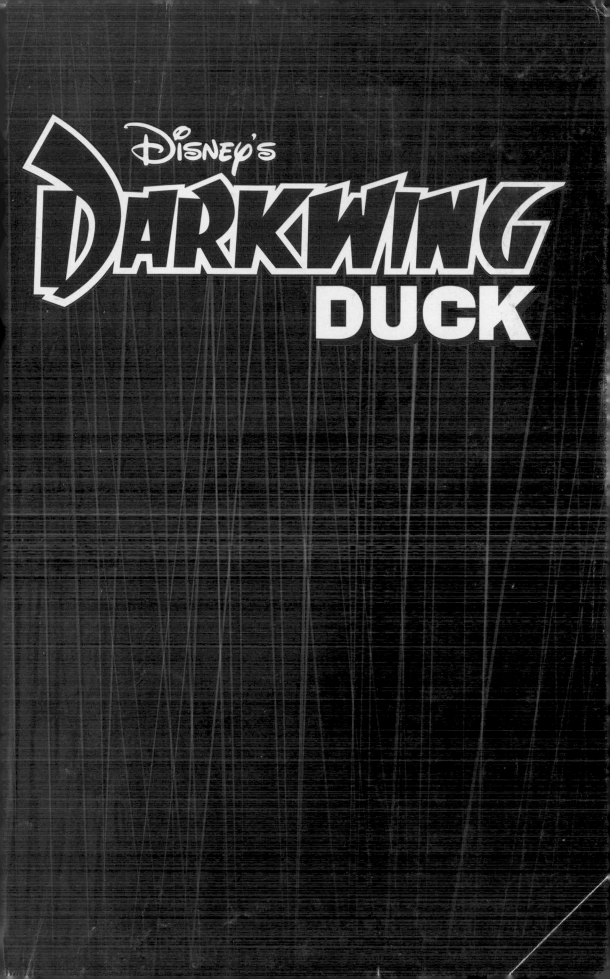

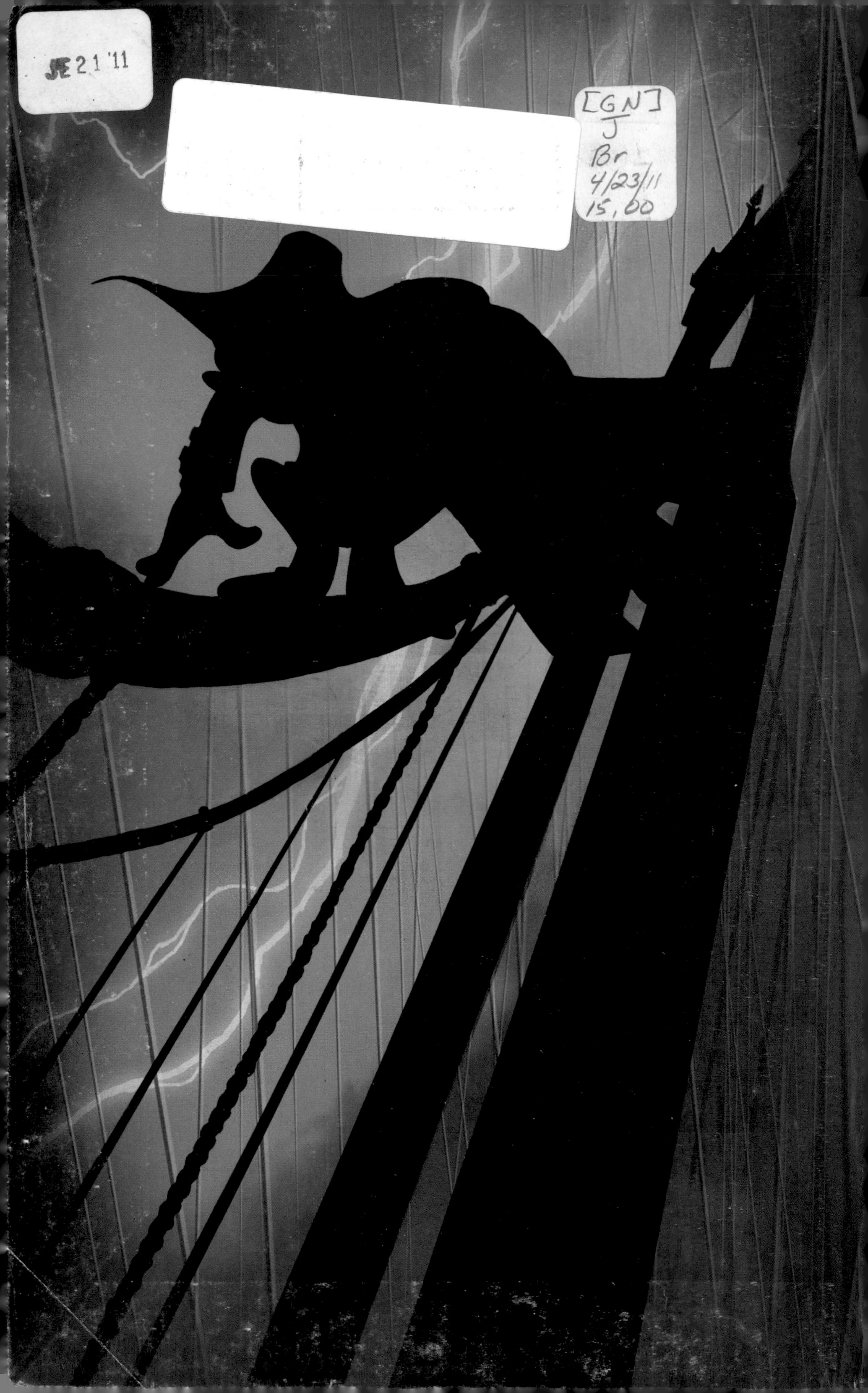